ROCOCO TO CUBISM

IN ART AND LITERATURE

ROCOCO
to
CUBISM
in Art
and Literature

By WYLIE SYPHER

VINTAGE BOOKS
A DIVISION OF RANDOM HOUSE
New York

FIRST VINTAGE EDITION, *February, 1963*

VINTAGE BOOKS
are published by ALFRED A. KNOPF, INC.
and RANDOM HOUSE, INC.

MANUFACTURED IN THE UNITED STATES OF AMERICA

ACKNOWLEDGMENTS

Once again I am indebted to the editorial advice of Jason Epstein and Andrew Chiappe, and also to The John Simon Guggenheim Memorial Foundation for the fellowship that enabled me to revisit European museums. Nor could I have written these chapters without the help always offered by librarians at the Fogg Art Museum of Harvard University. In addition I have enjoyed the advantages of all the care and wisdom of Evelyn Kossoff, in the Editorial Department at Random House.

The editors of *Kenyon Review* and *The University of Toronto Quarterly* have kindly given their consent to my using certain pages and materials from articles on "Gide's Cubist Novel," "Arabesque in Verse," and "The *Morceau de Fantaisie* in Verse," which originally appeared in these publications, copyright 1945, 1949, by Wylie Sypher.

Mr. Henry Pearlman of New York and Mrs. Frank G. Thomson of Haverford, Pennsylvania, have graciously and generously allowed me to reproduce paintings from their private collections.

Because of the scope of my discussion my debt to art historians and critics of literature can be only imperfectly indicated in the bibliographical note, or in the footnotes either, which never can specify all one owes to others. These chapters are rooted in the work of scholars like Pierre Francastel and Guy Michaud.

For permission to quote from copyrighted texts I am obliged to the following:

B. T. Batsford, Ltd. for passages reprinted from *Picasso* by Gertrude Stein

Dodd, Mead & Company, Inc. for passages reprinted from *Poems* by William Sharp

E. P. Dutton & Company, Inc. and the heirs of Luigi Pirandello for passages reprinted from *Each in His Own Way* and *Six Characters in Search of An Author* by Luigi Pirandello, from *Naked Masks: Five Plays*

Elek Books, Ltd. for passages reprinted from *A Love Affair* by Émile Zola, translated by Jean Stewart, copyright Elek Books Ltd., 1957

Farrar, Straus and Cudahy, Inc. for passages reprinted from *Selected Letters of Gustave Flaubert* translated and edited by Francis Steegmuller, copyright 1953 by Francis Steegmuller

Grove Press, Inc. for passages reprinted from *Selected Writings of Gérard de Nerval* translated with a critical introduction and notes by Geoffrey Wagner, Grove Press, 1957; from *The Voyeur* by Alain Robbe-Grillet translated by Richard Howard, Grove Press, 1958; and from "A Fresh Start for Fiction" and "Three Reflected Visions" by Alain Robbe-Grillet, appearing in *Evergreen Review,* Vol. I, No. 3, Grove Press, 1957

Harcourt, Brace and Company, Inc. for passages reprinted from *Film Form* and *Film Sense* by Sergei M. Eisenstein; from *Speculations* by T. E. Hulme; from "The Music of Poetry" by T. S. Eliot, copyright 1942; from "Burnt Norton," "The Dry Salvages," and "East Coker" in *Four Quartets,* copyright, 1943, by T. S. Eliot; from "The Waste Land," "The Love Song of J. Alfred Prufrock," "Preludes," "Whispers of Immortality," "The Hollow Men," and "Ash Wednesday," from *Collected Poems 1909–1935* by T. S. Eliot, copyright, 1936, by Harcourt, Brace and Company

Henry Holt and Company, Inc., The Society of Authors as the literary representative of the Trustees of the Estate of the late A. E. Housman, and Messrs. Jonathan Cape, Ltd., publishers of A. E. Housman's *Collected Poems,* for a passage reprinted from *A Shropshire Lad* by A. E. Housman

Houghton Mifflin Company for passages reprinted from *Mont Saint Michel and Chartres* by Henry Adams

The Johns Hopkins Press for passages reprinted from *Selected Prose Poems, Essays, and Letters of Mallarmé,* translated and edited by Bradford Cook

Alfred A. Knopf, Inc. for passages reprinted from *The Collected Poems of Wallace Stevens* by Wallace Stevens, copyright 1942, 1947, 1950, 1954 by Wallace Stevens; from *The Necessary Angel* by Wallace Stevens, copyright 1949, 1951 by Wallace Stevens; from *The Counterfeiters* by André Gide, translated by Dorothy Bussy, copyright 1927 by Alfred A. Knopf, Inc.; from *Journals* by André Gide, translated by Justin O'Brien, Vol. I, copyright 1947 by Alfred A. Knopf, Inc., Vol. II, copyright 1948 by Alfred A. Knopf, Inc., Vol. III, copyright 1949 by Alfred A. Knopf, Inc., Vol. IV, copyright 1951 by Alfred A. Knopf, Inc.; from *Lafcadio's Adventures* by André Gide, translated by Dorothy Bussy, copyright 1925, 1928 by Alfred A. Knopf, Inc.

J. B. Lippincott Company for passages reprinted from *Manet and the French Impressionists* by Théodore Duret

The Macmillan Company for passages reprinted from *Science and the Modern World* by Alfred North Whitehead, copyright 1925–26; and from *Pre-Raphaelitism and the Pre-Raphaelite Brotherhood* by William Holman Hunt

The Museum of Modern Art for passages reprinted from *Picasso: Fifty Years of His Art* by Alfred Barr; and from *Post-Impressionism* by John Rewald

W. W. Norton & Company, Inc. for passages reprinted from *The Modern Theme* by José Ortega y Gasset

Oxford University Press for "You Bid Me Try" by Austin Dobson

Phaidon Press, Ltd. for passages reprinted from *The Journal of Eugène Delacroix, A Selection* edited by Hubert Wellington and translated by Lucy Norton; and from *The Mirror of Art: Critical Studies by Baudelaire,* translated and edited by Jonathan Mayne

The Philadelphia Museum of Art for passages reprinted from *Creation of the Rococo* by Fiske Kimball

Philosophical Library for passages reprinted from "Immortality" in *Essays in Science and Philosophy* by Alfred North Whitehead

Random House, Inc. for passages from *Lectures in America* by Gertrude Stein; and from *Ulysses* by James Joyce

Rinehart and Company Inc. for a passage reprinted from "Blue Symphony" by John Gould Fletcher from *Preludes and Symphonies,* copyright 1930

Charles Scribner's Sons for passages from William Ernest Henley's "London Voluntaries"

Paul Theobald and Company for passages from *The New Landscape* by Gyorgy Kepes

Alice B. Toklas for passages reprinted from "Miss Furr and Miss Skeene" by Gertrude Stein

Viking Press, Inc. for passages reprinted from *Portrait of the Artist as a Young Man* by James Joyce

Auburndale, Massachusetts
October, 1959

TO LUCY

Contents

PART TWO
Picturesque, Romanticism, Symbolism

PART THREE
Neo-Mannerism

PART FOUR
The Cubist Perspective

LIST OF ILLUSTRATIONS

Foreword

The assumptions behind the following chapters have already been made by others, and I shall therefore repeat what they have written:

> In each period there is a general form of the forms of thought; and, like the air we breathe, such a form is so translucent, and so pervading, and so seemingly necessary, that only by extreme effort can we become aware of it.
>
> (Alfred North Whitehead: *Adventures of Ideas*)

> Systems depend wholly upon, or, better, derive directly from, the general mental attitude of a particular era. . . . The change of a system, moreover, does not concern merely a few elements, but affects the whole. . . . Forms recur; systems don't.
>
> (Emil Kaufmann: *Architecture in the Age of Reason*)

> Technique alone is powerless to account for the appearance of a new style, for a new style in art means the appearance of a new attitude of man toward the world.
>
> (Pierre Francastel: *Peinture et Société*)

These passages will suggest that I am concerned, as I was in *Four Stages of Renaissance Style,* with analogies—that is, cognate forms in literature and in painting, architecture, or other fine arts. I shall not attempt to defend this venture, which I tried to justify in the introduction to the earlier book dealing with renaissance, mannerist, baroque, and late-baroque phases of style from 1400 to 1700. In some ways the present essay is a continuation.

However, the problem of dealing with style since 1700 is more troublesome because we approach modern periods, where our perspective is much shorter than it is on the middle ages, the renaissance, or the baroque. After art historians have traversed these earlier periods by so many different paths, generalizations are possible, perhaps because history gradually determines which are the secondary developments. Then, of course, as our examination continues and we learn more and more, the problem complicates itself again, and there are continuing reinterpretations. The closer we are to any period, whether in knowledge or in time, the more intricate it seems. The nineteenth century is very close, at least in time, and the complications in its arts are very apparent simply because history has not yet been able to filter out the minor items.

Nevertheless if we are to discuss the arts from 1700 to the present, we must involve the notion of styles, and we need somehow to agree what the term style implies. The very use of the word has been thought, and with reason, an offence, and certainly no notion has caused more dispute in art history: we cannot seem to get along with it or without it. Perhaps nobody has dealt better with the theoretical problem of style than Arnold Hauser in his essay on "Style and Its Changes." Hauser takes the idea of style to be so essential to art history that without it we can have only a mere chronology or catalog of works and artists, and cannot even formulate the question how art changes, or why. Furthermore the notion of style is self-contradictory, since many artists working individually produce something that none of them intended: "Style is the ideal unity of a whole that consists in a lot of concrete and disparate elements." The heap, as Hauser says, is more than the grains of sand in it; yet the heap is only the sum of the grains. Thus a style has a dual nature: it takes its direction, form, or structure from many artists, no one of whom is necessarily aware of the style he is helping to create. If, I might add, the work of individual artists is too individual and too unlike the work being done by other artists, then the style may never find its common denominators. Something like this seems to have occurred among the romantics and impressionists, who have much in common, but might also be said to have too much not in common to have produced a style. In other words, a style brings a community of problems, methods, and solutions.

This remark proves that a style is an abstraction; it "is," Hauser notes, but it never "is" in the sense that a painting by any artist "is." A style is, in one way, only a figment of history that is written about the work of different artists. But it is a necessary figment, even if we do not agree in what mode it "is." The renaissance style is "at once more and less than what has actually been expressed in the works of the renaissance masters." Hauser shrewdly observes that a style is "like a musical theme of which only variations are known." The style exists—or at least appears—although no work by any artist actually attains it. So a style manifests itself almost in spite of the unconsciousness of artists that they are creating a style.

For my own part I should say that a style should be described rather than defined unconditionally, simply because an attempt to define with wholly convincing accuracy is liable to lead to dogmatism in matters where dogmatism is least needed and least helpful. Art history, like all history, arises from interpretation, and interpretation cannot, and should not, be final—a closed account.

During my discussion I have assumed that a genuine style is an expression of a prevailing, dominant, or authentically contemporary view of the world by those artists who have most successfully intuited the quality of human experience peculiar to their day and who are able to phrase this experience in forms deeply congenial to the thought, science, and technology which are part of that experience. This is an expression not easily achieved. A style is born slowly, after many efforts, false starts, and mistakes. All these difficulties, all these deviations, are inevitable, for any age comes only indirectly to a consciousness of what it believes about the world in which it exists; and there is always the inclination to phrase contemporary experience in the idiom of past experience—which, of course, is what gives continuity to the history of the arts.

Take, for example, the changing notion of the world that came when the mediaeval Ptolemaic order was altered by the Copernican renaissance order; this was a revolution in the conception of space—that is, in the conception of the universe itself and man's place in it. The first symptom in art of a changed conception came when sculptors, architects, and painters in the early renaissance began to represent reality by vanishing-point, orthogonal perspective. Such a perspective was in itself nothing beyond a mere technique, a special mechanism for organizing a painting or sculpture in the ratios of a new mathematic. Naturally this technique produced some whimsical effects at first, as in paintings by Paolo Uccello. It was only after Alberti and other Italian theorists of the quattrocento reasoned this technique into a closed system for treating space that an authentic renaissance style appeared in major painters. In spite of this slow birth of a new pictorial and architectural space, and in spite of the many conflicting and highly personal uses of vanishing-point perspective, the creation of a mathematically coherent space from a fixed point of view made possible Raphael's *School of Athens,* a work representing in achieved—almost in official—form a "grand" renaissance style, and summarizing in pictorial symbols the cultural experience of an age by techniques that were deeply in harmony with the thought and science of that age.

A style is more than the techniques that go into the making of the style, for a style expresses in adequate and, perhaps, classic form the whole consciousness of an age, an expression that goes beyond any mere manipulation of perspective. No style comes to maturity until all the techniques entering into it are fused into a coherent, or somehow compatible, method of representation.

Again, this does not mean that a style has no relation to past styles. On the contrary, every major style has a debt to past styles: the renaissance to the art of Rome, mannerism to the renaissance, baroque to the renaissance also, and cubism, probably, to nearly all known styles. The important point is not that a style is entirely new, but that it takes a *contemporary view* of past styles. Gothic took another view of antique art from the renaissance view; and both gothic and renaissance styles, deriving from the antique, were truly contemporary. The academic painting of the nineteenth century also derived from the antique, but the academic painter did not make past styles contemporary; and Picasso, by contrast, does, playing upon the past to stress its difference from the present. As T. S. Eliot puts it, the modern poet is modern precisely *because* he uses past poetry in his own way and with his own intents to deal with the present. Or, in Hauser's words, a style is a dialectic between works in progress and works that already exist. In the nineteenth century the painter or poet often tried to adapt new techniques to archaic composition, and thus did not use past conventions to exploit contemporary techniques but rather to make these techniques conform to past conventions. This was one trouble with impressionist painting, which found new techniques but tried to adapt these techniques to conventional composition. It was also a difficulty in romantic poetry, which discovered the technique of symbolism but hesitated to discard the rhetorical conventions of the ode, the ballad, and metre.

In the evolution of styles techniques appear in advance of the mature style. This was particularly true in the nineteenth century, an era when biology, physics, geology, astronomy, and machines were changing the basis of existence and belief. The technique of the artist is always developing concurrently with the changing technology of his culture—with the camera, for instance; and no century saw more rapid or complete revolutions in technology, applied arts, scientific theory, and the invention of new media like cast iron.

Under these circumstances one would expect the nineteenth century to show competing artistic techniques; and that was the case. The artist was affected by the thoroughgoing disharmonies behind nineteenth-century thought, like the clash between a mechanistic and a vitalistic explanation of life, the iron laws of physics *vs.* the organic forces of biology, the materialistic conception of society *vs.* the heroic, biological conception of the state. Accordingly, there is something mechanical in painting influenced by the camera, but there is something biological and organic about the rhythms in Renoir. Where this competition in techniques occurs, history becomes difficult. Chronology alone will not interpret what happened, for competing techniques are constantly interacting on each other.

Because of this competition I have tried to make a distinction between a genuine style and what I have called stylization, which is the use of a certain technique. To distinguish: a technique does not become a style until it can be used to represent adequately a contemporary view of the world, and like the arts of the early renaissance, the nineteenth-century arts are an area of competing techniques of representation. It is only in cubism—a style summarizing and conciliating the many techniques devised by impressionism, post-impressionism, and Art Nouveau—that an authentically modern style is achieved. Similarly, Uccello and Pollaiuolo and Fra Angelico, each using his own technique or stylization, finally made possible the grand style of Raphael. A style is based on the techniques it transcends. From this point of view impressionism was a technique—an invaluable, fruitful, ingenious technique—but hardly a style; or, more exactly, there were many differing techniques among the impressionists, each experimenting with his own method.

The last century yielded stylizations rather than a style. The distinction is useful in the nineteenth century above all centuries because so much of nineteenth-century art was an exhibition of new techniques that did not fuse into a style, possibly because the artist often resisted the technology of his day or else employed it only superficially. The Victorian artist hated iron, for example, because he hated industrialization; yet iron was the basis of the technology that determined his way of life. How striking it is to see a painter like Turner or Monet creating a work of art by a vision of the foundry or the railway. Thus the nineteenth-century arts showed a curious form of cultural lag Francastel calls "blockage." With the twentieth century and the appearance of cubism this blockage tends to disappear, for the cubist painter was able to accept and assimilate to his art not only the technology but the prevailing scientific theory of his day. Using the cinema, the machine, the theory of relativity willingly and intelligently—though not always with conscious intent—cubism manifests itself as an archetypal modern style, which the preceding century was not able to formulate. The Bauhaus simply continued this style into the technological field again—a form of return of the arts to society. Yet I do not wish to claim that there was any consistent or steady progress or evolution toward cubism, though it was, nevertheless, inevitable, or at least a consummation.

In a sense, too, the nineteenth-century arts showed a certain sort of primitivism, because so many painters and architects experimented with new techniques even if they did not attain a mature style. Francastel has noted that the real primitives are not those who try, like the pre-Raphaelites, to return to earlier forms of art, often archaic, but those who employ a new technique. So, also, the real primitives of nineteenth-century poetry were not those who tried to revive the ballad but rather those who explored the technique of the prose-poem and *vers libre. Vers libre,* we agree, never reached the status of a style; but it led to the authentically modern style of Valéry and Eliot, who have a relation to the cubists and the cinema. Degas, in the same way, is a primitive in his experiment with the daguerreotype view of things—notwithstanding the fact that, like many nineteenth-century primitives, he was a dandy and sophisticate. The realism of the nineteenth-century novel was a comparable form of primitive experiment—this time influenced by sciences like medicine, psychology or psychiatry, and laboratory, biological, or sociological observation—that never reached a satisfactory style. But realism made possible, by its very failures, the "pure" fiction ultimately written by André Gide, who dismissed from the novel whatever is not fictional.

All this will imply, in addition, that the nineteenth century was revolutionary in the arts as well as in society. And the real revolutionaries in art are not those who revolt or reject the past, but those who, in the course of their revolt, find a new technique. Rebellion is not in itself creative, as so much of romantic art proves, though it may lead to new techniques. The impressionists were rebels who were astonishingly creative.

In view of all these complications I cannot write a consecutive history of the phases through which a style developed in the nineteenth century, a period when competing techniques or stylizations developed concurrently and were adopted and adapted internationally almost as soon as they were invented. Instead, I am trying to distinguish some relation between stylizations—modes or techniques of representation in different media. Many different temperaments used these techniques for very different purposes and with very different effects. Yet there is a main trend; for at least one modern style has resulted from these competing techniques.

If a style is an authentic and acquiescent image of contemporary consciousness, a stylization is sometimes in one or another way a compromise, an evasion, a makeshift, a venture in adapting new techniques to past forms or subjects. In saying this I do not intend in the least to depreciate stylization. Some of the most valuable experimenting in the nineteenth-century arts took the guise of stylization, which historically and culturally may be as significant as any mature style. For a style is a maturation that is out-dated almost the instant it appears: it is contemporary for only a brief span; then it becomes a convention. Meanwhile the artist must continue to be contemporary—which means that he must not rest confidently in a style. The stylizations of the nineteenth century prove that many artists knew they were standing on a boundary. Art always thrives near boundaries, must always be pressing toward boundaries.

The various nineteenth-century stylizations make another distinction in terms advisable—the difference between illustration and decoration. By illustration I mean anecdotal or "literary" painting, using a canvas to tell a story or to present an episode. In contrast, the purest form of decoration is the motif, the design accepted for its own ornamental or aesthetic sake. For the most part nineteenth-century arts were illustrative, literary, anecdotal. The emphasis on plot in the novel shows how ineradicable was the wish for a "story." The reaction against illustrative art produced symbolism, Art Nouveau, and the French painting done by a small group of Nabis or "synthetists" gathered about Maurice Denis, who rejected realism and followed the flat decorative art of Gauguin. The trend of the whole decadent movement was toward decoration and abstract art. Illustrative art is subservient to its subject; decorative or ornamental art liberates itself from subject or else treats a subject—or an object in painting—chiefly as a vehicle for representing a motif.

I have tried to describe each style or stylization as clearly as possible by mentioning painters or poets whose work exemplifies the technique being discussed. However, I must insist that nearly every painter, poet, or novelist mentioned exhibits other aspects than those I choose to consider. Monet, for instance, is a realist who is an impressionist *and* a symbolist; Gide's early symbolist tales are quite unlike *Les Faux-Monnayeurs;* Turner has an early grey phase entirely alien from his luminist phase; Corot is sometimes an illustrator and sometimes a proto-cubist; Delacroix is sometimes a romantic and again a realist; Tennyson *can* write some very bare verse; Baudelaire is a belated romantic dreamer and an early symbolist; and I trust nobody would be foolish enough to place Picasso as being only a cubist—although I feel free to speak of him as such. Nearly every work I have cited stands in quite other relations with literary or artistic history than those I specify.

More important, stylizations are always intersecting each other throughout the whole period. Manet is an impressionist who has strong resemblances to Art Nouveau and even abstract art: his *Déjeuner sur l'Herbe* is at the same instant a simplification of color, a flat pattern, and an abstract design as bodiless as the later figurations in Gris. The *fauves* like Matisse are very close to Art Nouveau; but they are also congenial to the symbolists. How hard it is to say whether Gauguin belongs to symbolism, Art Nouveau, post-impressionism, or fauvism. I am compelled to choose instances arbitrarily, without implying that styles or stylizations can be—or should be—isolated from each other.

These blockages, interferences, and intersections granted, I shall try to indicate the relations between four or more identifiable styles or stylizations: rococo with its attendant *genre pittoresque;* picturesque with its attendant romantic-symbolist technique; neo-mannerism with its attendant pre-Raphaelite, impressionist, and Art Nouveau developments; and cubism. There are others; and it would be possible and legitimate to read the whole arrangement from other points of view. Nor do I wish to imply that the picturesque is more important than romanticism or symbolism, which are major developments in themselves but which avail themselves of a certain psychology first used in the picturesque. To study the relations between these four styles or stylizations gives an interpretation of the arts I trust can be maintained. The contradictory quality of nineteenth-century thought and experience, the many unsolved problems in nineteenth-century history and art, justify our approaching them from as many different angles as we can. To take these approaches is to see, also, that tendencies like romanticism, impressionism, realism, pre-Raphaelitism, symbolism, and Art Nouveau have more than one meaning, that they fall into a cluster of meanings depending on how they are seen. It is needless to repeat that since one cannot be isolated from the others, there must be a certain overlapping in any record of such artistic movements, which change their features as they are brought together. In any event some of the techniques of rococo reappear at the close of the century. That is why it is essential to begin by talking about a style thought to be frivolous and apparently foreign to our business.

My hope is that this discussion will be taken as an essay, not as a panorama of modern art and literature. In the preface to his discerning book on the stages of contemporary French painting, Bernard Dorival remarked that he was considering only special problems, and that his treatment was necessarily schematic, incomplete, and stylized. What he said of his three volumes applies more accurately and more obviously to what follows.

Part One

ROCOCO: THE IDEA OF AN ORDER

I

POPE AND THE ROCOCO SITUATION

It is hard to speak of rococo without either condescending or else seeming to take it too seriously, for it is not one of the major styles and appears during the first half of the eighteenth century as a fugitive manifestation in decorative arts. Ordinarily it is identified with the arts of the early years of Louis XV's reign, which reduced to a more intimate scale the over-magnified dignities of Louis XIV, the formalities of a late-baroque society. Whether or not rococo derives from baroque, it is a reaction against dilated baroque art, just as painting by Watteau is a reaction against academic painting by Le Brun. Fleming that he is, Watteau keeps the realistic note of the "little masters" and turns it to the melody of his *fêtes champêtres* by means of his personal touch, his modest palette. Watteau has his own cautious etiquette, and his vision is as sophisticated as the art of Versailles, but easier and more graceful. While he was painting, Parisian architects and decorators like Lepautre and Oppenord were designing the *hôtels* that were also giving a more informal manner to the grand decorum of Versailles. These *hôtels* kept many of the mirror-like illusions of the palace, and were planned, like Versailles, with exact symmetry. But the proportions were slighter; the atmosphere was more private, adapted to the spirited conversation of the salon groups which throve on the relaxation in regal bearing; the walls were reduced to a neat balance of simple planes that were sensitively decorated with fronds, tendrils, or little knots of weapons and hunting gear known as trophies. These delicate naturalistic details were used as ornamental motifs playing over the clear geometry of the architectural structure. The distinctive quality of rococo is taste, that indefinable but very responsive faculty referred to by the French as *je ne sais quoi.* Rococo shrinks the grandeurs of the preceding baroque, but without in the least vulgarizing the manners of a new middle-class society that could hardly take monarchy as seriously as it was taken in the splendid days of Louis XIV. This society needed a smaller, less pretentious theatre than was provided for the Sun King. After the pompous alleys at Versailles we see the quiet poetic vistas opening beyond Watteau's gay little parties, arranged in the diminished rococo activity which has the tempo of the minuet and the fragility of porcelain.

Rococo, then, seems to be an anti-climax. Unlike baroque, rococo produced very little theory since its artists were inclined by temperament to be unacademic and unpedantic: they had a touch rather than a system. Yet rococo is a legitimate—indeed, a recurring—style, and trifling as it may be, is singularly important because it is the last coherent style before the latter eighteenth century, and the nineteenth, lost a style and had, instead, only stylizations. In fact, the return to a style at the close of the nineteenth century came in part through the neo-rococo methods of Art Nouveau. This is why we must deal with rococo as a modern style. It is a watershed, possibly because it came with the enlightenment, the age when science began to affect deeply our view of the world. Sir Isaac Newton was still alive while rococo flourished.

There is the awkwardness, too, that the early eighteenth century is in many ways uncongenial to us, and rococo is an aspect of the very consciousness of that period. This consciousness is perhaps best represented by the only considerable poet of rococo, Alexander Pope, who is the least sympathetic to us moderns. It seems, then, unfortunate but unavoidable to approach the rococo problem by first dealing with Pope's particular kind of poetic sensibility, and, without claiming too much, putting him in a certain perspective. We had better admit at once that we need not like Pope; but this concession made, we must also admit that Pope was, quite in Gertrude Stein's sense, a contemporary artist—a poet in full harmony with the culture and thought of his day. It may help to repeat what Dr. Johnson said in answer to a question raised even in the mid-eighteenth century—"whether Pope was a poet." With great assurance Johnson replied, "If Pope be not a poet, where is poetry to be found? To circumscribe poetry by a definition will only show the narrowness of the definer, though a definition which shall exclude Pope will not easily be made."

Pope is unique—limited, perhaps, but able to write poetry because he brought to verse a singular mode of belief that made his art possible. It is a mode of belief no longer tenable, in spite of the curious affiliations between rococo and Art Nouveau, the bridge from the late nineteenth century to the abstract art of the moderns. The science of an age can influence belief, and each age has a prevailing science, which itself reflects a mode of consciousness. Pope was born into a Newtonian world.

To indicate more clearly Pope's rococo mode of belief we might try to distinguish it from ours. For a long while we have supposed that poetry can hardly be written unless the poet has at his disposal some myth; and we have often been told that science has deprived us of myth, and thus of a poetic vision of life, making the poet's task almost impossibly difficult. Science, we say, has "deprived man of his spiritual heritage" and "those basic fables and symbols" by which man lives. I. A. Richards' essay on *Science and Poetry* (1926) is somewhat dated; yet we seem to have accepted his opinion that our "universe of mathematics" has made obsolete "the magical view"—that is, "the belief in a world of Spirits and Powers which control events, and which can be evoked and, to some extent, controlled themselves by human practices." Richards went on to explain that poetry and other arts arose with this magical view—and "may pass away with it." How can poetry, he asked, deal with a God who is subject to a theory of relativity? So our poetic beliefs are "like a bed of dahlias whose sticks have been removed." To be sure, Ernst Cassirer has convinced us that a mythical view of the world is more ineradicable than Richards presumed; but even Cassirer grants that "in the new light of science mythical perception has to fade away." In desperation we have tried to find myth in Freudian symbols, in Grail romances, in Jungian archetypes, in the legendary adventures of Stephen Dedalus, or in Celtic twilights. True myth, however, is a belief unconsciously held, and we have been hyper-conscious about the poet's need for myth. Thus Richards was forced to say that the modern poet has only an ability to make pseudo-statements detached from any genuine belief.

This kind of lament about the difficulty of taking a mythical view is not new. At the opening of the nineteenth century Thomas Love Peacock quietly noted that there were no longer any Dryads in Hyde Park. Alexander Pope never supposed there were, or at Twickenham either. But he wrote poetry. And he made the scientific theories of his day directly available to his sensibility by a poetry of discourse, the verse essay. Rightly or wrongly we have presumed—for more than a century—that this is no way to write poetry. We have agreed that this is only verse at "the level of prose commentary." We hear, too, that Descartes and Newton killed poetry.

The simple truth is that they did not. They killed a certain kind of poetry, doubtless—but not poetry. As our closing chapter may suggest, Wordsworth was probably correct when in 1800 he said in one of the most enlightened passages anybody has written about poetry:

> If the labours of men of science should ever create any material revolution, direct or indirect, in our condition, and in the impressions which we habitually receive, the poet will sleep then no more than at present; he will be ready to follow the steps of the man of science, not only in those general indirect effects, but he will be at his side, carrying sensation into the midst of the objects of the science itself. The remotest discoveries of the chemist, the botanist, or mineralogist will be as proper objects of the poet's art as any upon which it can be employed, if the

> time should ever come when these things shall be familiar to us, and the relations under which they are contemplated by the followers of these respective sciences shall be manifestly and palpably material to us as enjoying and suffering beings.

Wordsworth himself "moved his wings" in the atmosphere of science—the eighteenth-century associationist psychology, which he continually employed to *discuss* the loss and recovery of his poetic vision.

Is there not a poetry of discourse, unmythical to the degree of being almost expository? Lucretius wrote such poetry. Much of Dante's *Comedy*—notably the culminating discussions in the *Paradise* on free will, grace, and sin—is such a poetry of discourse, an intense and accurate explication crystallizing the scholastic theorems of Aquinas in a language of the mind directed to the mind. (We have, however, preferred the drama of *Hell* to the intellectualism of the *Paradise*.)

Obviously Pope is not Dante in either intensity or intellect. Yet as the most successful poet of the enlightenment he faced a specifically eighteenth-century task in poetry: to make accessible to art the Newtonian rationalism which had caused a revolution in the life of man as a thinking and believing being. In his verse essays he wrote a poetry of exposition originating in ideas and using a special kind of verbal decoration: the poem as idea and ornament. Here we are concerned with this poetry only as it represents a legitimate style in the history of the arts. Pope is exceptional, if not anomalous, in English literature, and unquestionably the major poet of his age—the age after Boileau, producing so little verse in France that the historians apologize by saying this was an age of prose. Pope has a curious relation to the late-baroque sensibility and art of Dryden and Racine, since he seems to use their structure of balance, opposition, counter-statement, and antithesis. But Pope's language is not the language of Dryden or Racine, and his verse does not show a late-baroque mode of consciousness, which is more robust in Dryden and psychologically more inward in Racine's analysis of the self. Pope belongs to another tradition in art-forms, the rococo. And rococo is not merely a weightless or filagreed baroque. Rococo appears in an age of reason, which created the poem as idea and ornament, a departure from baroque.

In his prefatory note to the *Essay on Man* Pope gives us a hint about the rococo mode of consciousness: "The science of human nature is, like all other sciences, reduced to a few clear points: there are not many certain truths in this world." Pope's reduction of human nature to a few clear points is not like the reductions in Racine's dramas because it is thought first, then felt—the idea precedes the realization as poetic experience; it is rational rather than psychological reduction. The idea of Nature behind Pope's *Essay* is a concept as abstract, as neat, as theoretic as Newton's space-time system with its primary laws of motion:

> See worlds on worlds compose one universe,
> Observe how system into system runs,
> What other planets circle other suns. . . .
> Of systems possible, if 'tis confest
> That Wisdom infinite must form the best,
> Where all must fall or not coherent be,
> And all that rises, rise in due degree;
> Then in the scale of reasoning life, 'tis plain
> There must be, somewhere, such a rank as man.

To doubt this theodicy is to sin against the "eternal Cause" that has made "this frame" with all its "nice dependencies," its "gradations just":

> The general order, since the whole began,
> Is kept in Nature, and is kept in Man.

The enlightenment has a genius for conceiving naked intellectual structures like Pope's "ethereal frame," giving coherence to scientific, ethical, and aesthetic perceptions, and endowing rationalism with a peculiar sort of conviction:

> . . . the first Almighty Cause
> Acts not by partial but by gen'ral laws.

One of the improprieties of criticism has been to set Pope with Dr. Johnson among neo-classical poets. There are at least two differences. Johnson does not "number the streaks of the tulip" whereas Pope's verse abounds with particularities of every kind—the glitter of a necklace, the apparatus of the boudoir, the carp's luster, the sheen of a pheasant's crest, the sharp accents in casual dialogue, the sneer at this or that fop. Then too, if Johnson's *Vanity of Human Wishes* judges experience in summary and formal terms, it is not rationalist. If we ask which is the more doctrinaire poet, we do not hesitate to say Pope, not Johnson, just as we would say Voltaire, not Racine—the Voltaire who could write that morality is an abstract and cosmic system:

> La morale uniforme en tout temps, en tout lieu,
> A des siècles sans fin parle au nom de ce Dieu.
> C'est la loi de Trajan, de Socrate, et la vôtre.
> De ce culte éternel la nature est l'apôtre.
> ("*La Loi Naturelle*," I)

Johnson believes that human experience agrees; but he cannot think of it in this sort of logic. He surveys man from China to Peru, but he has no concept of a "law of nature," no deistic system of the universe. Voltaire, hoping to cleanse society of its infamies, is a more entirely thinking being than even Descartes. Johnson is a moralist who cannot rationalize his imperatives in Voltaire's abstractions. The atmosphere of Voltaire's poem, like the atmosphere of his *Philosophical Dictionary,* is ideational. It is the atmosphere of Pope's *Essay on Man,* which declares Nature to be a harmonious system:

> . . . jarring interests, of themselves create
> Th' according music of a well-mixed State.
> Such is the World's great harmony, that springs
> From Order, Union, full Consent of things.

This proposition is not like Johnson's conclusions drawn from moral experience; one is tempted to call it theoretic. It is a sort of thesis Johnson did not allow himself because it is a "notion." Here Pope shows himself to be an intellectualizing artist; he begins from a notion of a metaphysical order, then illustrates again and again how this order is manifest.[1] His ideas are his visions.

Far from caring about the beauty of any abstract order, Johnson bears the full weight of his own doubts, his own prejudices, his own defeats and pains. Soberly pondering his felt moral experience, he attempts to give some comprehensive judgment on life. Pope seems not to have begun with this sort of evidence: he found current the idea of a universal order, then exemplified its aspects. It is doubtful if anyone—least of all Samuel Johnson—could systematize Johnson's beliefs into an ideology. Moving slowly with a heavy-footed pragmatism toward his affirmations, Johnson struggles stubbornly with his own inconsistencies or illogicalities—which, however, do not budge him from his convictions though they cause him great trouble. Pope, also, is inconsistent, making contradictory or even paradoxical statements; but in the *Essay on Man* these contradictions are (he thinks) resolved within the framework of a clear idea of a Natural Order serving as premise to the poem. Or they disappear, plausibly, behind a merely verbal logic, and such employable notions as "Whatever is, is right." Here is a notion Johnson would not take as an axiom. Neither Dryden nor Boileau nor any late-baroque poets existed in Pope's bright but precarious system of ideas. Pope thinks faintly, but he thinks; and he is a poet—which Voltaire, for all his mental agility, is not.

Pope has been called a talented versifier, an exquisite designer in filagree, an inhibited romantic, a vessel of petty spite, an ardent moralist, and a metaphysical ironist. We have been told he cannot be judged by *The Rape of the Lock* but only by *The Dunciad;* or not by *The Dunciad* but only by *The Rape of the Lock;* or by neither, but by his conversation pieces, or his verse essays. Actually he is a great artist in the style known as rococo, which is why his mind often guided his poetic sensibility. Admittedly he did not have a first-class mind, and admittedly his notions were superficial; nevertheless, under the sanction of a special sort of poetic intelligence Pope nearly single-handed brought a counter-movement against baroque and late-baroque in verse. The significance of Pope's poetic method, of his own mode of poetic belief, can be seen by placing him in the enlightenment that finally produced Immanuel Kant, who said that human experience is possible only when we have an "idea of an order," a "concept of an intelligible world."

Pope's "idea of an order" reveals itself in his claim that "partial ill is universal good," which seems to be a platitude. But a platitude is a platitude mainly because the speaker is not aware he is oversimplifying. We should not consider Pope's idea of an order a platitude in this sense. Instead, Pope was practicing his own kind of poetic daring, for he was trying to make the best of current science, abstract as it was, available to the poetic imagination, and without benefit of myth. The daring does not, of course, seem very rash; yet Pope is an enlightened poet, and Kant put the whole spirit of the enlightenment into his phrase *sapere aude:* Dare to use your mind. A limitation, also, was in the ideas Pope found current, since they were, thanks to Bolingbroke and others, a facile version of Newton. Before, then, defining rococo as a style, we need to consider the kind of ideas Pope used—ideas that made possible rococo architecture and poetry.

II

FICTIONS
OF THE ENLIGHTENMENT

Whitehead once remarked that "in each period there is a general form of the forms of thought." That is, the mode of thinking in each age is also a mode of consciousness. The eighteenth century is usually called an age of reason without recognizing that its rational activity was almost identical with its imaginative activity. The enlightened imagination often expressed itself *as* ideas. Since the nineteenth century, imagination has usually been put in opposition to reason, and has meant emotional power, plastic representation, or a suggestion of what cannot be stated. This may be one cause for the disappearance of a poetry of ideas.

The special consciousness in the enlightenment was grounded, as Whitehead also noted, in a system of thought framed by seventeenth-century mathematicians, a system very abstract and presenting, on the one hand, precisely located bodies, and, on the other, mind, which succeeded in constructing a conceptual framework of time and space to enclose these simply located bodies.[2] Newton was the chief architect of this world-order, and his system inspired a religious attitude called deism, centering on a God who was a mathematical intellect. I. A. Richards has asked whether poets can be expected to deal with a God who is subject to a theory of relativity. Pope succeeded, under similar circumstances, in dealing with a God who was subject to Newton's three primary laws of motion. These laws have altered; but the poetic problem is the same.

The enlightened mode of consciousness appeared at least as early as Descartes, who (d'Alembert pointed out) was both philosopher and geometer. He had his greatest influence as rationalist—one who, in his own words, could employ "long chains of reasonings, simple and easy as they are, of which geometricians make use in order to arrive at the most difficult demonstrations." During the eighteenth century the mathematical method became an international mode of thinking. Fontenelle speaks for the enlightenment when, as devotee of Descartes and Newton, he remarks that "the geometrical spirit is not so tied to geometry that it cannot be detached and carried into other branches of knowledge."

Thus the enlightenment came to rely heavily on innate ideas, those primary notions or intuitions so clear that they cannot, any more than the axioms of geometry, be doubted—or disproved. These primal ideas are not built upon evidence from the senses; for whether we wake or sleep, Descartes assures us, a square can have only four sides: "truth so clear and apparent" we cannot question it. Descartes deprives reality of color, scent, and all sensuous qualities; the essence of any body is the mathematical idea we have of that body, its length, breadth, and height, features known only by thinking them. Descartes seemed to prove that reality is not the physical world but our notion of what that world is.

Newton completed the reconstruction of the world upon the basis of abstract ideas by making his universe a mathematical system governed by gravitational laws. He located all bodies within an ideational framework of absolute time and absolute space, which were like a conceptual envelope for all things existing here or there, now or then:

> Absolute, true, and mathematical time, of itself and from its

own nature, flows equably without relation to anything external, and by another name is called duration; relative, apparent, and common time is some sensible and external (whether accurate or unequable) measure of duration by the means of motion, which is commonly used instead of true time, such as an hour, a day, a month, a year.

Absolute space, in its own nature, without relation to anything external, remains always similar and immovable. Relative space is some movable dimension or measure of absolute spaces, which our senses determine by its position to bodies and which is commonly taken for immovable space. . . .

. . . All motions may be accelerated or retarded, but the flowing of absolute time is not liable to any change. . . .

As the order of the parts of time is immutable, so also is the order of the parts of space.

(*Principia,* I)

Regulated by absolute time, absolute space, and mathematical force, the planets revolve about the sun, the moons revolve about the earth and planets, in a "most beautiful system" framed by a "Lord God, Pantokrator, or Universal Ruler" who is an abstract principle "utterly void of all body and bodily figure, and can therefore neither be seen, nor heard, nor touched; nor ought He to be worshipped under the representation of any corporeal thing." Newton's universe is a mathematical construct, and his God cannot be mythologized any better than Einstein's God of Relativity: He cannot be incarnated, but only thought. The fleshly baroque image of God—Milton's Father smiting Satan, hurling him into the abyss—has been abstracted to an *idea* of God. Even Newton's "force" is not a personal will of the deity, but a mathematical law.

Finally John Locke in his *Essay Concerning Human Understanding* (1690) decided that although there are no innate ideas in the mind, nevertheless knowledge is "nothing but the perception of the connection of and agreement or disagreement and repugnancy, of any of our ideas." Locke is a rationalist as well as an empiricist; for if the senses give us materials for knowledge, knowledge itself is a result of abstracting this sense experience to ideas and adjusting these ideas in clear relationships. So Locke, like Descartes, comes to identify knowledge with notions of size, figure, number, motion. These are the "primary qualities" of our world. The "secondary qualities" are colors, sounds, taste, and odor, the "sensible" impressions bodies make on us. We feel the world through the sensorium; but we know it only when ideas are disengaged from this sensed experience.

Locke, not Descartes, is the *doyen* of the enlightenment, which was erected upon a few simple notions—a "coherent body of underlying assumptions, widely accepted as too self-evident to need, as a whole, formal exposition or defense."[3] These preconceptions were premises to the thought of the eighteenth century, much as evolution became a premise to the thought of the nineteenth century.

The notion of a self-evident order in nature, in the mind of man, in society, caused the enlightenment to be doctrinaire in nearly all its beliefs. By the close of the seventeenth century Leibnitz conceived his universe as a system of formal atoms (monads) moving freely but regularly in a pre-established harmony, the premise of an order "so reasonable" that he can state:

> It follows farther, from the perfection of the supreme author, that not only is the order of the entire universe the most perfect possible, but also that each living mirror representing the universe in accordance with its point of view, that is to say, that each *monad*, each substantial center, must have its perceptions and its desires as well regulated as is compatible with all the rest. . . .
>
> For all is regulated in things, once for all, with as much order and harmony as is possible, supreme wisdom and goodness not being able to act except with perfect harmony.
>
> (*Principles of Nature and Grace,* 1714)

The faith of deists was based on this order, where each relation is as clear as in a geometric system; these relations, remarks Samuel Clarke, are "notoriously plain and self-evident." The world is a concord of free atoms.

Similarly the idea of a self-evident order founded by pre-established "contract" is the premise of Locke's civil government, which derives from a law of Nature, a pre-condition to polity:

> . . . it is certain there is such a law, and that too as intelligible and plain to a rational creature and a studier of that law as the positive law of commonwealths, nay, possibly much plainer; as much as reason is easier to be understood than the fancies and intricate contrivances of men.

The clarity of this law is precisely due to its being *un*written and "nowhere to be found but in the minds of men." The state of Nature, the basis of civil society, has its own law, for it is not a state of license but of reason:

> The state of Nature has a law of Nature to govern it, which obliges everyone; and reason, which is that law, teaches all mankind who will but consult it, that being all equal and independent, no one ought to harm another in his life, health, liberty, or possessions.

Locke never intended to "turn man loose to an unrestrained liberty, before he has reason to guide him"—that would be not liberty but a contest for power. "The freedom then of man, and liberty of acting according to his own will, is grounded on his having reason, which is able to instruct him in that law he is to govern himself by." Baroque politics were founded on authoritarian power; Locke's politics are based upon reason, which is the law of Nature. Like Leibnitz's formal atom moving by its own will in a pre-established accord with other atoms, Locke's civil man has a "natural liberty to be free from any superior power on earth, but to have only the law of Nature for his rule." Leibnitz's monads, Locke's free man, Newton's planets each rushing with its own force in its own orbit but obeying the "natural" laws of gravity—all are parts of a "most beautiful system."

The various Declarations of the Rights of Man could hardly have been phrased without primary political concepts that could be held only in the ideational atmosphere of the enlightenment. At the close of the century Adam Smith brought this idea of order into economic life as well. Each acquisitive member of society obeys his "natural" impulse to buy in the cheapest market and sell in the dearest, asserting his freedom in an open exchange self-regulated by the "natural" laws of supply and demand. These economic principles resemble the literary principle that—as Rymer and Dennis said—poetry submits to a law of Nature: namely, that "man is everywhere the same" and that poetry "can neither have greatness or real beauty if it swerves from the laws which reason severely prescribes it." For Pope, also, Parnassus is a kingdom of Reason, since the poet's judgment must "follow Nature."

Alexander Pope was no philosopher; but he assumed the existence of certain primary notions—standards that seem to be innate in a nearly Cartesian way. Critics may blunder, he admits—

> Yet if we look more closely, we shall find
> Most have the seeds of judgment in their mind:
> Nature affords at least a glimmering light;
> The lines, tho' touch'd but faintly, are drawn right.

The categories of judgment are there. I have intentionally used the word categories, for the verses remind us that the rationalism of the enlightenment was, ironically, justified by Immanuel Kant, who was able to show that only our notions of time, space, cause, and effect enable us to deal with a world we cannot understand by the senses or in itself; and our mind by means of "categories of experience" brings among our confused impressions "the idea of an order" which alone makes experience intelligible, usable, or even thinkable. The enlightenment was sure that knowledge is rational knowledge, and in his own way Kant affirmed the worth of ideas.

When we seek a name for this "general form" of the forms of enlightened thought, we find it in Jeremy Bentham, one of the last thinkers of the enlightenment and one of the harshest critics of its rationalism. He would call it a *fiction.*[4] As Bentham uses the term, a fiction is not a "perceptible entity" but an invention of the mind and language, created "by the grammatical form of the discourse employed in speaking of it." Our ideas of Right, Obligation, Power, Prerogative, Possession, and

Property are fictions, for actual "existence is not meant to be ascribed" to them; they are affirmations. "To language then—to language alone—it is, that fictitious entities owe their existence—*their impossible, yet indispensable, existence.*" We do not intend fictions to have the sort of reality we ascribe to objects in nature. Yet they are necessary to the activity of the mind. "Of nothing, therefore, that has place, or passes in our mind, can we speak, or so much as think, otherwise than in the way of *fiction.*" Surfaces and lines, Bentham notes, are fictions; and we cannot have a geometry without them. They are "feigned for the purpose of discourse," a "contrivance but for which language, or, at any rate, language in any form superior to that of the language of the brute creation, could not have existence."

No better comment has been made on the enlightened mode of belief, its "formation of ideas." Bentham understands that in his age moral and political imperatives took the form of fictions—"the furniture of minds" he calls them—notions which, once conceived, are spoken of as "real," not as "pneumatic," entities. For instance, "the word *right* is the name of a fictitious entity; one of those objects the existence of which is feigned for the purpose of discourse—by a fiction so necessary that without it human discourse could not be carried on." And there is "a considerable degree of sameness" in the ideas with which the human mind is furnished. Bentham realizes that the concept of right, having no objective existence in the course of history, is a means by which man orders his own existence in history and imposes upon history a principle of justice.

The enlightenment was thus able to live in a world of ideas very consciously, being aware that its fictions were contrivances of the mind, a particular mode of belief. It gave rational meaning to sense data by the fictions it imposed on them.

This enlightened mode of consciousness has been reinterpreted recently by Vaihinger, who regarded fictions as rational structures invented by the self to assist it in mastering experience.[5] Vaihinger classified various sorts of fictions more carefully than Bentham. First there are *legitimate fictions* which we consciously hold in the released condition of assumptions or agreements we know are empirically unprovable but nevertheless useful; we regard these fictions, says Vaihinger in his famous phrase, *as if* (*als ob*) they were verifiable. Most of the "self-evident" truths of the enlightenment were held *as if* they were verifiable: the equality of men, the state of nature, the social compact, the inalienable rights and truths. Then there is the *semi-fiction,* Vaihinger says, which is only partially verifiable or "referential." Adam Smith's economic laws are semi-fictions. The *hypothesis* is a fiction needing to be supported or proved by objective evidence (nineteenth-century science was developed from hypotheses). The *dogma* is a fiction we accept as an arbitrary affirmation necessary to quell fear or doubt, or to relieve tension in the self. Behind the dogma is some urgent need.

The essential genius of the enlightenment was its ability to erect fictions or semi-fictions. We need not, for our purposes, ask whether the fictions of natural right, natural law, and natural order may not at times have been phrased under dogmatic pressures; perhaps they were in Locke—certainly they were in ardent revolutionary minds like Paine and Condorcet. The main point is that Vaihinger is describing the general form of enlightened thought when he says that "ideational constructs are in the strict sense of the term real fictions when they are not only in contradiction with reality but self-contradictory in themselves." Geometry, for instance, rests on a basis of real fictions, for the very concepts of point, line, plane, circle, and sphere are all grounded in "unreal" situations and are also self-contradictory: a point is a logical absurdity, and we can hardly build a solid world from points, lines, and plane surfaces. Yet these fictions are, like the value 3.1416 . . ., essential to rational discourse even if we never see a point, a line, a plane, or a circle. The geometer must believe these fictions; and, in a special sense, he does, although he knows they are self-contradictory. Pope's *Essay on Man,* like Locke's *Civil Government,* Smith's *Wealth of Nations,* or Jefferson's Declaration of Independence, is filled with real fictions such as "the general order," "universal good," and "Nature."

Having achieved this fictional view of the world, the enlightenment found it could dispense with myth, that magical view of the "Spirits and Powers which control events, and which can be evoked and, to some extent, controlled themselves by human practices." Milton tried to take a mythical or magical view of the world in the baroque theatre of *Paradise Lost,* where the universe was not yet neutralized by science, where anthropomorphic images of God and Satan could still be invoked. For Milton as poet the gods are still, in a sense, on Olympus, and he could still animate his world—Eden, at least—by human agencies. But even Milton was having trouble with these magical images and supernal agents, and after the enlightenment set in, all such mythological figures became either the sprites of Pope's *Rape of the Lock* or the personifications of eighteenth-century verse. The language of myth is, prevailingly, metaphor, since metaphor dramatizes the world, anthropomorphizes reality. Pope uses the simile, not the metaphor, as his usual poetic device.

Whatever we believe myth to be, there is a difference between a baroque and a fictional view of the world. Here is the importance of rococo as a style—to this extent the first modern style. The enlightenment dispensed with Milton's plastic and magical theatre. Milton's baroque cosmogony becomes Addison's spacious firmament on high, a "spangled frame" where God is an astronomical principle and the universe is a radiant system of mathematical law. The worlds are still a divine order; but the planets run in Newtonian orbits—"In Reason's ear they all rejoice." If there is drama in Addison's universe, it is the action of disembodied forces, not a mythical drama played by baroque gods and heroes.

The fictional view of the world means a new situation in poetry, a new relation between the poem and the mind. Is it unfair to say that Milton's resplendent Eden and Heaven were already anachronistic, a poetic scene ill suited to Milton's rationalizing theology? Unfortunately at times Milton's intellect seems superior to his poetic myth. Thus *Paradise Lost* was written under adverse poetic conditions, since its myth—however triumphantly successful as baroque art—was incapable of enlisting the full belief of Milton's great intelligence. His poetic world-picture was not fully capable of representing his rational world-picture. He tried to take a magical view of the world at the threshold of an age tending toward a neutralized scientific view.

As poet of the enlightenment Pope came to terms with his intellectual milieu. He did not try to create (or even to believe in?) Milton's sort of myth. Somewhat like Dante when he wrote the *Vita Nuova,* Pope showed a new poetic mentality. By means of his fictions of Order and Nature—grounded as they were in the "best thought of his age"—Pope wrote a verse that enabled him to express his convictions without making the universe an anthropomorphic theatre. His poetic medium is adequate to his world-picture:

> Look round our world, behold the chain of love
> Combining all below and all above.
> See plastic Nature working to this end,
> The single atoms to each other tend,
> Attract, attracted to, the next in place,
> Formed and impelled its neighbour to embrace.
> See matter next, with various life endued,
> Press to one center still, the general good.

These fictions are naïve (certainly we can no longer believe them); yet Pope solved his poetic problem by accepting a poetry of discourse, a medium that required, for Pope, no "suspension of disbelief," no artificial mechanisms or inventions. It is a medium that assimilated poetry to the prevailing culture without exacting any self-deception. In a certain way, then, Milton's poetic mechanism compared with Pope's causes a kind of obscurantism, a dread of being contemporary. All good poetry is, of course, traditional; however, it may be questioned whether any poetry is successful if it is not as contemporary as it can be, intellectually as well as technically. Otherwise there is a sad truth in Peacock's sneer that the poetic mind marches, like a crab, backwards, living "in the days that are past." If we are to reject Pope there must be other grounds for contempt; at least his belief and his medium are not anachronistic. We are not, howbeit, concerned with the truth of poetry—only with the singular importance of rococo in the development of modern styles. It does represent a break with the past.

Pope is contemporary in a still further sense, for the eighteenth century was not only rationalist but also empirical: as

Hazard puts it, the age was rational by temper but empirical in its activities. The enlightenment arose in Locke's rationalism and Newton's mathematic; but it also produced the botanical observations of Buffon. There is a similarity between Pope's poetic method and Buffon's scientific method, since Buffon has a rationalist system of Nature but is also a close student of flora (botany is a characteristic eighteenth-century science, as the intense interest of Thomas Gray and others having such a fine eye for flowers proves). In discussing "Truth" Buffon shows the two sides of the eighteenth-century mind, its theoretical temper and its empirical activities:

> There are many kinds of truths, and we are used to placing in the first order the mathematical truths, which are, however, only truths of definition; these definitions are based on *simple suppositions, but abstract,* and all the truths of this kind are simply the logical but always abstract consequences of those definitions. . . .
>
> On the contrary, physical truths are not arbitrary, and do not depend upon us; instead of being grounded on suppositions we have made, they are *founded only on the facts;* a succession of similar facts. . . . The word truth includes both, and consequently indicates two different "truths". . . .
>
> (*Natural History*)

In physical science, Buffon holds, one proceeds "from observation to observation." The journals and letters of the time have passage after passage of the most delicate and personal examination of nature. If Pope is the poet of enlightened fictions, he is also the designer of toyshops of the heart with an eye for every sharp detail:

> Here files of pins extend their shining rows,
> Puffs, powders, patches, bibles, billet-doux.

His foreground is filled with minute perceptions. He is sensitive to colors, sounds, textures, and all the "secondary" qualities of things. In a quite technical sense Pope is rococo—the almost unique poet in a style that is neither Milton's nor Johnson's. It is a minor style, to be sure, but groundwork for the towering, cloudy romantic dreams that followed.

III

ROCOCO

AS A STYLE

A great many loose definitions of rococo have been made, probably because this style expresses a very transitory situation. Behind it, at the close of the seventeenth century, was the authoritarian and resplendent baroque, which had sobered into a formal and, at times, grave late-baroque art. All the while, the Cartesian spirit was having its effects, for, as Cassirer notes, after the mid-seventeenth century a rationalist mentality "permeates all fields of knowledge until it dominates not only philosophy, but also literature, morals, political science, and sociology." This rationalism did not, however, paralyze the arts until the close of the eighteenth century, when the generation of the French Revolution devoted itself to the "elementary geometry" of Directory art, the Adams, Hepplewhite, and the hollow classicism of Jacques Louis David. Serving as a transition or a point of intersection at the beginning of the eighteenth century, rococo was affected by the Cartesian spirit, but did not capitulate to its geometry; it was also affected by the proprieties of late-baroque art, and by the taste and almost feminine sensibility of La Rochefoucauld, La Fontaine, and French artists who had an *esprit de finesse.* This perishable style is hard to define because it is, paradoxically, both lively and formal. It accepts the decencies with a personal touch and expressiveness; it is artful and natural; it is a public and conventional style with an inalienably private note; its formulas allow ease and freedom. It is an art that makes the most of slight materials without overstraining them.

We cannot do better than to heed the definitions in Fiske Kimball's *Creation of the Rococo,* a strictly historical description of this style.[6] Properly speaking, rococo belongs to the age of Louis XV and to France, and even if it appeared in architecture, it is not so much an architectural style as a development within the decorative arts: "the primary sphere of the movement was, to a degree almost unique in artistic history, in the realm of decoration: in the interior, whether domestic or religious, and in ornament, chiefly the ornament of surface." This ornament of the surface did not spring from baroque, nor in spite of its oriental fantasy is it directly indebted to *chinoiserie.* Instead, it is an architectural use, by designers like Pierre Lepautre and Oppenord, of the arabesque motifs invented by decorators and painters like Berain and Watteau. Collections of trophies and other ornaments—for example, Watteau's *Recueil d'arabesques, trophées, et autres ornements décoratifs*—were engraved and published while rococo was appearing in architecture. The arabesque design had been used earlier in gardening and in "compartments of ornament" painted by Le Brun. In any case, rococo is first of all a style of ornamentation—not, it is to be noted, basically illustrative, but decorative. This distinction is important in view of the decorative Art Nouveau, the neo-rococo of the latter nineteenth century. Rococo treated the ornamental motif as an end in itself.

Baroque architecture had often used the cartouche, a highly plastic and sculptural form. The arabesque was unlike the cartouche, which was moulded from heavy baroque masses. Rococo decoration was a play of intricate and sharp naturalistic detail upon a flat or empty surface, and as arabesque motifs extended into architecture, the baroque emphasis on columns, pilasters, and richly plastic orders diminished. The shift from baroque pompousness to rococo taste in decoration can be seen by comparing the materialism of Grinling Gibbons' choir stalls in Saint Paul's (1695–97) with the fastidious naturalism of Pierre Lepautre's choir stalls in Notre Dame (1710–11).

During the rococo period, covering roughly the first half of the eighteenth century, the architectural framework was no longer massive, but reduced to thin pilaster strips defining the simple panels of walls, the room becoming a symmetrical space with a balance of central and diagonal elements, a skeleton of almost gothic frailty. In Lepautre's rooms designed at the opening of the century,

> . . . one of the most striking qualities was the abandonment of plasticity: in architectural members and decorative motifs alike. The column soon completely vanished from his work, the pilaster, greatly attenuated and reduced in relief, survived only as a strip, its cap and base dissolving. The wall panels, increased in height, had their mouldings likewise diminished in projection. . . . Interlaces and scrolls . . . invaded the panels themselves at top and bottom and around the central rosette. Not the plastic baroque cartouche, which survived only as a shield of arms, but a smooth surface with surrounding bands and scrolls became the typical field for decorative enrichment.
> (*Creation of the Rococo*)

The walls became a field for the ornamental motifs that required exquisite workmanship—finely executed bands, interlaces, palm branches, leafage, stems, acanthus scrolls, flowers, sprays, and tendrils carefully presented upon a neutral plane [1].

These fragile passages, very sharply cut, with involved detail, overspread the panel to create a "delicate linear organism" replacing the lavish columns, heavy light and shadow, and bulky architectural members that baroque had used. In rococo the firm, thin architectural skeleton, which almost vanished, was like a Newtonian world-order erected by mathematical concepts, those colorless mental fictions behind the intricate appearances of things; or, perhaps, like Locke's idea of a state of Nature as the invisible design beneath the social order. To heighten the fictional quality of rococo space the architect often

Archives Photographiques, Paris

I HÔTEL DE MATIGNON, PARIS: *Interior*

used mirrors. In the Hôtel de Soubise mirrors not only empty the walls but also wipe away volumes until one seems to move through a constantly changing infinity—which, however, is firmly ordered by the balanced central and diagonal elements. Behind all this illusion there are equations. The individual decorative details in this rococo space are freed or liberated, yet repeated, restated, with a regularity that recalls Pope's world of

Windsor Forest, "Where order in variety we see / And where, though all things differ, all agree."

As Fiske Kimball points out, Oppenord and other rococo architects used a highly conventional ground plan—"the pre-existing walls of rooms of simple and indifferent form." Having simplified and regularized the fabric of their walls to a framework of symmetrical planes, they embroidered decorative fields on these neutral surfaces by C-curves, reverse curves, interlaces, and swirls. Thus the face of the wall became organic although the architecture was basically a geometric abstraction of uncomplicated rectangles and cubes. The brilliant arabesque inscription releases itself with a spontaneous vitality from the invisible and unpretentious mathematic of the walls; yet the mathematic of the walls was always there as a supporting fiction, a pre-established harmony taken for granted—posited without any great attempt at originality but with perfect clarity.

In general, then, the rococo substructure is rationalized in simplest terms, and on the surface the bright precise naturalistic decoration develops with occult balance rather than with mathematical symmetry. Among the reasons for the vitality of rococo ornamentation is the fact that one side of a panel never exactly repeats the design of the opposite side; there is equivalence, not mere restatement. The interlace continuously varies its pattern, and the variety of naturalistic detail is so spirited that without the symmetry of the substructure it would look confused. Walls curve into ceilings by ornamented covings that give an illusion more cunning than the baroque theatre. In a sense rococo is exoskeletal because it ramifies upon a surface—"lives along the line," like Pope's intricately moving spider. As in flamboyant gothic, the wall becomes imperceptible behind leafage, sprays, tendrils, and scrolls so finely executed that they dazzle. The rococo artist has exquisite facility in recording the secondary qualities of things, as Locke would call them. The plain order of the rectangular room, with balance of memberings and windows, is an abstract framework capable of sustaining the brittle naturalism springing from the framework itself.

These developments in rococo came between 1700 and 1740

in the interiors of the Petit-Luxembourg, the Hôtel de Toulouse, the Hôtel de Roquelaure [2], the Hôtel de Soubise, and elsewhere in Paris—for rococo is an essentially urban art, like the art of the *Spectator* and the Addisonian essay. It is an art of a middle class that has not yet been entirely hemmed in by the metropolis. It is, quite literally, urbane: in a way baroque was not. The city had not yet become a prison; and the middle class had not yet been deprived of tradition by a machine age. Hence the note of taste and politeness in rococo. These classes needed an art less domineering than baroque. Pope was one of the poets to earn his living by writing for this new class. He came at a moment when he could be on easy terms with Bolingbroke, and he wrote a verse unequalled in decorative finesse. Rococo is a sign of an interim social condition, with the new individualism of a Newtonian world.

Meanwhile, also, rococo painters like Watteau, Lancret, Pater, and Bigari were situating their volumes in a new sort of space. If baroque concentrates its masses and tends to crowd its bulky figures into the foreground, rococo painting breaks up its masses, allows empty space into the foreground, and opens infinite distances behind its artificial little *fêtes champêtres*. Rococo space has its own sort of vacancy because the bodies in it are located casually, in *nodules,*[7] leaving them in a very free situation so they can move spontaneously. It is almost as if the persons in Watteau's small garden scenes were endowed with a "natural liberty"—a freedom they can assume without asserting any baroque force or will. "As those move easiest who have learned to dance," says Pope, conveying the impression we have of these emancipated shepherds and shepherdesses in rococo panels, who express their mood without constraint and without effort.

In mid-century the Italian Bigari created in his paintings a remarkable visionary architecture where puppet-like figures move gracefully in a space that seems emptier than powerful baroque spaces. It is as if the sense of a vast but orderly Newtonian system had naturally penetrated this rococo world, tempering the baroque stress, isolating bodies, atomizing the episode, and making space dominate mass instead of having mass dominate space, as it did in baroque. The rococo foreground

Archives Photographiques, Paris

2 HÔTEL DE ROQUELAURE, PARIS: *Panel*

may be intricate; but it is never crowded. Yet small as these figurines are, rococo space is not overwhelming; the sprightly personages in Watteau and Lancret are perfectly at ease in these great vacancies; at their own pleasure they collect into groups; they move here and there readily, though their progress is never disorderly. They have the manners of the amateur; and the pose of the amateur—the distaste for pedantry—is a rococo attitude. The nonchalance in Watteau, Bigari, or Lancret is due partly to rococo skill in *locating* bodies tactfully—almost as Newton successfully located the bodies in his universe by periodic law or periodic intervals. The scale in Guardi's Venetian scenes [3], for instance, is so nicely managed that although the dimensions are trivial, the effect of emptiness and room for movement is almost miraculous. The most intricate rococo ornament has, like rococo painting, an atmospheric freedom; every detail has its own individuality. For rococo art and culture have a strong sense of personal identity, or tempera-

The Samuel H. Kress Collection, National Gallery of Art, Washington, D.C.

3 GUARDI (FRANCESCO): *Campo San Zanipolo*

4 GASPARI (PIETRO): *Prospettiva*

ment, that is not aggressive but a private and intimate consciousness of distinctions that are understood rather than argued. *The Rape of the Lock* is a curiously personal poem, considering its deliberate artificiality. Watteau's scenes are curiously intimate, considering their deliberate affectations.

Rococo painting inherited from *genre* in the Low Countries a special non-heroic or even anti-heroic note, not only in Watteau and the French *conversation galante* but, more significantly, in landscapes that *play* with nature in the Italian *veduta fantastica,* notably the waterfalls painted by Giuseppe Zais. Rococo landscapes suggest that man's relation to the world has changed. Ruysdael and Hobbema had subordinated man to nature—at the cost of almost ignoring the figures, who are negligible in their version of *paysage.* By contrast, the drama in Fragonard's parklike scenes centers on small gallants who are drenched in smoky sunshine. The innumerable fantasies by Marieschi, Ricci, and Zuccarelli are enlivened by miniature peasants dispersed amid immense ruins. Sometimes, with Moretti, Gaspari, or Battaglioli, they appear in an architectural *prospettiva* [4]. Everywhere the human being is brought into personal but unheroic relation with the scene. This is also true in Guardi, whose Venetian courtyards are seen through archways saturated with bronze light; the marble of his *Dogana* or *Santa Maria della Salute* shimmers through shadows cast up by the torpid green waters of the canal, for Guardi was already "touching" his scenes like the impressionists. These perceptions of waterfalls, ruins, and canals are capricious, dreamlike, and momentary, showing how the rococo *veduta* is an early variety of the picturesque, placing man in an atmosphere. In handling the vistas of *The Champs Élysées* [5] or *Fête in a Park* Watteau uses the rococo formula for clustering figures, making them exist in a quality of light or air, just as they are clustered slightly off axis in Pope's *Windsor Forest,* where nymphs and their lovers linger amid groves that half admit and half exclude the day. Immersed as these figurines are in a climate, they do not lose their individuality. Guardi's fine rococo eye sees each of the citizens of Venice personally as they parade in myriads through the vast Piazza San Marco during festival seasons.

Since rococo space is emptier than baroque space, it seems to

5 WATTEAU: *The Champs Élysées*

be merely an area for motion, giving rococo environment an elasticity lacking in the more monumental baroque arena. Tiepolo's ceilings open up the baroque mythologies, dispersing them airily across new celestial voids. By their vivacious gathering, the rococo figures in Watteau's *Embarkation for Cythera* or in *fêtes champêtres* by Lancret or Pater make the space about them resilient until nature appears to be alive. But the rhythms in rococo nature—easy as they are—do not suggest the heavy biological forces pulsing through post-Darwinian nature, felt by Whitman as a "procreant urge." The reigning nineteenth-century science was biology; the reigning eighteenth-century science was astronomy, the Newtonian system. The colloquial periods in rococo conversation and letters, like the intervals in rococo painting, suggest liberty without collision or confusion.

Yet deep within the geometry of Newton's system the deists thought they could find some animation, a "sense sublime" of something interfused. This subtle motion seems to play through the tendrils and fronds of rococo ornament. Rococo begins as decoration of an abstract system by naturalistic details; but it leads, with its delicate spray and leafage, to a sense of "natural piety." God is not only a mathematical mind; He is soon felt to be a spirit, a cosmic breath. Thus the Newtonian system gave rise to a rococo paradox: the geometry of the universe became animated with organic rhythms (not yet felt "in the blood"), and Pope, accepting a deistic vision of nature, reaches an intermediate state between Newton and Wordsworth:

> See thro' this air, this ocean, and this earth,
> All matter quick, and bursting into birth:
> Above, how high progressive life may go!
> Around, how wide! how deep extend below!
> Vast chain of being, which from God began;
> Natures ethereal, human, angel, man,
> Beast, bird, fish, insect, what no eye can see,
> No glass can reach; from infinite to thee;
> From thee to nothing . . .

The rococo artist, like Pope, finds himself in an interregnum between baroque and the oncoming romantic pantheism. None the less Pope's verse, like Lepautre's architecture and Watteau's painting, belongs to a distinguishable style.

IV

ARABESQUE IN VERSE

When the *Essay on Man* appeared in 1733–34, Pope wrote a prefatory note on "The Design" in which he claimed that the merit of the poem was "in steering betwixt the extremes of doctrines seemingly opposite." He hoped to show that he could harmonize social rank with equality, self-love with benevolence, reason with passion, and partial ill with universal good. He believed he could reduce these seeming contradictions by means of an idea of Nature, one of the luminous fictions of the enlightened mind as self-contradictory as any of the axioms of geometry. Pope was aware of the simplifications in this fiction, for he insists throughout the poem how necessary it is to believe that

> The least confusion but in one, not all
> That system only, but the Whole must fall.

His theodicy is a concept as doctrinaire, and as consciously held, as Newton's space-time system: the "mighty maze" has a "plan"—

> . . . this frame, the bearings, and the ties,
> The strong connexions, nice dependencies,
> Gradations just.

Pope did not need to draw on Leibnitz, Bolingbroke, Shaftesbury, or the other deists, since the fiction of an order was already accepted at the opening of the century, the notion that "All are but parts of one stupendous Whole." Not compromise, but a balance of extremes, is the principle behind this Order. This overruling sense of order was congenial not only to the Cartesian mind but also to late-baroque art.

The tectonics of Pope's *Essay* are those of the rococo chamber, where there is a perfect balance of vertical and diagonal elements with median symmetry serving as an inconspicuous framework for the flat, neutral surfaces like the "few plain truths" in which Pope has such confidence. "Order is Heaven's first law." In his *Anecdotes* Spence reports Pope as saying that "all the rules of architecture would be reducible to three or four heads. The justness of the openings, bearings upon bearings, and the regularity of the pillars." This fiction of equilibrium enabled Pope to translate Milton's myths into "higher levels of abstraction"[8] so that poetry could deal conceptually with religious themes.

The fiction of an order was especially valuable in a universe that was becoming atomized. While the astronomers were discovering a "plurality of worlds," as Fontenelle had it, the moralists were finding how "the whole duty of man" makes problems for the private conscience—since protestant individualism was being extended into the ethics of daily life; and the literary critics were finding that in spite of all the rules everyone has his own personal taste, a faculty liable to be erratic unless one has a correct idea of the "just standard" of Nature:

> . . . which is still the same:
> Unerring Nature, still divinely bright,
> One clear, unchanged, and universal light.

In science, ethics, society, and art it was necessary to seek some sort of unity amid all this diversity. So in the *Essay on Man* all the minutely seen objects in a "mighty maze"—"weeds, oaks, spiders, bees, halcyons, lawns, floods, roses, rills—are held in place by their relation and meaning to a divine and universal plan."[9] The Third Earl of Shaftesbury had the same concern to unify "Glorious Nature":

> Now, in this which we call the *Universe,* whatever the perfection may be of any particular systems, or whatever single parts may have proportion, unity, or form within themselves; yet if they are not united all in general, in *one* system, but are, in respect of one another, as the driven sands, or clouds, or breaking waves; then there being no coherence in the whole, there can be inferred no order, no proportion, and consequently no project or design. But if none of these parts are independent, but all apparently united, then is the *Whole a system* complete, according to one *simple, consistent,* and *uniform Design.*
>
> (*The Moralists,* Part II, sec. iv)

Rococo is an art very attentive to the individual within the abstract plan. As literary critic Pope appreciates individual talent, a "lucky license," those "nameless graces which no methods teach," and all the personal tastes going like our watches—"none just alike." Still he is able to reconcile personal tastes and talents with an abiding law of Nature:

> Those rules of old, discovered, not devised,
> Are Nature still, but Nature methodized;
> Nature, like Liberty, is but restrained,
> By the same laws which first herself ordained.

Nature, then, proves to be the classics, which are a fiction in Pope's criticism analogous to the fiction of a state of Nature antecedent to Locke's social compact, a fiction that has as little to do with what Homer or Horace actually wrote as the history of Athens or Rome has to do with the fiction of a primal civil society. Both fictions insure the freedom of the individual within a presupposed order. Together with Locke, Pope can close in from the harmony of the whole to the tastes and conduct of each person:

True wit is Nature to advantage dressed,
What oft was thought, but ne'er so well expressed;
Something whose truth convinc'd at sight we find,
That gives us back the image of our mind.

Pope's "rules of old,"—discovered, not devised—are not grounded in classic texts but in a formula of correctness held almost *a priori* in the critic's mind by a consensus, agreement, or unwritten compact. Thus those who would climb Parnassus must first "follow Nature." As moralist, too, Pope accepts a fiction of an order: "The state of Nature was the reign of God."

For Pope even the passions were fictions. One of his most remarkable poems, *Eloisa to Abelard,* translates the emotions to a level of abstraction perhaps unknown until Freudian concepts began to affect modern literature. It is sometimes said that Pope was unable to deal with strong feeling, and that therefore this poem is merely rhetorical. It would be more accurate to say that Pope deals with strong feelings thematically, for *Eloisa to Abelard* is a *study* of strong feeling. The poem is dramatic, especially in its movement; but it is a form of discourse *about* passion rather than a recreation of passionate experience. Pope is not so concerned with Eloisa herself as he is with a fiction of a ruling passion which he mentioned in the *Essay on Man,* saying the passions are modes of self-love, a gale driving us across the ocean of life; and each of us suffers, or can suffer, a master impulse, the mind's disease. In the prefatory note Pope explains that Eloisa's letters "give so lively a picture of the struggles of *Grace and Nature, Virtue and Passion.*" So *Eloisa to Abelard* becomes another of the Moral Essays, in one of which Pope describes the various "Characters of Women," holding that the ruling passion is more uniform in women than in men. By means of Eloisa, Pope shows what happens when a woman is dominated by love instead of by the two usual master impulses of the female temperament—"The love of pleasure and the love of sway." Eloisa *discusses* her emotions, remarking on her divided mind in a commentary that reduces her confused feelings to explicable form:

How happy is the blameless vestal's lot!
The world forgetting, by the world forgot;

Eternal sunshine of the spotless mind,
Each prayer accepted and each wish resigned;
Labour and rest that equal periods keep;
Obedient slumbers that can wake and weep;
Desires compos'd, affections ever ev'n;
Tears that delight, and sighs that waft to heav'n. . . .
Far other dreams my erring soul employ,
Far other raptures of unholy joy. . . .
O curst, dear horrors of all-conscious night!
How glowing guilt exalts the keen delight!
Provoking demons all restraint remove,
And stir within me every source of love.

But we do not live with her through her dreams; they are talked of, not represented. We know that she is in a state of conflict; yet we do not experience the conflict with her, as we do with Othello.

There is a difference between these alternating states of mind and the geometry of passion in Racine's plays. The soul of Phèdre actually moves from one pole of feeling to another; but Eloisa is *meditating* upon the contrary effects of her master passion. She is caught between a *state* of Grace and a *state* of Nature, and Pope does not render the drama of her alternating moods, but, instead, only her remarks upon her alternating moods. Pope is exact in saying that the poem is a struggle between Grace and Nature, Virtue and Passion—and these are not emotions but ideas of psychological states, or fictions by which Pope deals with Eloisa's experience. Racine did not begin with an idea of what a state of Love is; he began with Phèdre suffering the impulses of a divided will. In Racine passion is discourse; in Pope passion is the topic of Eloisa's discourse.

That is, Pope intellectualizes emotion. His poem is doctrinaire in the sense that it originates in the fiction of a master passion. Eloisa is not by any means a romantic or pre-romantic poem of feeling. If we compare Eloisa with Clarissa Harlowe, we see that Richardson, for all his moralizing, renders the texture of his heroine's feelings as Pope does not. Clarissa meditates on her lot; but her experience is treated from within, and her feelings are so valued for their own sake that her very sentimentality is a solvent for whatever thoughts she has about her condition. Clarissa's ability to immerse her notions in feeling gives a somewhat Proustian atmosphere to her melodramatic account. *Eloisa to Abelard* is closer, oddly enough, to some of our stories illustrating Freudian theories. The Oedipus complex is really a fiction not unlike Pope's fiction of a ruling passion. Indeed, we have tried to read Freudian theory as myth; but perhaps we should admit that Freud has afforded us only fictions: the Freudian topography of the self—the Id, the Ego, the Superego—is a fiction. How many recent novels seem to originate, like *Eloisa to Abelard,* in an idea of a certain psychological state? How many such novels *regard* states of feeling?

No one, of course, would take these novels as rococo for this reason; however, the idea of a passion is a neutral field, so to speak, upon which Pope can develop the expressiveness of Eloisa's language, so that the poem is another form of rococo wit. In fact rococo wit often amounts to a kind of verbal illusion —"What oft was thought, but ne'er so well expressed"—a play on the surface. "Expression is the dress of thought," says Pope— "It gilds all objects but it alters none." The verbal quality of Pope's wit, like the slight relief of the rococo arabesque, appears in many couplets in the *Essay on Man,* the surface sparkle appearing within a symmetrical membering:

> Fear to the statesman, rashness to the chief,
> To kings presumption, and to crowds belief.

The plausible notions behind these couplets are a substructure just adequate to sustain the verse. Pope is superficial in a quite technical way, for his "phonetic texture," his suiting sound to sense, his occult balances, contrasts, inversions, and cross-echoes inside the stave, are the literary counterpart to rococo decoration of a neutral field.

It is true that Pope was not impelled by passion; but to say that he is merely a versifier is like calling Lepautre and Pineau merely interior decorators, not architects. Rococo is, legitimately, a style of organic surfaces with sharply worked-up details, its technique concealing an underlying simple geometry by superficial designs. The sustaining fiction allows a surprising and even capricious freedom in "single parts." A rococo interior frees itself from its geometry by flowing lines. It has been said that no one has ever confined himself so strictly as Pope to an exacting metre and yet so often surprised us with the unpredictable.[10] In the same way Oppenord freed the elements of his fantastic designs without imperilling the architectural system. Here rococo is comparable to gothic, where there was a tension between the frail, conceptualized architectural frame and the individual details within the system—naturalism, expressiveness, and intimacy appearing inside an abstract scheme.

Nervous—yet not strained—Pope's art has the external intricacy and naturalism of the rococo-arabesque, where the sensitive execution of details is more apparent than the total unity, the coördinations. The waving rococo line of beauty resembles the movement of Pope's verses, which have been called a "growth along a line." Pope was a specialist in transition—"a grace which the 18th century practiced with care."[11] In his verse-essays he passes easily from one unit of structure to another not by logic but merely by the illusion of his verbal texture. The prose summaries he prefixed to his *Moral Essays,* the *Essay on Criticism,* and the *Essay on Man* show how his major topics follow each other with a sort of "horizontal continuity" like the membering of a rococo chamber; and their verbal surface is one continuous transition like the fluently decorated walls of the Hôtel de Matignon designed by Pineau. The architectural divisions of these walls are suppressed so that the logic of the larger units is less evident than the virtuoso quality of the ornament and the vitality of individual passages. In the rococo garden the *parterre en broderie* has the same horizontal continuity, a passage from intricacy to intricacy within a field, a linear organism spread across a levelled neutral surface. The finespun arabesque coheres because it is held on the negative plane of the panelling.

The logic behind Pope's verbal surface is sometimes so invisible a plane that the verses themselves can be read, like some finely decorated rococo panel or an ornamental *parterre en broderie,* either down *or* up, this way *or* that. To take a somewhat extreme instance, I quote in reverse order a passage from *Epistle to Mrs. Blount:*

But that for ever in his lines they breathe,
The smiles and loves had died in Voiture's death.
Voiture was wept by all the brightest eyes,
The truest hearts for Voiture heaved with sighs,
And the gay mourned who never mourned before;
Ev'n rival wits did Voiture's death deplore.

Dr. Johnson said that Pope "hangs upon the ear." Line by line his phonetic texture is an organic play of antithesis and parallel, a rebound of term against term, phrase against phrase, with occult balance inside the couplets, which, however, usually have a median axis:

Self-love and reason to one end aspire,
Pain their aversion, pleasure their desire.

Even in *The Dunciad,* where Pope uses the "sacred weapon" of ridicule more sternly than in the lighter satires, he keeps his glittering rococo surface, the dazzling play of lapidary verse:

We nobly take the high *priori* road,
And reason downward, till we doubt of God:
Make Nature still encroach upon his plan,
And shove him off as far as e'er we can:
Thrust some mechanic cause into his place,
Or bind in matter, or diffuse in space.

In such passages it is hard to say whether the thought inspires the language or whether the language provokes the thought. In spite of its larger scale and intent, *The Dunciad* is rococo in its art of the surface, its closely woven texture of allusions, which are minutely contemporaneous and far more topical than in Johnson's satire, or Dryden's. It reminds us of the art of the first book of *Gulliver's Travels,* when Swift was presenting his own plain truths behind precise allusions to local affairs. This Lilliputian technique is also rococo.

Pope's rococo surface does not consist, as is sometimes believed, of poetic diction, a "gaudy and inane phraseology." On the contrary, rococo has a marked distaste for the pedantic, the labored, the pretentious, the learned or over-stated. It may be doubted whether poetic diction is a rococo device at all, for rococo is simplified, reduced, minutely precise. Milton's epic verse, not Pope's, carries the weight of an excrescent language, a polysyllabic, sonorous, latinate tongue like the bulging high relief in Grinling Gibbons' carvings with their swags, consoles, garlands, and baroque cartouches. If we set aside certain passages in his translations from Homer, where Pope was intentionally being epical, his language is like the simple, almost prosaic, language of grasses, fronds, and tendrils in rococo panels, used flexibly, distinctly, attentively:

> Thus critics, of less judgment than caprice,
> Curious, not knowing, not exact, but nice,
> Form short ideas, and offend in arts
> (As most in manners) by a love to parts.

Here is a language of common life Wordsworth wished to use. Pope's verse has a different sort of surface tension than poetic diction can give; it has the low relief, wiry fibre, and decorative isolation of the rococo interlace, trophy, and acanthus swirl, often with the finespun observation that is empirical. Pope sees a pheasant as clearly as Buffon:

> . . . his glossy, varying dyes,
> His purple crest, and scarlet-circled eyes,
> The vivid green his shining plumes unfold,
> His painted wings, and breast that flames with gold.

This naturalism is not romantic. It has the exactitude, frailty, and grace of the flowers, trees, birds, and trellises in Watteau's *ornements décoratifs* like *May* [6] or *Le Berceau* with tendrils of some local vine and transparent leafage. Or there is the passage in *Windsor Forest* where in the genial spring, the quivering shade, larks are shot:

> They fall, and leave their little lives in air.

Pope's rococo sensitivity shows itself when he confesses to Spence: "I was always particularly struck with that passage in Homer, where he makes Priam's grief for the loss of Hector

6 WATTEAU: *May*

break out into anger against his attendants and sons; and I could never read it without weeping for the distress of that unfortunate old prince"—whereupon the poet, reading the passage, was interrupted by his own tears.

Rococo art has its own sensibility, which is like an atmosphere about the arabesque design. But rococo design is not sentimental because this art, with its touch of the amateur, always keeps its appearance of play; and play, being self-conscious, prevents sentimentality yet allows feelings. Watteau's arabesques like *L'Heureux Moment*—a kind of diminished *Embarkation for Cythera*—show that a great deal of rococo sensibility appeared in the pastoral, an urban taste for landscape, a taste responsive to nature without being romantic. Pope's garden and grotto at Twickenham must have been like those asymmetrical arabesques designed by Lepautre before the wilder *contraste dans les ornemens* became fashionable in the 1740's. *Windsor Forest,* as Pope saw it, resembles one of the carefully arranged pastorals in Watteau's parks:

> Here waving groves a chequer'd scene display,
> And part admit and part exclude the day;
> As some coy nymph her lover's warm address
> Nor quite indulges, nor can quite repress.
> There, interspers'd in lawns and op'ning glades,
> Thin trees arise that shun each other's shades.

Watteau's pastoral is nowhere gentler than in his designs for *Autumn, Spring, Summer:* lovers in tender little panels, their poses natural, casual, animated, but a trifle melancholy because their joys, they know, are brief; their tiny dramatic scene, filled with discreet pathos, is enclosed in the fronds of some ornamental tree; or they sit apart from some amusing *partie de chasse* cultivating their feelings in a small dialogue. If we can judge from his prefatory note, Pope had the same feeling for his own *Pastorals;* at least he says, as if writing a text for Watteau's slim designs:

> A pastoral is an imitation of the action of a shepherd, or one considered under that character. The form of this imitation is dramatic, or narrative, or mixed of both: the fable simple, the

> manners not too polite nor too rustic; the thoughts are plain, yet admit a little quickness and passion, but that short and flowing: the expression humble, yet pure as the language will afford; neat, but not florid; easy, and yet lively.

Neat but not florid, easy and yet lively—this is the authentic rococo tone in an art that is "polite," an art answerable to the feelings, but able to temper them. Pope has the rococo tone. He carefully sets all his scenes at a certain distance from his own feelings so that a sufficient interval is kept between himself and his poem, himself and his reader. In *The Rape of the Lock* he runs with an easy gait over a wide emotional scale—hope, grief, mockery, pathos, doubt, gaiety; but none of these emotions means more than any other. The focus does not shift. Having set his tone, his moral plane or equilibrium in which no feeling is allowed to weigh too heavily, Pope can allow himself every sort of response: from bitterness ("The smiles of harlots and the tears of heirs") to compassion ("And little hearts to flutter at a beau") to amusement ("They shift the moving toyshop of their heart") to mockery ("When husbands, or when lapdogs, breathe their last") or earnestness ("Unless Good Sense preserve what Beauty gains"). Pope's attitude—his tone—is another fiction. The same polite interval is kept in the very personal dialogue in the *Epistle to Dr. Arbuthnot,* when Pope seems to be playing with his own spite; that is, unlike the romantic poet, he remains in control of his anger, his ridicule, his contempt. The poem is private without being a confessional. The movement is a *capriccio*—the animated variable tempo of the *Satires,* "snipsnap short, and interruption smart" with "major, minor, and conclusion quick."

The eye of the rococo artist catches life at its minor tensions, its minor exchanges. One of these is Watteau's *Enseigne de Gersaint,* a small incident in Paris business, painted in eight days, with little groups of men and women intently discussing some pictures to be sold. There is no great baroque action, but an accent on the impromptu gesture, an intimate appreciation of the poetry in ordinary transactions. It has the diminished theatre of Pope's dialogues:

P.—Then better sure it charity becomes
To tax directors, who (thank God!) have plums;
Still better Ministers, or if the thing
May pinch ev'n there—why lay it on a King.
F.—Stop! stop!
P.—Must satire then nor rise nor fall?
Speak out, and bid me blame no rogues at all.
F.—Yes, strike that Wild, I'll justify the blow.
P.—Strike? Why the man was hang'd ten years ago.
(*Epilogue to the Satires*)

These scenes belong to an art that makes the most of its limited scale and motif, an art that does not divorce the mind from sensibility. When this divorce happens, later, we have sentimental anecdotes by Greuze and the stereotyped rhetoric of mid-century poets. With its neutral geometry and its ornamental surfaces, rococo is the last style before the arts become various modes of emotionalism, antiquarian pastiche, or literal description. The reaction against this loss of a style finally caused a modern revolution which brought symbolism and the formalities of neo-rococo design, Art Nouveau, and cubism.

Before rococo vanished it went through an eccentric phase that looks forward to picturesque and symbolist art. The latest moments of rococo are pivotal in the history of modern styles, for the so-called *genre pittoresque,* a brief closing variation on rococo design, is an early phase of a new subjective art that tries to suggest, not to state. Nothing could better prove that the history of styles is discontinuous, or that affinities between artists occur where they are least to be expected.

V

GENRE
PITTORESQUE

If we catch them at informal moments, the most "correct" artists of the eighteenth century are likely to surprise us by their oddity. Pope filled his gaudy little cavern at Twickenham with stalactites and stalagmites fetched from the caves of Somerset. The chill, self-contained Addison wrote a series of papers in the *Spectator* upon the pleasures of imagination, which, he said, can entertain us with "ideas of visible objects when the objects are not actually before the eye, but are called up into our memories, or formed into agreeable visions of things that are either absent or fictitious." The imagination "bestows charms on a monster"; it can excite "a pleasing kind of horror in the mind" and amuse by strangeness and novelty. In Italy the "imaginary landscape" or "imaginary view" appeared as ornament over doors, a variety of *capriccio* given to rearranging architectural motifs or recognizable buildings into a fantastic topography often with some nostalgic appeal for those

Courtesy, Museum of Fine Arts, Boston

7 PIRANESI: *Baths of Caracalla* (etching)

who knew Venice or Rome. The format of these "pieces over doors" was often irregular, and little-known painters like Marieschi, Giuseppe Moretti, Pietro Gaspari, and Francesco Battaglioli created the almost surrealistic *vedute di fantasia.* Other rococo artists like Canaletto, Guardi, and Bellotto at times painted imaginary views. In the theatre the Bibbienas were designing great fanciful perspectives influenced by the *capriccio;* and by mid-century Piranesi was engraving his sinister visions of classic architecture, his shadowy prisons, his nocturnal Roman ruins[7]. Meanwhile in England Chippendale, another rococo artist, was releasing his fancy in strange, distorted designs for brackets, shields, frames, and other ornaments. Toward the close of the era came the horrors of "gothic" novels.

Such eighteenth-century capriciousness is usually treated vaguely as an aspect of early romanticism. But in its first phase, at least, it is a bizarre facet of rococo—the *genre pittoresque,* a technical development in rococo design.[12] Its history is brief, and must not be confused with the larger romantic developments or with the picturesque. As a phase of rococo decoration *genre pittoresque* appeared in France about 1730 in the work of Nicolas Pineau, and by 1754 in France, at any rate, it came to an end after Cochin attacked this sort of caprice.

Strictly speaking, this fantasticality in rococo design evolved in decorative arts in the France of Louis XV as a "new taste"—a *goût nouveau*—for irregular contrast in ornament, and it was called *le contraste dans les ornemens.* In effect it is an exaggerated asymmetry; but it also yields those wilder inventions of imaginary architecture that are described by Fiske Kimball as "half-plastic, half-visionary." Apparently this new taste was partly a reversion to the motif of the baroque cartouche, which a group of French engravers and painters transformed into illusory structures known as *morceaux de caprice* and issued as *cahiers* of ornamental designs for canopies, trellises, fountains, and freakish landscapes that distort baroque columns, walls, and statues almost beyond recognition. The *morceau de caprice* looks like the ruins of a baroque imagination, or a baroque imagination struck mad.

A taste for irregular forms—*rocaille* or *coquillage*—appeared in some of Watteau's arabesques, his designs for *singeries,* grottoes, dens, and elements. Then in 1734 J. A. Meissonnier, designer of silverware, issued his *Livre d'Ornemens,* a collection "des Fontaines, des Cascades, des Ruines, des Rocailles, et Coquillages, des morceaux d'Architecture qui font des effets bizarres, singuliers et pittoresques, par leurs formes piquantes et extraordinaires, *dont souvent aucune partie ne répond à l'autre.*" Among these extraordinary forms where one feature fails to correspond with another, there were also designs for ceilings with figures and animals, with "borders extremely ingenious and varied." Small as they are, Meissonnier's half-plastic, half-visionary scenes create an illusion of structures in huge scale, with bulbous pavilions, sweeping reverse curves, broken scrolls, distorted columns and balustrades, airy trellis-like canopies, portentous cascades, and titanic spiral or reversed stairways seen from an oblique angle or from far below. Shortly afterward appeared another collection of fantastic pieces by Jacques de la Joue—giant asymmetrical fountains, terraces, and flights of stairs in acute perspective, half-oriental sultanas' baths, exotic thrones, improvisations upon architectural orders, broken monstrous car-

8 CUVILLIÉS (FRANÇOIS DE): *Morceau de Caprice*

touches, and all kinds of allegorical figures dramatically surrounded by the wreckage of a half-baroque world, as if Piranesi were translated into an unintelligible dialect.

There were many other *cahiers:* by Boucher (who did a series of fountains), Peyrotte, Blondel, Mondon, Babel, Girard, and de Cuvilliés [8]. These designers were fond of architectural chaos, as if the great Roman fountains were seen by some deranged mind—lofty aqueducts bent out of scale, gigantic balustrades louring like ramparts, cartouches used as archways, ruined obelisks rising near grotesque temples, shepherds gathered below tumultuous geysers spouting as though they would flood this insane world. Boucher's *Recueil de Fontaines* is a wild display of magical conchlike basins amid which appear fauns, classical gods, and amoretti—a pastoral gone crazy. All this is characteristic of the *morceau de caprice:* full but broken volumes, agitated statuary, a proscenium of architectural elements or ruins opening into asymmetrical grottoes or vistas of fountains, canopies, or other *formes piquantes,* sometimes with a note of *singerie,* sometimes with nymphs, loves, or allegorical personages. Yet this fantasy has, actually, little to do with *singerie* or *chinoiserie;* it is, instead, the rococo asymmetrical designs given a strange and irresponsible dimension. The occult balance of rococo art is changed into the freakish contours of a dream.

The British *genre pittoresque* is no less whimsical than the French, even if it is less frequent. Hogarth's reaction against symmetry, his liking for agreeable monsters, shapeless forms "leading the eye a wanton kind of chase," is probably related to the growth of *genre pittoresque* within rococo. His serpentine line of beauty reappears in Chippendale's girandoles and shields for pediments—"compartments of ornaments"—that are as eccentric as almost anything in the *morceaux de caprice;* and engravers like J. Ingram reproduced Jacques de la Joue's suites of ornaments and figures—Architecture, Eloquence, Music, Optics, and so on. For the many Englishmen fond of prints Mathias Lock prepared in 1752 his *New Drawing Book of Ornaments, Shields, Compartments, Masks, &c.* Hogarth's *Analysis* (1753) illustrating "the waving line, or line of beauty, varying still more, being composed of two curves contrasted," was a rather disorderly grammar of winding, twisting forms explained by some incoherent theories. George Bickham's designs for songs like "Bright Cynthia" and "The Inamour'd Swain," and Thomas Johnson's *One Hundred & Fifty New Designs* (1761), particularly his designs for clock cases and frames, show the same distortion of rococo as the fantastic views being painted in Italy at the same time. In many cases the "English" garden with its Chinese-Gothic devices is related to the *morceau de caprice,* as we can see in Halfpenny's collections, William Wrighte's *Grotesque Architecture,* and the long series of *Jardins Anglais-Chinois* edited by Le Rouge.

This romantic aspect of the British temperament, its liking for "gothick" irregularity and surprise, is well known. What has not been suspected is that the poetry of William Collins, written chiefly between 1740 and 1750, exactly while rococo was creating *morceaux de caprice,* is also a form of *genre pittoresque.* If Collins had written in France, the affiliation would doubtless be clearer; but the French seem to have produced no poetry in this mode. As it is, we have not known how to judge the strange work of this English poet, who sometimes wrote a mechanical sort of eighteenth-century verse but who plainly has a "poetical character" of an irregular kind. His half-plastic, half-visionary imagination, his subjective landscapes inhabited by violent and deformed allegorical creatures have disconcerted critics, who have asked whether his disordered classical forms were not due to his confused wits or his slipshod habits of composing and correcting his texts. Dr. Johnson spoke of the "grandeur of wildness" in Collins, who, he said, "delighted to rove through the meanders of enchantment."

Collins peoples his "unreal scene"—the "visions wild" of fancy—with "the shadowy tribes of mind." Almost like the surrealist he "confronts incongruities," and his "shadowy shapes" seem to inhabit landscapes of the dream. Take, for instance, a passage from his "Ode on the Poetical Character," which seems like a psychic displacement of one of Milton's scenes in "Il Penseroso":

> High on some cliff, to Heav'n up-pil'd,
> Of rude access, of prospect wild,
> Where, tangled round the jealous steep,
> Strange shades o'erbrow the valleys deep,

> And holy genii guard the rock,
> Its gloomes embrown, its springs unlock,
> While on its rich ambitious head,
> An Eden like his own lies spread;
> I view that oak, the fancied glades among,
> By which as Milton lay, his evening ear,
> From many a cloud that dropp'd ethereal dew,
> Nigh spher'd in Heav'n its native strains could hear. . . .

The language is here and there merely a version of the poetic diction of the age; but the subjective atmosphere, the oblique allusions, the incoherent syntax give the poem a certain psychic hazard, which Coleridge was later to translate in "Kubla Khan" into "a vision in a dream." Then too, the inspiration is obviously baroque, as it was when the French designers reworked the cartouche.

As if he were under some spell Collins is prone to repeat his phrases and rhythms; his recurring "O Thou" invocation abruptly lifts the poem by an unaccountable excitement:

> Thou, to whom the world unknown
> With all its shadowy shapes is shown;
> Who see'st appalled th'unreal scene,
> While Fancy lifts the veil between:
> Ah Fear! Ah frantic Fear!
> I see, I see thee near. . . .

The ode is charged with an alarm that the stereotypes of academic verse cannot express. The bat in the "Ode to Evening" flies so darkling it has been called[13] a sign of melancholy that "verges on disorder," and "far too profound to arise from an evening landscape alone":

> Now air is hush'd, save where the weak-ey'd bat
> With short shrill shriek flits by on leathern wing. . . .

This leathern creature exists in a climate of some poem by Baudelaire after he was brushed by the cold wing of madness. In the "Passions" ode some frantic allegorical shapes are fixed in strained poses within a conventional classical framework—

the "just designs of Greece"; yet "madness rul'd the hour" as Fear, Hope, Revenge, and other sculpturesque figures occupy in turn the unearthly scene of Fancy, where Collins can "gaze her visions wild." The conventions of pseudo-classic verse have not fully censored the meanings of this irrational poem.

We must agree with Dr. Johnson, then, that Collins indulged "some peculiar habits of thought," and

> . . . was eminently delighted with those flights of imagination which pass the bounds of nature. . . . He loved fairies, genii, giants, and monsters; he delighted to rove through the meanders of enchantment, to gaze on the magnificence of golden palaces, to repose by the waterfalls of Elysian gardens.
>
> This was however the character rather of his inclination than his genius; the grandeur of wildness, and the novelty of extravagance, were always desired by him, but not always attained. . . . This idea which he had formed of excellence led him to oriental fictions and allegorical imagery. . . .
>
> (*Life of Collins*)

In mentioning Collins' oriental fictions Dr. Johnson is doubtless referring to the *Persian Eclogues.* These poems are not the usual *chinoiserie.* At some vague distance we see in them Tefflis' towers, secret vales, and the long shadows of the mind's twilight. Nor are they like the rococo pastorals of Pope or Watteau. They have an air of estrangement like the illusory scenes invented by de la Joue, Cuvilliés, or Boucher.

In fact, Collins is master of the literary *morceau de fantaisie,* with its classic and baroque elements thrown into such disorder that decorative asymmetry takes on the subjective dimensions of *genre pittoresque.* However shadowy Collins' forms may be, his imagination is highly plastic, yet decorative rather than architectural. His array of personifications is sculpturesque, although these figures do not appear with "regularity." The structure of his odes on "The Passions" and "The Manners" is a train of allegorical personages arranged as a loose procession of figures making melodramatic gestures or fixed in outlandish poses. Collins himself was amused by prints and was skilled in drawing; he once contrived as decoration a medallion with "two elegant Heads à l'antique"—

> . . . over the lower part of the necks of which there shall be a veil thrown, from under which a little *Art* shall appear writing on a Roman scroll, & a Satyr either in contrast holding up another, or writing on part of the same, or suppose the veil to be upheld by Friendship, who may at the same time point to the Relievo of the medallion while she discovers the ornaments of the base by supporting the veil.

With its plasticity, its animation, its bemused character, and its asymmetrical arrangement this design is almost a *morceau de caprice.* The prose sketch by Joseph Warton from which Collins evidently drew the "Passions" ode might appear in the *oeuvre* of Meissonnier as a *jeu d'artifice.*

Collins' extravagance is a visionary distortion or confusion of classical, gothic, and oriental forms. His shrine of Liberty is like one of the architectural caprices invented by Cuvilliés:

> In Gothic pride it seems to rise!
> Yet Graecia's graceful orders join,
> Majestic thro' the mix'd design.

The "Highland Superstitions" ode has an astonishingly mixed design, and the "world unknown" of the "Ode to Fear" is crowded with deformed shapes of the *maîtres ornementistes,* who had explored some of Collins' "dim-discover'd tracts of mind" where the decorative is changed into a rococo romanticism:

> For lo what monsters in thy train appear!
> Danger, whose limbs of giant mold
> What mortal eye can fix'd behold?
> Who stalks his round, an hideous form,
> Howling amidst the midnight storm,
> Or throws him on the ridgy steep
> Of some loose hanging rock to sleep:
> And with him thousand phantoms join'd,
> Who prompt to deeds accurst the mind. . . .

No matter what Collins owes to Milton (the monstrous Danger, for example) the "Ode to Fear" suggests that Rimbaud was right in saying, "The first romantics were *seers* without quite realizing it." Odes by Thomas Gray have some of this fine visionary confusion of gothic and grecian, and some of his personifications ("Pale Grief, and Pleasing Pain,/With Horror, tyrant of the throbbing breast") are akin to Collins' haunted figures; but Gray's perspective is not fantastic.

For all this, *genre pittoresque* is not really romantic even if it ventured a short way into the alien terrain of dreams. Collins is not *voyant* in Rimbaud's sense of the term, nor were the *maîtres ornementistes,* who nevertheless wrought some strange variations on the decorative motifs of rococo art. The *genre pittoresque* is a technique of extravagant asymmetry, *le contraste dans les ornemens.* The magical irregularities of the *morceau de caprice* appeared inside the neat framework of rococo architecture with its exact balance of members. Thus also the framework of Collins' odes—for the ode was his usual form—is regular; as regular as the external features of Georgian architecture. But the regularity of the large units does not control the negligent asymmetry inside the system. Collins wanted to "revive the just designs of Greece" by using a traditional sequence of strophe, antistrophe, and epode, and also, probably, by using classic machines, conventional apostrophe, personification, and epithets. Similarly the *compartment d'ornement* used traditional classic orders and allegorical figures of gods and nymphs; its vocabulary was customary enough, but it used this vocabulary queerly. Collins' themes were bookish: tragic fear, pity, simplicity. However, all this academism does not affect the internal movement of the poem, the development being erratic, indirect, fickle.

The "Ode on the Poetical Character" progresses by obscure allusion and free association; in spite of the purported three divisions, the poem as a whole is perplexing, if not distracted. The first unit is a tissue of very oblique allusions to Spenser in the form of an excited apostrophe to Young Fancy. The second unit, presumably also an apostrophe, does not have the advantage of coherent syntax and apparently alludes to the moment in the creation of the world when God put Young Fancy on his throne while the shadowy tribes of mind rejoiced. The final unit—again elliptical, the phrasings being private—seems to be a tribute to Milton, whose "evening ear" catches, among "fancied glades," some unearthly strain. The "Ode to Fear" likewise uses the regular framework of strophe, epode, and antistrophe, and again progresses through erratic personifications into an improvisation upon Sophocles and a final suspended exhortation to the figure of Fear herself.

Of course the Pindaric ode in English is usually irregular; yet Collins uses a "tectonics of caprice" like those of the *genre pittoresque*. The references are not only ambiguous; they are haphazard. The images—genii, monsters, waterfalls, and golden palaces—are visionary and plastic. The personifications are sculptural, but their presentation is exclamatory:

> Whilst Vengeance, in the lurid air,
> Lifts her red arm, expos'd and bare:
> On whom that rav'ning brood of Fate,
> Who lap the blood of Sorrow, wait;
> Who, Fear, this ghastly train can see,
> And not look madly wild, like thee?

Like the *cahiers d'ornement* these odes "font des effets bizarres, singuliers et pittoresques, par leurs formes piquantes et extraordinaires, dont souvent aucune partie ne répond à l'autre." Both are an asyntactic form of rococo.

The figure of Vengeance appears "in the lurid air." One of the subtler pictorial values of the *compartment d'ornement* was aerial or atmospheric perspective, to which Collins was very sensitive. In his "Verses to Sir Thomas Hanmer" he imagines an "expressive picture"—

> Methinks ev'n now I view some free design,
> Where breathing Nature lives in ev'ry line:
> Chast and subdu'd the modest Lights decay,
> Steal into Shade, and mildly melt away.

The hamlets brown, the dim spires, the gradual dusky veil of night in "Ode to Evening" transpose rococo into a poetic vision that obviously owes a good deal to painting by Claude. Those "robes of tend'rest blue" in "Ode to Pity" have the rococo *bleu Nattier* of which French portraitists were so fond. Yet this sensitivity to color was everywhere in the poetry of the day, and Collins is *genre pittoresque* rather because of his half-plastic, half-visionary designs.

If Pope's verse can be said to correspond to the early rococo—an arabesque ornament of surface—Collins with his fine madness represents the *genre pittoresque,* a minor and transient mode of a transient style. In 1754 Cochin wrote the obituary for *genre pittoresque* when he spoke of it as *désordre.* About 1779 Dr. Johnson repeated what he had said before: that Collins' poems were a "deviation in quest of mistaken beauties." *Genre pittoresque* found a new dialect in the polite language of rococo art, and in this dialect was already making allusions not understood by the eighteenth century.

Part Two

PICTURESQUE, ROMANTICISM, SYMBOLISM

I

THE LOSS OF A STYLE

The years between 1750 and 1900 produced those embracing trends known as romanticism, from which sprang symbolism, and realism, none of these becoming a style if we mean by style conformity to techniques adequately expressing the consciousness of an era and accepted nearly by agreement among artists who are most sensitive to their contemporary world. Romanticism and realism were alike symptoms of revolt against outworn conventions; they were necessary artistic reactions that never found an artistic canon and thus remain essentially negative. T. E. Hulme did not seriously overstate the case when before World War I he said that a hundred years of romanticism had brought only disorder and that we must get "a new convention." He was seeking a "classic" convention, and cubism was precisely this. All styles are classic so far as they find a convention that is truly contemporary.

Romanticism is urgent feeling rather than a style. In his *Salon of 1846* Baudelaire rightly said that romanticism is "only to be found within."

> Romanticism is precisely situated neither in choice of subjects nor in exact truth, but *in a mode of feeling*. . . . To say the word Romanticism is to say modern art—that is, intimacy, spirituality, color, aspiration towards the infinite, expressed by every means available to the arts.

The romantics found that reality is subjective. That is why they look forward to the existentialists. Romanticism has been fruitfully defined as a special kind of empiricism, an experiment to test all values by the emotions.[1] When this sort of experiment is made, the response always exceeds the ability of the writer or painter to formulate; thus the diversity of romantic techniques. In his essay on "Poetry in General" Hazlitt gives an indispensable definition of romanticism, which is intensity of experience rather than art—or, as Wordsworth put it, a spontaneous overflow of feeling. Hazlitt writes:

> The poetical impression of any object is that uneasy exquisite sense of beauty or power that cannot be contained within itself; that is impatient of all limit . . . the imagination will distort or magnify the object. . . . The province of the imagination is principally visionary, the unknown and undefined.

The inexpressible must be conveyed, as Baudelaire says, "by every means available." In his aesthetic Hegel exalted this romantic internality (*Insichsein*) to an absolute artistic value. Delacroix, the archetypal romantic painter, says in his *Journal* (March 26, 1854):

> Fine works of art would never become dated if they contained nothing but genuine feeling. The language of the emotions and the impulses of the human heart never change; what invariably causes a work to date, and sometimes ends by obliterating its really fine qualities, is the use of technical devices that were within the scope of every artist at the time the work was executed.

Here Delacroix points to the romantic dilemma in art: the conflict between consciousness and representation, as Francastel calls it when he notes that romantic painters in spite of their emotional revolt remained faithful to conventional form. Delacroix [9] returns to Rubens to represent his lion hunts and

Louvre, Archives Photographiques, Paris

9 DELACROIX: *Death of Sardanapalus*

harem scenes, and in spite of his bravura a great many technical problems in his painting remain unresolved—eventually to be settled by the "formal vibrancy" of Van Gogh's methods. Artistically the romantics often give us the reality of temperament—the "characteristic"—instead of new formulas of vision. There is abundant promise but incomplete performance—which means that anything one says of romantic art sounds like a half-truth.

Their acceptance of emotion as art should have led the romantics to expressionism, and Turner, in fact, did discover expressionist light and color, just as Shelley has passages resembling Rimbaud's fantasies. Daumier's lithographic vision of Don Quixote shows how far he could go toward a new pictorial grammar—already used by Goya for his own purposes in commenting upon war and folly. Yet for all this enormous talent and inventiveness in Turner, Constable, Géricault, Blake, and Goya—and in Delacroix too—the real revolution in technique did not come until later, with the impressionists, who in turn begot the post-impressionists and the cubists. Romantic painting, especially, seems like a chaos of astounding faculties, disappointing in its formal legacy, but creative in the quality of its experiences. The same would be true of literature.

Romanticism often means exactly what Victor Hugo said it meant when he wrote in his preface to *Cromwell* (1827) that the art of the new century would not be judged according to old rules but only by "the special laws of individual temperaments." The extreme diversity of the so-called romantic achievement in the arts is apparent in the radical differences between painting by Ingres and painting by Delacroix, one using a decorative line, the other the sweeping free rhythms of color and "touch." It would be hard to name two painters inherently more unlike in method and effect. In England Constable and Turner are equally dissimilar, the one opening up his composition by a brushwork that fractures space and light into their structural rudiments, the other dissolving everything in palpitating color that burns and fades in musical crescendo and diminuendo. Goya belongs with Géricault and Daumier because he discovered the grotesque as Hugo understood it and as Browning, a retarded romantic, exploited it. Hugo insisted that romantic drama would present the "abnormal and the horrible, the comic and the burlesque," the beast as well as the beauty. The diversity of talent in romantic painting is different from the equally extreme diversity of talent in the early renaissance, when painters as unlike as Angelico and Piero della Francesca were both addressing themselves to similar problems, the task of representing the existence of things in a new kind of space and light. However uncongenial the faculties of these two artists, their interests, artistically, had a common area; but the romantic painter worked from his temperament, and the problems in his art arose from his disposition, which was often moody. This is why romantic irony—the sudden fluctuation in feeling—is so characteristic in the painting and poetry of the early nineteenth century.

We can hardly expect a style to result from this play of temperament, since different artists were not concerned with the same problems further than to revolt, to reject, to cast off precedent. The mutiny and methods of painters and writers were personal. Hugo's poem "Response to an Accusation," for example, shows how correct Camus is in saying that the nineteenth century opened to the sound of falling bastions—not only politically but artistically:

Oui, je suis ce Danton! je suis ce Robespierre!
J'ai contre le mot noble à la longue rapière,
Insurgé le vocable ignoble, son valet. . . .
J'ai pris et démoli la bastille des rimes.
J'ai fait plus: j'ai brisé tous les carcans de fer
Qui liaient le mot peuple, et tiré de l'enfer
Tous les vieux mots damnés, légions sépulcrales. . . .
J'ai fait un jacobin du pronom personnel. . . .
J'ai dit à Vaugelas: Tu n'es qu'une mâchoire!
J'ai dit aux mots: Soyez république. . . .
J'ai jeté le vers noble aux chiens noirs de la prose.

To make a "jacobin" of the personal pronoun, to cast dignified verse to the black dogs of prose, is not really to find a new poetic formula. That had to wait for Baudelaire, the prose poem, and *vers libre.*

The art of the romantics is a strange spectacle of jacobinism and conformity—a struggle for liberation that was not completed until much later. Wordsworth cast into the highly conventional and exclamatory form of the ode his deepest personal intimations, and the result is a clash between those passages in which he does actually write a new kind of meditative verse—

Fallings from us, vanishings;
Blank misgivings of a creature
Moving about in worlds not realized—

and passages of gaudy, perhaps inane, rhetoric that bears the stamp of eighteenth-century mechanical verse—

Now, while the birds thus sing a joyous song,
And while the young lambs bound
As to the tabor's sound. . . .

"Fallings from us, vanishings": this is entirely different from the language in the meditative poetry of the day. Wordsworth said he sought a new language—"the very language of men"—but he never actually discovered what that language was; the consequence is that *The Prelude* has passages of incantatory power and simplicity along with clumsy lines like "My drift, I fear, / Is scarcely obvious." In speaking thus of his erratic performance, one sounds as if one expected every line of a poet's work or every canvas of a painter to be successful. The point, rather, is that there is an abiding discord in much romantic art between the vision and the medium, which accentuates the inequality in romantic performance. Later in the century performance is also uneven; but after impressionism, *vers libre,* and the constellations of symbolist verse the discord between vision and medium diminishes. Baudelaire at least had at his disposal "little poems in prose" to express "the undulations of the dream." Wordsworth wanted to change poetic language but accepted a "regular and uniform metre" because, he said cautiously, "there is some danger that the excitement may be carried beyond its proper bounds." In short, like other romantics he had a limited confidence in any new medium; and poetry waited more than a century before Eliot insisted that the poet insofar as he is a poet should not use his passions but, instead, rely on his medium, not his personality. Wordsworth held verse to be merely the "external testimony" of poetry. For Eliot, the verse, the medium, is the substructure of poetry, and for the cubist a painting is a number of planes assembled in a certain order. In other words, the formal problem was not sufficiently important to the romantic artist.

The uncertainty and incompleteness of romantic experiments in technique are also evident in Shelley, whose intensely emotive art should, logically, have led him to the wild music of Rimbaud's illuminations. Instead, Shelley revolutionizes his technique in relatively few passages. *Prometheus Unbound* is an ascent to the incandescent heights of romantic freedom by the somewhat devious approach through "Lyrical Drama." The Aeschylean legend, of course, Shelley consciously alters to suit his rebellious and platonic spirit, and the form of the drama is nearly symphonic in its four movements or acts. However, only the fourth act is symphonic or, perhaps, choral in technique, the other three being neither successful drama (there is no action even when Jupiter, confronted by Demagorgon, falls) nor entirely successful lyric (the ineffectual dramatic struggle weakens the force of the triumphant vision of the free human mind). With the fourth movement, when the drama is done, there is a truly orchestral tribute to deified man, and Shelley reveals the possibilities inherent in romantic verse for performing the incantations of the poet-*voyant.* In such passages Shelley ventures to use the vehicle that later carried Rimbaud to invisible splendors. Or again, a poem like "The Cloud" purifies Shelley's verse to an abstract musical notation that liberates an aural formula from logical statement. Here he anticipates the decadent music of Swinburne and the *fin dė siècle.* But in much of his verse Shelley is almost ferociously devoted to his revolutionary message rather than to creating a new poetic medium.

What is true of Shelley is also true of Byron, whose insurgent, mercurial temperament was able to treat with virtuosity the Spenserian stanza and *ottava rima.* By one of the most egregious romantic feats Byron's satanic melancholy, resembling Hugo's unruly moods, becomes articulate in Spenserian *stanzas* (not, really, Spenserian *verse*). It is a daring anachronism, like Canova's sensuality expressing itself in the treatment of Pauline Bonaparte as a Venus Victrix ȯr Ingres' presenting his odalisques in Raphael's line. In poetry especially the romantics intended to break with the past but offered only variations on conventional techniques. Shelley, for instance, attempted Jacobean drama in *The Cenci*—a feat that did not come off, since the play shows how perilously close the romantics could come to mere plaster-historical effects in their quest for a style. This drama is a museum of Jacobean horrors and language.

Occasionally, to be sure, they did find a technique that is adequate. Blake discovered the poem-in-prose, a bardic method adapted from Ossian and the Bible enabling him to convey Baudelaire's new rhythms. In his shorter lyrics, too, Blake, rather than Wordsworth, succeeded in concentrating romantic feeling into forms and images that anticipate the half-symbolist verse of Baudelaire. "Kubla Khan" alone would prove that Coleridge was capable of writing a thoroughly new kind of poetry. This "vision in a dream" is also proto-symbolist in its images, its suggestion, its hallucinatory range and composition; and its iambic metres have the quality of *vers libre.* By contrast, "Christabel"—supposedly based on a "new principle" of counting accents, not syllables—seems like an artifice; and "The Ancient Mariner" with its ballad-form is a venture like

Byron's *Childe Harold,* a tactic that is usable once but not affording a very durable technique.

The inherent inconsistency or competition in romantic techniques is striking in Keats, in many ways the most accomplished artist of his generation because he was also, by intent, the most derivative. Steeped in the poetry of the past, eager to *find* his style, intelligently aware of his methods—like Baudelaire—Keats is the most mature, the least predictable, of the romantics. Like Baudelaire he set about transforming his *volupté* into *connaissance:* sensation into recognition. The question is often asked what Keats would have done had he lived. One is tempted to guess he would have become the T. S. Eliot of romantic verse because he, like Eliot, deliberately explored the resources of the past in hope of achieving a contemporary style. Artistically, Keats is the least temperamental and best disciplined of the romantics, the poet of his day most concerned with technique as such, even though he cannot be said to have found a technique. He returns to Spenser, to Shakespeare, to Elizabethan drama, to Milton, to Boccaccio, to the sonnet, to the ballad, to marble urns and Homer, to the dim untrodden regions of his dreams where strange pains fledge the steeps of his thought, to cold pastorals, to the ode and epic, or the melancholy poison of his senses. One of the most heartening failures in romantic art is Keats's vain effort to use Milton's inversions and thunderous pace. Technically there is a deep similarity between Keats and Delacroix, both enormously enriching conventional forms of composition by a poetry of fine excess. Keats belongs to a generation of poets represented by Lamartine, who remarked he wanted to be romantic in feeling but classic in form.

The truth is that technically speaking there is no such thing as romantic art; there are only romantic artists. No poets, painters, architects, or sculptors could be less compatible in technique than Wordsworth and Byron, Ingres and Turner, Nash and Pugin, Canova and Rude. The outburst called romanticism is a mode of consciousness rather than a style with a canon, a common body of usages and interests. The romantic problem of expressing feeling was not solved until the symbolists, a second generation of romantics, attempted a special technique in poetry, painting, and music. The difference between the first and second generations of romantic artists is chiefly that the early romantics rested within conventional forms whereas the symbolists found new forms—their "execution," as Baudelaire said. The watershed between the two generations can be located quite accurately: at Baudelaire, who compared art to a mathematic. Baudelaire shared the feelings of the first romantics, but he had an unremitting care for composition that enabled him to transcend his sexual and other emotions and reach an aesthetic, impersonal level of beauty.[2] If the early romantics were more concerned with their emotion than with their verse, Baudelaire and his symbolist followers like Mallarmé and, finally, Valéry, seem first to have conceived their poetry as "a movement, a contour, a rhythm" to be imposed upon feeling.

It would be possible to hinge the history of the nineteenth-century arts on the turn that came when Baudelaire wrote about his sympathy for Wagner's music in 1861, in his essay on *Tannhäuser.* At first he responds like any romantic to the overpowering tumult of Wagner's music, which rouses in him dreams of "everything excessive, immense, aspiring," leading him to visions of infinite horizons. Then he says, "Je résolus de m'informer pourquoi, et de transformer ma volupté en connaissance. . . ." The phrase summarizes the difference between the first and second generations of romantics. The second romantics were more critical—that is, more self-conscious, if not more intelligent. Baudelaire is rejecting the earlier romantic surrender to feeling so that he may be more entirely aware how feeling becomes art, for *connaissance* surely means "consciousness" as well as "knowledge." From the first, Baudelaire was attracted to Gautier and Poe, who cultivated a style "pur et fleuri," cold, calm, like diamond. In one sentence Baudelaire is saying what Matthew Arnold later explained in his essay on "The Function of Criticism"—namely, that the creative activity of the first quarter of the century was premature because in spite of its creative energy it "did not know enough." Arnold remarks, "This makes Byron so empty of matter, Shelley so incoherent, Wordsworth, even, profound as he is, yet so wanting in completeness and variety." Baudelaire the poet was also Baudelaire the critic; and his critical sense is inalienable from his poetic talent. The same is true of Mallarmé and Valéry—and T. S. Eliot.

For Baudelaire feeling is not enough. Like Arnold, like Valéry and Eliot, he needs an aesthetic. This is the real revolution in the history of romanticism: the shift from sensation to a consciousness of how sensation transforms itself to art. Such consciousness is liable, of course, to bring with it a sense of difficulty, even a paralysis, along with over-developed theories of art, aestheticism, byzantine effects, and decadence. But aestheticism and decadence are a price to be paid for the revisions of romanticism that produce stylizations and, eventually, a style. The history of impressionism and symbolism (since the two blend), the most significant development in the arts of the century, is determined by Baudelaire's need to translate *volupté* to *connaissance*. Pater the critic (only a critic) completes the translation, furnishing the aesthetic without the poetry. It is Valéry the critic-poet who brings the aestheticism of the symbolists to the activity of the modern mind—the Valéry who says in *Pièces sur l'Art* that there is a *mystique* of sensation. Baudelaire cultivates this mystique, which often paralyzed Mallarmé. The impressionists, fortunately, always trusted their eye, their *volupté,* without sacrificing too much to theory, although they too were led by their revolt from academic formulas to a high degree of self-consciousness.

The impressionists were realists, and what is called realism is another sort of nineteenth-century empiricism, another means of testing values pragmatically—in this case objectively instead of subjectively. It is an effort that could not have been made without romanticism, which had within it a great deal of realism, as we see in Wordsworth's notions about language, in the painting of the Barbizon group, or in Keats's effort to burst Joy's grape against his palate. Some of this realism is a form of revolt from the academic, the outworn. The opposition of the realists to the academicians was social as well as artistic: the Count of Nieuwerkerke, who controlled official patronage, said the Barbizon painters were "democrats who don't change their linen."[3] Géricault shows the realism inherent in romantic painting. His study of the insane—the haunting face of *La Folle*

—is a very intense observation that is "independent." It is quite in contrast to the insurgent romantic drama of his *Raft of the Medusa,* which is only a flamboyant variant of academic mechanisms: his figures are "antique" nudes, his light is a studio glare, and his waves are from the palette only—especially that preposterous arching billow about to break over the shipwrecked. Here the romantic heroics are only a form of journalism—like Delacroix's *Liberty Guiding the People.*

The realism inherent in the whole romantic period is clearly evident in portrait-painting, a hard core of prose within the poetry of painters like Delacroix and Géricault. In his portraits Ingres returns from his stucco mythologies to severe naturalism. David's imperial displays and his revolutionary classicisms are totally unlike his portrait of *Madame Chalgrin* with its red-brick background, its elementally simple figure in gray dress and blue sash. (In this "realistic" work David uses Van Gogh's swirling color and brushwork.) Portrait and landscape were alike a return to nature. In the same way, perhaps for the same reason, there was a return in the novel from Scott and Hugo to Maupassant's *Une Vie* and the Goncourts' *Germinie Lacerteux.* Wordsworth made his return to "common life" in a poem like "Goody Blake."

Inconsistently enough, this realism leads, like Baudelaire's romanticism, back to a consciousness of style. Flaubert the anti-romantic writes to Louise Colet: "The more Art develops, the more scientific it will be, just as science will become artistic." The more scientific, the less the personality of the artist matters; or as Flaubert says about writing *Bovary:* "No lyricism, no comments, the author's personality absent." Along with Baudelaire, Flaubert moves toward an aesthetic of Beauty. Of course the artist's personality was never absent, as Flaubert too well knew when he endured his agonies (*les affres de l'Art*): "25 pages in six weeks. . . ." "Last week I spent *five days writing one page. . . .*" "It amounts to thirteen pages, no more, no less, thirteen pages in seven weeks. . . ." Or again: "I am studying the theory of clubfeet. . . ." "I am still struggling with clubfeet." Flaubert may protest that "Passion does not make poetry, and the more personal you are, the weaker"; but he knows that he hates the very reality he is compulsively forced to analyze.

"Axiom," he states: "hatred of the Bourgeois is the beginning of virtue." Realists often passionately despised the actuality that fascinated them. Often, too, they were more devoted to art than the romantics. However intently Flaubert studies clubfeet, he also confesses: "What seems beautiful to me, what I should like to write, is a book about nothing, a book dependent on nothing external, which would hold together by the strength of its style." He repeats he is "no man of Nature—her 'wonders' move me less than those of Art." Baudelaire might have said this. Here Flaubert the realist meets Delacroix the romantic, who noted in his *Journal* (February 22, 1860): "Realism should be described as the antipodes of art." Realism is only a theory, not a style—an attitude, not a method, in spite of many definitions given during the century: "exact imitation of nature as it is," "a disregard of all the quests for elegance," "the study of the ugly."[4]

If there is no realism? There is only a succession of painters as unlike as Courbet, Manet, Degas, Meissonier; and writers as unlike as Balzac, Flaubert, Zola, Ibsen, George Eliot, and Hardy. Realists were always transcending mere accuracy, creating their own aesthetic effects. Witness Courbet's great *Atelier du Peintre* [10] with its Titian-like wealth and assurance and its olympian nude, all in a resonant gray tonality. Realism is a highly unstable condition, giving rise to other, more personal, values than reportage. Paradoxically the very realists who wanted to cancel out the personality of the artist give us the most personal and temperamental forms of nineteenth-century art. Probably there are more brands of realism in the nineteenth-century novel and painting than of any other so-called style. Realists wished to present the expected, the banal; but the really banal painting was academic—that is, in the "classic" tradition. Courbet's nude in the *Atelier* or Degas' ugly females scrubbing their backs as they sit in tin tubs are not banal; but Cabanel's Venus floating on academic spindrift in the Salon of 1863 is the cliché of calendar art. George Moore pointed out that the Academy was a "mere commercial enterprise" run by painters who offered the public landscapes like tea trays and figures from bon-bon boxes.

Both realism and romanticism were revolts against the offi-

10 COURBET: *Atelier du Peintre*

Louvre, Archives Photographiques, Paris

cial, against Montalembert and the Institute, the academicians who were always admiring the "big" subject, the antique stereotypes with "literary" meanings exhibited year after year in the salons. At the dead center of nineteenth-century painting was the academic machine like Couture's *Romans of the Decadence* (1847) [11]. The esteem for these machines was partly due to the ease with which they could be "read." Until Baudelaire wrote his *Salons,* criticism was literary or moralizing, stressing the subject just as Diderot did when he praised Greuze for the moral of *The Prodigal's Return* and blamed Boucher for his sensuality. A century later Ruskin was still asking what makes one subject "greater" than another, what "makes one truth greater than another, one thought greater than another"? Or why is painting a peach "nobler" than painting hawthorn or nightshade; or why is the emotion in Wordsworth's "Ellen" nobler than in Shenstone's "Jessy"; or why are Dutch genre painters inferior to Angelico in "spiritual beauty"? Ruskin laboriously comes to the decision that "high art" must seek in nature "whatsoever things are lovely, and whatsoever things are pure."

Endlessly debating how to define "a higher and lower range of beauty," Ruskin cannot say which is more necessary: a "grand" subject, intense emotion, or accuracy of depiction. In discussing the "moral of landscape" he ends by choosing "truth" instead of "beauty." The utter confusion of moral with aesthetic criteria is illustrated by Ruskin's praise of Landseer's painting, *The Old Shepherd's Chief Mourner,* which he reads exactly as critics tried to read Géricault's *Raft of the Medusa,* Courbet's *Bonjour M. Courbet,* or Manet's *Olympia.*

> Take, for instance, one of the most perfect poems or pictures (I use the words as synonymous) which modern times have seen:—the "Old Shepherd's Chief-mourner." Here the exquisite execution of the glossy and crisp hair of the dog, the bright, sharp touching of the green bough beside it, the clear painting of the wood of the coffin and the folds of the blanket, are language—language clear and expressive in the highest degree. But the close pressure of the dog's breast against the wood, the convulsive clinging of the paws, which has dragged the blanket off the trestle, the total powerlessness of the head laid, close and motionless, upon its folds, the fixed and tearful fall of the eye in its utter hopelessness, the rigidity of repose which marks that

Louvre, Archives Photographiques, Paris

11 COUTURE: *Romans of the Decadence*

there has been no motion nor change in the trance of agony since the last blow was struck on the coffin-lid, the quietness

> and gloom of the chamber, the spectacles marking the place where the Bible was last closed, indicating how lonely has been the life—how unwatched the departure of him who is now laid solitary in his sleep;—these are all thoughts—thoughts by which the picture is separated at once from hundreds of equal merit, as far as mere painting goes, by which it ranks as a work of high art.
>
> (*Modern Painters,* Part I, sec. i, chap. 2)

Is it any wonder that Baudelaire reacted against "vulgar and banal ideas," as he called them, in criticism and painting—this sort of melodrama, which is romanticism diluted by middle-class "thoughts"?

Ruskin's criticism shows how hard it is to distinguish romantic from realistic attitudes. The romantics were always trying to transcend nature by feeling; yet they succeeded no better than the realists in detaching themselves from nature. This is one reason why they did not find a style. The symbolists, however, succeeded in detaching feeling from objects, treating it as a "pure" rhythm, a "constellation," a crystallization that borrowed a minimum from what is seen. Reacting against realism and photography and reportage, the symbolists isolated feeling as an artistic value quite apart from the representation of things, so that consciousness could exist in the image, as a poetic or pictorial motif. At this point symbolism draws close to other experimental techniques in the later nineteenth century—notably Art Nouveau—and prepares the new formalism of an authentic modern art.

The symbolist technique originated in that misunderstood development known as the picturesque, which has a resemblance to *genre pittoresque* but is inherently different from that strange phase of rococo. After he printed *Creation of the Rococo* Fiske Kimball wrote a letter to the *Times Literary Supplement* (June 8, 1946) remarking "The mere fact that . . . the English landscape garden was a creation contemporary with Watteau and Oppenord does not make it Rococo, in any just or established usage, nor does it make the Rococo Romantic." Rococo, he goes on, is a decorative style, basically architectural, that "cannot be absorbed into Romanticism." He closes with the bold notion that the various romantic movements of the eighteenth century should, in fact, be characterized by the term *picturesque*.

Actually the picturesque is a technique—not a style—running under the romantic surface currents, developing into symbolism in poetry and painting, and mediating between different arts and different periods. The technique of this picturesque-romantic-symbolist tradition is to suggest rather than to state; the artist in this tradition has a psychology instead of a style, and he often refuses the world outside, using it only to evoke certain feelings. Wordsworth believed that the process of writing his own poetry was evoking a complex of feelings: "the emotion is contemplated till, by a species of reaction, the tranquillity gradually disappears, and an emotion, kindred to what was before the subject of contemplation, is gradually produced, and does itself actually exist in the mind." The poet, he says, is different from others because of "a greater promptness to think and feel without immediate external excitement." This is an art of private excitation, and among the symbolist painters late in the century Odilon Redon attempted this sort of evocation by his misty forms rousing *le sens du mystère*. Redon worked from the interior, reaching the spirit by intimations:

> The sense of mystery: that is to be continually amid the equivocal, double, triple aspects—intimations of aspects (images within images), forms about to be, or forms existing only in a certain state of soul in the beholder. (1902)[5]

Wordsworth was on the verge of this sense of mystery when by a kind of auto-excitation he felt "thoughts that do often lie too deep for tears."

One of the originators of this technique was John Milton, that prodigy in various poetic styles, for "L'Allegro" and "Il Penseroso" are evocative to the extent of being almost proto-symbolist. These verses are, to be sure, an academic exercise, but the rhetoric is saturated with a mood—a mood that is transient and gives each poem its intonation.

> Right against the eastern gate,
> Wher the great sun begins his state,

Rob'd in flames, and amber light,
The clouds in thousand liveries dight. . . .
Russet lawns and fallows gray,
Wher the nibling flocks do stray,
Mountains on whose barren brest
The labouring clouds do often rest:
Meadows trim with daisies pide,
Shallow brooks and rivers wide.
Towers and battlements it sees
Boosom'd high in tufted trees . . .

This is like painting by Claude, whose thin light bathes the conventional pastoral, vibrating with a tone more private than the baroque sunburst. The two poems are studied excitations or suggestion: the secluded reading of romance and tragedy, the great bell resounding over some wide shore, the minute drops falling in the clear dawn. We think, too, of Giorgione's subjective vision of classic landscape. "L'Allegro" and "Il Penseroso" are tone poems, their unity coming from Milton's intimate pleasures, the prospects opening before his inward eye that is his solitary bliss, like Wordsworth's. Also like Wordsworth, he is in a vacant mood, a reverie. Form in the two poems is an emotional drift or direction as well as a rhetorical structure. Admittedly these verses are a source of the picturesque and the eighteenth-century meditative poem. But picturesque is not merely an eighteenth-century, pre-romantic episode in the arts. It has its nineteenth-century phases, including calendar art, and it also impinges on symbolism. If it is not a style, it is a trend with implications that Ruskin is one of the few critics to notice. It is one transition between rococo and modern styles.

As we might guess from Milton's two poems and Claude's paintings, the origins of picturesque must be sought in the seventeenth century, or earlier in the phases of gothic, renaissance, or baroque art which used light and shadow, color, and broken contours for painterly effects. There are picturesque passages in Altdorfer, and the "little masters," Ruysdael, and Hobbema caught the quick sunlight and shadow sweeping across the Low Countries; they saw painterly values in scenes from humble life. Along with Rembrandt, Salvator Rosa, Magnasco, Piranesi,

Hubert Robert, they belong to a mode of vision that appears almost continuously through the history of art north and south of the Alps. But it was not until this painterly manner in art and literature consciously used the associationist psychology devised by John Locke that picturesque had a coherent history leading toward the symbolist art of Mallarmé and Maurice Denis at the close of the nineteenth century. Denis wrote: "Symbolism is the art of translating states of soul into color and images. These images, either invented or borrowed from nature, are signs and symbols of states of mind." Symbolist poets move beyond the mechanical associationist memory to the creative dream.

In sum, the picturesque appears during two centures in two different aspects: first an appeal to the eye alone as a painterly technique, then as an art in which an emotive state is translated (to use Denis' phrase) into a visual image that becomes a "hieroglyph" for a mood, feeling, or "dream." Originally a mode of expression that was entirely visual—arising from and agreeable to the sense of sight—the picturesque during the eighteenth century changed, under the influence of the prevailing psychology, into an art in which visual impressions are signs or symbols for consciousness ("states of soul," as the symbolists had it). The course of this development is confused, yet discernible if we keep in mind the shift in focus from the exterior to the interior world. Symbolism is an extension of picturesque.

II

VISUAL PICTURESQUE: THE PLEASURES OF IMAGINATION

John Locke in the *Essay Concerning Human Understanding* (1690) took sight to be "the most comprehensive of all our senses, conveying to our minds the ideas of light and colors." What we have seen, can be recalled, for memory has "the power to revive again in our minds those ideas which, after imprinting, have disappeared, or have as it were been laid aside out of sight." Memory of what has once been seen brings with it, too, a sense of recognition: "the mind has a power in many cases to revive perceptions which it has once had, with this additional perception annexed to them, that *it has had them before.*" Thus memory adds a new human dimension of time—the sense of one's past—a dimension that gives to recovered impressions, though Locke does not say so as clearly as Proust, a personal meaning. However, Locke does say that these recollected sights become identified with our feelings: "those which naturally at first make the deepest and most lasting impressions, are those which are accompanied with pleasure or pain." The way is already open for Proust's research into that great "solid" psychology of the past, which is the domain of romantic experience.

Locke, indeed, seems more modern than Addison, his popularizer, who in 1712 wrote a series of *Spectator* papers on "Pleasures of Imagination," papers which for practical purposes inaugurate the history of picturesque as an art-form. Addison assumes that "our sight is the most perfect and most delightful of all our senses. It fills the mind with the largest variety of ideas, converses with its objects at the greatest distance, and continues the longest in action without being tired or satiated with its proper enjoyments." Sight "brings into our reach some of the most remote parts of the universe," and furnishes us with ideas because "we have the power of retaining, altering, and compounding those images, which we have once received, into all the varieties of picture and vision that are most agreeable to the imagination." The primary pleasure of imagination, he goes on, is actually seeing objects before our eyes. The secondary and more fruitful pleasures "flow from the ideas of visible objects when the objects are not actually before the eye, but are called up into our memories, or formed into agreeable visions of things that are either absent or fictitious." This secondary or creative imagination can "enlarge, revise, or vary" images to satisfy us with "strangeness and novelty" of visions appearing on its "spacious horizon." Among the eighteenth-century secondary pleasures of imagination were the half-plastic, half-visionary forms of the *morceau de caprice.* Yet the *morceau de caprice* and the *genre pittoresque* remain only a form of ornament, a subdevelopment in the rococo decorative field, even if they had psychic overtones, as in Collins' poetry.

For a long while critics, poets, and painters thought of the picturesque as an art of the sight only. As Richard Payne Knight wrote, the picturesque is a "mode of vision," a way of looking at scenery that recalls certain paintings we have seen and liked. A picturesque landscape was simply one that imitated paintings—especially paintings by Salvator, Claude, or the Dutch masters. The English "gothic" garden was picturesque in this sense. If a picturesque scene arouses memories, says Knight, they are only memories of paintings once seen by "those acquainted in that art." The topographical poem, too, was picturesque because it had "that kind of beauty which belongs exclusively to the sense of vision," though it could recall scenes from the classic georgic or eclogue. A picturesque poem like John Dyer's *Ruins of Rome* doubtless stimulated the imagination of the reader to transform Italian scenery into a landscape peopled with antique figures and weighted with memories of history.

Ordinarily the eighteenth century distinguished three kinds of style: the beautiful, the sublime, and the picturesque. Edmund Burke's famous essay identified the beautiful as what is small, smooth, round, mildly colored, and capable of giving pleasure. The sublime, on the contrary, is loud, rugged, gloomy, titanic, and able to inspire awe or terror. Though Burke did not discuss the picturesque, it was usually assumed to be a category between beauty and sublimity, having the roughness of the sublime along with an air of decay or antiquity. Uvedale Price thought that "Qualities of roughness and of sudden variation, joined to that of irregularity, are the most efficient causes of the picturesque." The picturesque has a quality that might be called (though the word was not used) quaint.

William Gilpin explains that "among all the objects of art, the picturesque eye is perhaps most inquisitive after the elegant relics of ancient architecture; the ruined tower, the gothic arch, the remains of castles and abbeys. These are the richest legacies of art. They are consecrated by time." Here is a "sentiment of age" Ruskin later sought in gothic. The luxuriant vistas of Thomson's *Seasons* with the golden hues of Claude or the heavier tones of Rubens, are also picturesque—a pleasure for the eye, and also emotive landscape. Dyer's topographical poems show how the irregular pleasures of the "vista" excited eighteenth-century sensibility:

> Temples! and towns! and towers! and woods!
> And hills! and vales! and fields! and floods!
> Crowding before me edg'd around
> With naked wilds, and barren ground.

Ruskin said that Claude first set the pictorial sun in the pictorial heaven. The radiance of Claude's light glowing over his artificial landscape induced the eighteenth-century "picturesque traveler" to carry a "Claude glass" with him when he went to the Lake Country; by means of this colored mirror the landscape was transfused with "that mellow golden hue so beautiful in itself, and which, when diffused, as in a fine evening, over the whole landscape, creates that rich union and harmony so enchanting in nature and in Claude." About 1756, when Dr. John Brown wrote to Lord Lyttelton, he took a Claude-view of the Lake Country:

> . . . the ruling tints of the valley being those of azure, green, and gold, yet ever various, arising from an intermixture of the lake, the woods, the grass, and corn fields: these are finely contrasted by the grey rocks and cliffs; and the whole heightened by the yellow streams of light, the purple hues, and misty azure of the mountains.

Reproduced by courtesy of the Trustees of the Tate Gallery, Millbank, London

12 GAINSBOROUGH: *Landscape—Sunset*

Such picturesque color is almost a state of feeling; the azure of the landscape is almost an inner vibration. The sight, said Addison, is the instrument of the imagination.

Even in the narrowest eighteenth-century sense of the word the picturesque is really more than a way of seeing. The picturesque scene is usually saturated with a mood—particularly that vulgar form of eighteenth- and nineteenth-century picturesque, the "cottage art" of Oudry and Morland, where shaggy oak trees, thatched roofs, domestic clutter, and the pastoral tasks of the submerged but honest poor are associated with a sentiment that survives in our calendar art. This debased version of picturesque deserves a moment's regard since it is one of the socially significant modes of vision—the Kitsch of picturesque art. It appears in Gainsborough's *Cottage Door* and his *Landscape: Sunset* [12] with their sentimentality about the life of the poor, expressed in a pictorial pastiche that probably traces back to the broken tones and shadows in Salvator, the roughness in Magnasco, the chiaroscuro of changing weather in Giorgione, and the peasant scenes of the Low Countries. Cottage art is also related to the fancies of *vedute* painters like Marieschi and to the "imaginary landscape" with ruins and peasants seen in atmospheric light. A great deal of mid-eighteenth-century painting was swept by the cloudy sunshine that glowers and fades in Fragonard, Richard Wilson, Gainsborough, Hubert Robert, and even in boudoir mythologies by Boucher. The eighteenth-century eye was extremely responsive to light and shadow, which became almost a signature for "landscape instinct" in poetry and painting.

The cottage art of Oudry, Gainsborough, and Morland is a form of pastoral diluted to a waterish level of sentiment, a daydream of the simple pleasures of rustic life that appears like a new Eden during the eighteenth century. Goldsmith's "sweet Auburn" with the sheltered cot, the brook, the busy mill, the sober herd, the mouldering wall and shapeless ruin, is a special kind of idyl that changed *genre pittoresque* from rococo decoration to a social fantasy:

> Sweet was the sound when oft at ev'ning's close,
> Up yonder hill the village murmur rose;

There, as I past with careless steps and slow,
The mingling notes came soften'd from below;
The swain responsive as the milkmaid sung,
The sober herd that low'd to meet their young,
The noisy geese that gabbled o'er the pool,
The playful children just let loose from school;
The watch-dog's voice that bay'd the whisp'ring wind,
And the loud laugh that spoke the vacant mind;
These all in sweet confusion sought the shade,
And fill'd each pause the nightingale had made.

This landscape is as ideal as Milton's visions in "L'Allegro" and "Il Penseroso," but marked by realistic details. It is not, however, realism; for the details are seen in a general tone of feeling such as Wordsworth sought, later, to throw over the incidents of country life. It is an emotive landscape that eventually becomes calendar art. The slovenly scene at Auburn is a middle-class illusion arising from a stereotyped sympathy for the "honest poor," who become eligible for pity or even admiration when they appear in a pastoral landscape. The urban poor do not lend themselves to this sort of nostalgia. Hogarth treated London guttersnipes by caricature, not by cottage art. A great deal of romantic social feeling worked itself off in cottage art, which placed the peasant against the emotive "ground" of picturesque landscape.

Ruskin called this painting a debased form of contemplation, as surely it is. During the eighteenth century, and the nineteenth, the urban middle class found it could not forget the simple pleasures of the poor, so attractive at a distance—the distance of the daydream. Ruskin remarks that this is a "parasitical" variety of picturesque appealing to someone not altogether unvirtuous but able to regard misery and ruin only at a remove that makes pleasurable feeling possible:

Through all his enjoyment there runs a certain under current of tragical passion,—a real vein of human sympathy;—it lies at the root of all those strange morbid hauntings of his; a sad excitement such as other people feel at tragedy, only less in degree, just enough, indeed, to give a deeper tone to his pleasure, and to make him choose for his subject the broken stones of a cottage wall, rather than of a roadside bank . . . : and, together with this slight tragical feeling, there is also a humble and romantic sympathy; a vague desire, in his own mind, to live in cottages rather than in palaces; a joy in humble things, a contentment and delight in makeshifts, a secret persuasion (in many respects a true one) that there is in these ruined cottages a happiness often quite as great as in king's palaces. . . . And thus, being nowise sure that these things can be mended at all, and very sure that he knows not how to mend them, and also that the strange pleasure he feels in them *must* have some good reason in the nature of things, he yields to his destiny, enjoys his dark canal without scruple, and mourns over every improvement in the town, and every movement made by its sanitary commissioners. . . .

(*Modern Painters,* Part V, chap. 1)

There is no better passage to interpret the mood of this middle-class version of pastoral where the inertia of reverie conceals a social compromise. Cottage art is an opium of the middle class, filled as it is with a desire for good works and sympathy for the unfortunate, yet able to deflect these genial feelings into an appreciation of poetry, painting, and novels in which the poor looked comfortably and reassuringly picturesque. This kind of art is a perverted form of realism—perverted because it bathes its clutter of barnyard details in complacency and reverie. The good eighteenth-century gardener, the Reverend William Mason, suggested that poverty has a picturesque effect if the children of the Poor—"in many a tatter'd fold"—are given rush hats and leather scrips and set to wandering through the vales of some great estate. Sir William Chambers, who devoted himself to laying out picturesque English gardens, hinted that wherever there are collieries and mines and famished cottagers, the addition of "a few uncouth straggling trees, some ruins, caverns, rocks, torrents, abandoned villages, in part consumed by fire, solitary hermitages, and other similar objects, artfully introduced and blended with gloomy plantations, would compleat the aspect of desolation, and serve to fill the mind." To Chambers' eye this would be very "Chinese." The scene of picturesque poverty—otherwise, the art-view of misery—is an eighteenth- and nineteenth-century pastoral often found in novels where, as one churchman put it, the poor come to their frugal repasts with an appetite the rich cannot often enjoy.

Cottage art is not in the main current of picturesque, which is a much wider manifestation in all the arts. Unfortunately, however, the picturesque has been so entirely identified with this debased or diluted calendar art and feeling that it has not been seen for what it is: an early phase of a subjective technique that gradually changes during the course of romanticism to the symbolism of the later nineteenth century. The Kitsch we have just mentioned is a minor and particular channel to release the pseudo-social, pseudo-artistic feelings of a middle class that was without a style and therefore resorted to the pastiche, of which cottage art was a brand. When cottage art was stripped by Courbet of its picturesque atmosphere in paintings like *Stonebreakers* or *Funeral at Ornans,* realism appeared. When the pastoral mood vanished under the bold eye of someone like Courbet, the creature values of humble life appeared in all their crudity. There was a note of realism in cottage art; but the random details—the roughness of oak trees, the shaggy thatched roof, the bucolic apparatus of poems and paintings—were picturesque only because they were seen in a self-indulgent, reminiscent mood: "In that sweet mood when pleasant thoughts Bring sad thoughts to the mind," as Wordsworth wrote.

Wordsworth is much in point here, for his poetry was by intent a form of cottage art, throwing a color of feeling over common incidents: "the feeling therein developed gives importance to the action and situation," he insists, "and not the action and situation to the feeling." So he tells the story of Martha Ray and Michael. Wordsworth was a great artist of the picturesque who was transitional between the earlier picturesque of the eighteenth century and the nineteenth-century development of picturesque toward symbolist art. He looks back to the eighteenth-century idyl, the topographical painters and poets. He looks forward to Proust, who also recognized in the language of the senses an intimation of unknown modes of being and who, like Wordsworth, could be laid asleep in body and through an intermittence of the heart could translate a sensation into a timeless recognition.

Wordsworth tried to explain his intermittences—when the

light of sense goes out and his mind feeds upon infinity—by the prevailing "associationist" psychology; and next we must consider this psychology as a mechanism by which picturesque changed from a merely visual pleasure to a shaping imagination that could read into objects of the outside world the revelation of the absolute. Even the diluted picturesque we have called cottage art needed to be seen emotively, for it was, as Ruskin noted, a debased form of contemplation. Wordsworth is contemplative in a higher vein.

III

PSYCHOLOGICAL PICTURESQUE: ASSOCIATION AND REVERIE

To go back for a moment to Addison's papers on the imagination: it is already clear that picturesque is an activity not only of the primary imagination but also of the secondary—what Coleridge was later to call in his own jargon the "esemplastic" or shaping imagination, the coloring of a remembered or a present scene by a mood. The activity of the secondary imagination causes Wordsworth to see a sunset in a new way: for the very clouds "take a sober coloring" from "an eye that hath kept watch o'er man's mortality." Picturesque can be a kind of scenery giving pleasure to the eye or resembling painting; but it can also, and more creatively, be a way of projecting moods into scenery until landscape becomes a symbol. Byron wrote that "high mountains are a feeling," and Amiel remarked in his *Journal* (October 31, 1852) that a landscape is a state of soul. Romanticism often seems to be a way of using the world as an instrument to express feeling.

The broader agreements between picturesque and romantic

art are shown in a passage from lectures given in Paris in 1826 by Théodore Simon Jouffroy, which indicates how romanticism was leading toward Baudelaire's proto-symbolism:

> So each thing, each notion, is, in a certain way, a symbol. . . . The art that represents sounds, forms, colors, words arouses in us not only an idea of what it imitates but also other ideas that gather about them by association. . . . Everything is symbolic. . . . This is the difference that separates the realm of things from that other realm we do not see, the visible and the invisible. . . . In style, in discourse, what one calls an image is the representation of the invisible by visible objects. . . .
>
> (*Cours d'Esthétique,* xviii)

Jouffroy is defining a Copernican revolution in the arts, resembling the revolution in philosophy Kant wrought when he showed that we cannot know the absolute by the senses or by reason but must transcend both by vision; thus an understanding of reality cannot be gained "objectively" but only "subjectively." An object must not be taken for a thing-in-itself but only as a sign in another order of being. The change brought about by the romantics was to make the mind not a mirror of the outside world but a source of analogies—a means of reaching the invisible by means of the visible.[6] Using objects only as symbols, the mind is creative, and its creative action begins in the feelings that cluster about sounds, forms, colors, words by association. The associationist psychology was as influential in the eighteenth century as Freudian psychology is in the twentieth.

In its early phases this psychology is mechanistic—nearly behavioristic; but it was changed by Coleridge and the romantics to an "organic" theory of imagination, a power to envision another higher order of reality; or even to create it, as in a dream. Reality for Baudelaire is often "a vision in a dream." His "artificial paradise" was an "architecture of dreams" like De Quincey's *Confessions of an English Opium Eater,* which was written while the romantics were discovering the powers of the imagination. De Quincey tells us that in 1817 as a result of drugs his dreams were "a theatre suddenly opened and lighted up, which presented nightly spectacles of more than earthly splendor," with vast extensions of space and time. Some of these spectacles were inspired by Piranesi's fantastic views (De Quincey must be referring to the *Prisons*):

> . . . vast Gothic halls: on the floor of which stood all sorts of engines and machinery, wheels, cables, pulleys, levers, catapults, &c &c. . . . Creeping along the sides of the walls, you perceive a staircase. . . . Follow the stairs a little further, and you perceive it come to a sudden and abrupt termination, without any balustrade, and allowing no step onwards to him who had reached the extremity except into the depths below. . . . But raise your eyes, and behold a second flight of stairs still higher. . . . Again elevate your eye, and a still more aerial flight of stairs is beheld.

This architecture of dreams is a romantic version of *genre pittoresque.* It leads De Quincey toward Baudelaire's long imaginary voyages and "the expansion of things infinite." Meanwhile Coleridge had taken his own imaginary voyage into the kingdom of the great Khan Kubla. The associationist psychology is a key to the *genre pittoresque,* but also to the romantic dream and, at last, to symbolism itself.

We need not trace the course of this psychology through the many followers of John Locke, but summarize its rather naïve theory as it appears in David Hartley, whose *Observations on Man* (1749) were so popular that Coleridge named his son David Hartley Coleridge. Hartley explains that once sense impressions are recorded in the mind, they "run into clusters and combinations by association," so that sensations become identified with passions or affections, which can be "excited by objects, and by the incidents of life . . . till at last, by the numerous reciprocal influences of all these upon each other, the passions arrive at that degree of complexness which is observed in fact, and which makes them so difficult to be analyzed." In short, feelings become identified with objects or events, which in turn can stimulate these associated feelings. As Wordsworth said later, our thoughts inscrutably represent our past feelings; for memory is always resurrecting feelings obscurely in clusters. Eight years after Hartley printed his work Mark Akenside wrote a poem,

The Pleasures of Imagination, suggesting how a scene becomes an indelible symbol for associated feelings:

> For when the different images of things
> By chance combin'd have struck the attentive soul
> With deeper impulse, or, connected long,
> Have drawn her frequent eye; howe'er distinct
> The external scenes, yet oft the ideas gain
> From that conjunction an eternal tie
> And sympathy unbroken.

The sympathetic association of scenes with feelings led Wordsworth to identify the sight of the Wye valley near Tintern Abbey with his experiences when, five years before, his sorrow had been eased by seeing the same landscape. The place becomes for him a symbol of emotions so deeply embedded in his consciousness that he gropes to define them "with many recognitions dim and faint / And somewhat of a sad perplexity." His earlier view of Tintern has not been to him like a landscape to a blind man's eye, but has returned amid the din of cities with a strange restorative power, felt in the blood and along the heart. The recollection of these hallowed and pure motions of the senses—an organic sensibility that caused his retinal impression of a scene to remain as a Proustian residue of experience—is like a spell, disturbing him with elevated thoughts and some intimation of a motion interfused through his life and through the world. The Wye has become symbolic of a past state of consciousness and resurrects "thoughts of more deep seclusion"—his alienated mood of 1793. The topography of the valley conforms to his passions, past and present, as he interpenetrates nature with his feelings, and his seeing becomes a creative act, a shaping imagination excited by the senses but transcending the senses. Baudelaire said that the world is a forest of symbols. Wordsworth speaks of

> . . . all the mighty world
> Of eye and ear,—both what they half create,
> And what perceive.

The only means at his disposal to account for his moods of exaltation was Hartley's theory of associationism, which did enable him to write about these experiences even if it could not explain them satisfactorily:

> The scenes which were a witness of that joy
> Remained in their substantial lineaments
> Depicted on the brain
> . . . .
> and by force
> Of obscure feelings representative
> Of things forgotten, these same scenes so bright,
> So beautiful, so majestic in themselves,
> Though yet the day was distant, did become
> Habitually dear, and all their forms
> And changeful colors by invisible links
> Were fastened to the affections. . . .
>
> (*The Prelude,* I)

Hartley did for Wordsworth what Plato could not: that is, furnish some reason why sensuous experience was elevated to rapture—because a scene, a tree, a flower became associated with primal affections and feelings.

The most influential book on associationist aesthetic was printed in 1790, just before Wordsworth began to write. Archibald Alison's *Essays on the Nature and Principles of Taste* illustrates the psychology available to Wordsworth and underlying the deeper picturesque that, as Rimbaud implied, made the romantics symbolists "without knowing it." In these *Essays* Alison holds that the arts must use objects as "signs or expressions of qualities capable of producing emotion," and that art is able to transform the appearances of things by evoking in us an emotion to color the world by our mood: "Our minds, instead of being governed by the character of external objects, are enabled to bestow upon them a character which does not belong to them." Things can serve as "signs" for feelings. In an astonishing remark Alison seems to imply Baudelaire's notion that colors, scents, and sounds can "correspond" in harmonies: ". . . by means of the connexion, or resemblance, which subsists between the qualities of matter, and qualities capable of producing emotion, the perception of the one immediately, and very often irresistibly, suggests the idea of the other; and so early are these associations formed, that it requires afterwards some pains to separate this connexion, and to prevent us from attributing to the sign, that effect which is produced alone by the quality signified."

Beauty and sublimity, like the picturesque, are due, says Alison, to "a variety of images in our minds, very different from those which the objects themselves can present to the eye." By such evocations the scenes of common life are tinged with the feelings they arouse:

> Trains of pleasing or of solemn thought arise spontaneously within our minds; our hearts swell with emotions, of which the objects before us seem to afford no adequate cause; and we are never so much satiated with delight, as when, in recalling our attention, we are unable to trace either the progress or the connexion of those thoughts, which have passed with so much rapidity through our imagination.

Accordingly the sunset for Wordsworth's eye becomes a "sign" for a primal sympathy too deep for tears. Or as the symbolist Ernest Raynaud put it in 1883, "a river corresponds to a destiny; a setting sun to a glory being destroyed."[7]

Anticipating Proust's intermittences, Alison says there is no man who does not have private associations to enhance particular scenes and books; and the imagination is freest during the relaxations of the "vacant and unemployed"—those who enjoy Wordsworth's "wise passiveness"—

> In such trains of imagery, no labor of thought, or habits of attention are required; they rise spontaneously in the mind . . . and they lead it almost insensibly along, in a kind of bewitching *reverie*.

This is the word we have been expecting, since the picturesque is a reminiscent imagining. Alison quotes, in fact, the Abbé Delille (Jacques Delille) on the subject of gardening, an excerpt that might stand as epigraph for a Proustian novel on the Guermantes or Méséglise "ways":

> N'avez-vous pas souvent, aux lieux infrequentés,
> Rencontré tout-à-coup ces aspects enchantés,

Qui suspendent vos pas, dont l'image chérie
Vous jette en une douce et longue rêverie?

There were many passages of reverie in eighteenth-century novels and poems; but this enchantment with a certain place, bringing a sense of obscure harmonies, is also an early moment in the history of symbolist art: an image from the outside world overwhelms us by its suggestion, its note of "correspondence," perhaps; then there occurs some interruption or intermission of ordinary perception while the scene before us takes on the value of metaphor, gathering about itself a whole state of consciousness. Unwittingly, of course, the Abbé stands on the verge of what today would be called depth-perception in contrast to surface-perception, and hints that some of our most valuable experiences are formless and inarticulate, incapable of being structured in conventional forms of art. This proto-symbolism is based upon the associationist psychology as Alexander Gerard and other aestheticians of the day explained it: "A number of distinct perceptions being thus united, by co-existence, in the imagination, any one of them occurring to the mind, suggests the rest." So there is a "constant vibration of thought between the objects immediately connected with the passion." Delille's sense of affinities is more than an enchantment with place; it is a premonition of Wordsworth's sense of something deeply interfused.

The Abbé deserves another word since his poem on *L'Imagination,* begun in 1785 and finished in 1794, devotes eight books to "les effets réciproques de l'imagination sur les lieux, et des lieux sur l'imagination." Delille finds that our thoughts, "always contagious," run into "secret clusters," a *marche involontaire* stimulated by sensations stored in the memory:

En images sans fin une image est féconde:
Tel un caillou tombant forme une cercle dans l'onde;
Un autre lui succéde, et tous les flots troublés
Étendent jusqu'aux bords leurs cercles rédoublés. . . .
Enfin, par le hasard d'un heureux voisinage,
Une image souvent éveille une autre image. . . .

These recognitions and correspondences emancipate us, the Abbé finds, from place and time:

> Dans un espace étroit, et dans un temps borné,
> Son magique pouvoir ne fut point confiné.

The imagination prefers what is past to what is present, and *les traits indécis* to *contours précis.* For the Abbé imagination springs, as it does for Proust, from memory, *notre âme en silence amassant ses trésors:*

> Ainsi les souvenirs, les regrets et l'amour,
> Et la mélancholique et douce rêverie,
> Reviennent vers les lieux chers a l'âme attendrie,
> Où nous fûmes enfants, amants, aimés, heureux. . . .

As a generalization we may say that the earlier eighteenth-century imagination was captured by space—the spaces that had been found by Newtonian astronomy and by the explorers of distant places of the earth. The deists especially were drunk with the thought of the spacious universe; and rococo is an art that is spatial. But the sentimental eighteenth century was enchanted by time; and perhaps the essence of romanticism is the discovery that the field of human experience is time,[8] especially the sense of the past, which brings a new meaning to fatality, and the sense of the future, which brings a new meaning to destiny. Time remembered—or else the desperate dream of the future, the spring that cannot be far behind, the wonder of the world that is to be. Romantic sadness, romantic revolt, romantic ecstasy are aspects of this new consciousness of time. And always for the romantic there is a sense of the inadequacy of the present: "For in life there is no present," says Manfred, bitterly. In "Le Lac" Lamartine hopelessly asks: Can we not hold even an hour? "O temps, suspends ton vol!" It is useless. Then love; the hour ceases, and we die. But there is always the solace of memory. The eighteenth-century reverie is antechamber to the terrible new expansion of nineteenth-century time. So reverie, by its subtle and silent associations, brings to the Abbé a release from the present.

The images in the mind cluster *par le hasard* in the green shade of reverie when sense impressions often mingle in a sort of synaesthesia; the Abbé finds it easy to associate the experience of sight with the experience of hearing or taste:

> . . . chaque sens, par un heureux concours
> Prête aux sens alliés un mutuel secours;
> Le frais gazon des eaux m'embellit leur murmure;
> Leur murmure, à son tour, m'embellit la verdure.
> L'odorat sert le goût, et l'oeil sert l'odorat. . . .
> Ainsi tout se répond, et, doublant leurs plaisirs,
> Tous les sens l'un de l'autre éveillent les désirs. . . .

Ainsi tout se répond: this is not, to be sure, precisely Baudelaire's sense of correspondence when *les parfums, les couleurs, et les sons se répondent* with long echoes in a shadowed and deep unity; but it is a first venture toward those mysterious and ineffable analogies which the symbolists discovered. Dugald Stewart in 1810 uses the very term analogy in explaining how the sublime is due to association: "The ideas thus associated may be conceived to bear some distant analogy in their mutual communications with each other."

In reading such statements we must remember that for the eighteenth century an idea is a residue of a sense impression. That is what Keats supposed when he exclaimed "O for a life of sensations rather than of thoughts." Like Wordsworth, he wished to reduce poetry to primary experience, proving it on the pulses. Wordsworth thought of the poet as a man speaking to men because he could more sensitively than ordinary persons study how "our continued influxes of feeling" are influenced by thoughts which are themselves "representatives of all our past feelings." Thus in *The Prelude* Wordsworth hoped to trace "the primary laws of our being" by describing his

> . . . observation of affinities
> In objects where no brotherhood exists

for the average mind. These affinities are the fruit of the poet's extreme sensitivity, his "organic sensibility":

> Those hallowed and pure motions of the sense
> Which seem, in their simplicity, to own
> An intellectual charm.

Again, this is not precisely Baudelaire's venture in transforming *volupté en connaissance,* but it does show how the associationist psychology transformed sensation into imagination, and how imagination became a creative power by means of association, an activity which explored, as Wordsworth said, "obscure feelings representative / Of things forgotten" and gained from reverie recognitions or revelations of what is beyond time and place. The creative poetic act begins in wise passiveness, organic pleasures, and animal sensibilities; but it leads to a vision when "the light of sense goes out" and the invisible world reveals itself with a flash like

> Characters of the great Apocalypse,
> The types and symbols of Eternity,
> Of first, and last, and midst, and without end.

So from Alison's "bewitching reverie" and associations most "loose and general" there comes a proto-symbolist poetry in which a tree, a particular field, that Wordsworth has seen, can suggest a sense of loss inexpressible, a moral crisis:

> But there's a tree, of many, one,
> A single field which I have looked upon;
> Both of them speak of something that is gone;
> The pansy at my feet
> Doth the same tale repeat.

In these moments Wordsworth has touched one of the octaves along *l'immense clavier des correspondances* on which Baudelaire set himself to compose. During Wordsworth's revelations picturesque transforms itself to romanticism; and soon romanticism is to transform itself to symbolism.

As a romantic, Wordsworth casts over the world the light of his imagination, suggesting an equation between the sun's afterglow and his sorrow. The equation is more obscurely written in Mallarmé, more hieroglyphic; but it is the same kind of equation, interpenetrating the world by "many recognitions dim and faint." Both Wordsworth and Mallarmé felt an equivalence between a moment of duration in them and a moment of duration in things, bringing a sense of affinities almost mystical:

> . . . there is a dark
> Inscrutable workmanship that reconciles
> Discordant elements, makes them cling together
> In one society.
>
> (*The Prelude,* I)

In sum, "Tintern Abbey," identifying a "sad perplexity" with the Wye valley, is in a tradition of picturesque art that arose with Milton's "Il Penseroso," developed through the landscape poets of the eighteenth century, and reached transcendental intimations in Wordsworth, these intimations later inspiring Mallarmé's flight to the azure of the Absolute. Wordsworth's verse is the highest achievement of the picturesque in literature, which, in Alison's sense, is a way of seeing the world emotively, a means of associating a mood with objects until the contour of a landscape becomes the image of one's consciousness.

Here it will be objected that Wordsworth was inspired by what the eighteenth century knew as "the sublime." However the sublime and the beautiful—as defined by Burke, at least, and treated by most other critics—do not depend so heavily upon the emotional state of the beholder, but rather upon the traits of the scene itself—rough or smooth, dark or light, broken or gently curving. By contrast the picturesque is a *way* of seeing, the structuring of the scene depending on *how* we see what is before us rather than what kind of scene it is. To be sure, beauty and sublimity elicit emotions; yet they are categories of scenery rather than responses to scenery. Certain kinds of scenery, admittedly, are apt to rouse associations that cause the "psychological" picturesque we have been discussing. Alison says, for example, that we may see "an old tower in the middle of a deep wood, a bridge flung across a chasm"—one of the vistas devised for the "English" garden:

> If I am not mistaken, the effect which such objects have on every one's mind, is to suggest an additional train of conceptions, beside what the scene or description itself would have suggested. . . . They are, in general, such circumstances as coincide, but are not necessarily connected, with the character of the scene or description, and which, at first affecting the mind with an emotion of surprise, produce afterwards an increased or additional train of imagery.

The object itself, Alison explains, is only a "hint to awaken the imagination, and to lead it through every analogous idea that has place in the memory." By recovering the past, picturesque fancy is able to give a romantic amplitude to the scene before us. Whately, writing on picturesque gardens, remarked, "For such is the constitution of the human mind, that if once it is agitated, the emotion often spreads beyond the occasion."

The "ground" of a picturesque painting, poem, or scene is a mood, a feeling of unity in color or tone. Alison's term for this harmony is "unity of expression" or "unity of emotion," and he thinks that any contrast in a scene will only "strengthen the effect of the general emotion." Coleridge's theory that a poem reconciles opposite or discordant qualities extends Alison's notion that a work of art must inspire "one unmingled emotion." The gist of Coleridge's theory of imagination is in one of his letters to Southey (August 7, 1803): "I almost think that ideas *never* recall ideas, as far as they are ideas, any more than leaves in a forest create each other's motion. The breeze it is that runs through them—it is the soul, the state of feeling." Coleridge saw that Hartley's association was a mechanical composite; the deeper, creative association comes when artistic vision "diffuses a tone and spirit of unity that blends, and (as it were) *fuses* each into each by that synthetic and magical power to which we have exclusively appropriated the name of imagination." Coleridge is well along the way toward a symbolist theory of de Wyzewa, who in 1886 said that a poem should express a "total emotion."

The more mechanical sort of picturesque association led to the artificial gothicism of the early romantics; and, in general, after rococo, the arts of the eighteenth century adopted the pastiche. Witness Horace Walpole's *papier-mâché* gothicism at

Strawberry Hill, or Beckford's showy middle-class antiquarianism at Fonthill, or the Grecian, Palmyran, Roman, Egyptian fads of the early nineteenth century, and the ersatz classicism of Canova, David, and Walter Savage Landor, and the whole Empire period. Or there is Chatterton with his Rowley poems—and the ballad like "The Ancient Mariner." Once the principle of associationism was accepted, the artist had unlimited credit to draw on past styles. This credit resulted in the lavish historicism that overtook architecture along with all the so-called styles of the century between 1750 and 1850; by 1851, if not before, signs of an authentic modern style appeared—with the iron-and-glass Crystal Palace.

Historicism, especially in its gothic aspects, is a form of nostalgia, which in turn implies a sentimental attitude toward architecture. Much of the historicism was picturesque insofar as the architect intended to evoke associations by means of antiquarian references or pastiche. Dreaming of the middle ages was one of the shortest ways out of Manchester. Notoriously architecture of the nineteenth century was without a style, chiefly because the middle classes refused to accept the machine, iron, brick, and glass as basic materials for design. Consequently architecture was a continual adapting of past designs to present uses, and, as Pevsner has said, "associational values were the only values in architecture accessible to the new ruling class."[9] The upper middle class particularly, not choosing to recognize the worth of its own industrial arts, and without any cultural tradition of its own, borrowed its styles from the past or from afar; and in its concern to have "elegance" in building, painting, and poetry utilized whatever history or geography put at its disposal: parliamentary gothic or commercial greek. The parvenus could freely associate "culture" with these designs; that is, their architecture and decoration became a mode of picturesque. The pastiche allowed a maximal range of association with values they yearned for. In 1850 the Royal Panopticon of Science and Art built for itself in Leicester Square "the finest example of Moorish architecture ever erected in England."

Along with this quest for a usable past rose a cultural problem of vulgarity, on which Ruskin has an enlightening chapter in *Modern Painters.* A notion of vulgarity does not arise in any society where the class structure is so closed that everyone has his place and knows it—and keeps it. The hierarchical society of the middle ages produced a number of *arrivistes,* its bounders; but the feudal system was still rigid enough to provide a sanctioned and public ritual by which these few could climb: marriage, conquest, or the accolade of chivalry. These rituals were still available in the renaissance to the despotic Medicis, who made business a princely enterprise; and the regime of Louis XIV still preserved a social hierarchy. But the nineteenth century produced a horde of parvenus who were obliged to discount the older rituals and who were a culturally discontented class like our prosperous "workers." The cultural malaise attending the rise of these shopkeepers, as Macaulay frankly called them, is disclosed in the whole uneasy notion of vulgarity, which becomes a category in upper-middle-class values. The Victorian fear of being vulgar is an unpleasant symptom of an ineffectually aristocratic order penetrated in great numbers by a new and ambitious class; it is a penalty for being successful. The successful man must be "refined." As Ruskin notes, the readiest means of proving one is not vulgar is an exquisite sensitivity: "A gentleman's first characteristic is that fineness of structure in the body, which renders it capable of the most delicate sensation." This reliance on sensitivity as a mark of "breeding" also, ironically, opens the way for the dandy, who is a bohemian exquisite living at the very core of the new middle class. We must not pause to consider the many implications of the notion of vulgarity; but Henry James, for example, would be impossible without an idea of vulgarity. When Strether, with his heightened impressionability, finds he must be one of the people upon whom nothing is lost, he lifts the "breeding" of an old-world order to a moral imperative that enables him to be really human and to transcend the gentility of Woollett. There is also Gide, the ultimate dandy, carrying Ruskin's sensitivity to a decadent "refinement."

The loss of a style in the nineteenth century was involved generally with this prevailing dread of vulgarity—not only because it produced a decadent art for art's sake, but also because the arts accepted elegance as a means of avoiding vulgarity. The wish to have "rich" designs fostered the pasticheurs. The pastiche disguised, ornamented, and distorted; and it likewise encouraged a free range of association with past art, past values—history, in short. There is an episode in Disraeli's novel *Coningsby* when Oswald Millbank, son of an industrial baron, first visits Hellingsley, lately purchased by his father, and is delighted to see that it offers "better recollections of English manners, than that to which we would now introduce our readers. . . . It stood a huge and strange blending of Grecian, Gothic, and Italian architecture, with a wild dash of the fantastic in addition. The lantern watch-towers of a baronical castle were placed in juxtaposition with Doric columns employed for chimneys, while under oriel windows might be observed Italian doorways with Grecian pediments." More seriously, Richard Payne Knight confessed at the opening of the nineteenth century, without any sense of shame at all, in his *Inquiry Into Taste:*

> It is now more than thirty years since the author of this inquiry ventured to build a house, ornamented with what are called Gothic towers and battlements without, and with Grecian ceilings, columns, and entablatures within; . . . having at once the advantage of a picturesque object, and of an elegant and convenient dwelling.

The eighty thousand who went to see the Eglinton Tournament, held in August, 1839, at Eglinton Castle near Glasgow, and paid for by Archibald Montgomerie, also evidently went without embarrassment—or even a sense of the ridiculous.[10] There was a Grand Procession with men-at-arms, trumpeters, banner-bearers, heralds, and a King of the Tournament, a Queen of Beauty, a Black Knight, along with Knights of the Griffin, Dragon, Black Lion, Red Rose, White Rose, and Burning Tower. The tilting took place in a drenching rain. But the whole affair was painfully like a scene from the *Idylls of the King,* a pastiche of Malory and country-house theatricals:

> O brother, had you known our mighty hall,
> Which Merlin built for Arthur long ago!
> For all the sacred mount of Camelot,

And all the dim rich city, roof by roof,
Tower after tower, spire beyond spire,
By grove, and garden-lawn, and rushing brook,
Climbs to the mighty hall that Merlin built.
And four great zones of sculpture, set betwixt
With many a mystic symbol, gird the hall;
And in the lowest beasts are slaying men,
And in the second men are slaying beasts,
And on the third are warriors, perfect men,
And on the fourth are men with growing wings. . . .
(*"The Holy Grail"*)

This is the brand of pseudo-mediaevalism that made Ruskin despair of using gothic to solve the problems of taste, tradition, and function in architecture. The irony is that Ruskin, too, interpreted gothic picturesquely; but in so doing he introduced a deeply modern sense of History and enlarged his picturesque view of architecture by a modern sense of Time as a measure of human experience. Ruskin's chapters on gothic are prefatory to Henry Adams' great passage on the Virgin and the Dynamo, and to Eliot's quest for some usable past to give us a tradition while we dwell amid the chaos of a Waste Land. Ruskin's appreciation of gothic is a facet of his Landscape Instinct, for he sees architecture against its geographic setting, as a feature of Landscape.

In the fifth volume of *Modern Painters* and in *Seven Lamps* Ruskin says that one of the true orders of painting is the Contemplative, which records "the historical associations connected with landscape, illustrated by, or contrasted with, existing states of human life." These historical associations are a noble form of picturesque, the baser form of which is only a taste for broken lights, irregular lines, and the "accidental or external qualities" of a "parasitical sublimity." The spurious picturesque is "rather the degradation (or sometimes the undeveloped state) of the Contemplative." If a landscape is "dyed by the deep colors of human endurance" and recalls "the most precious inheritance, that of past ages," it belongs to the higher picturesque. If a major pathos of History is associated with landscape, Ruskin calls the painting Contemplative; but if the associations are merely of "the eye," not of "the heart," then the painting belongs to the lower order of picturesque we have previously related to calendar art. Ruskin admires gothic as a noble architecture because it is, like a Contemplative Landscape, an exponent of History and Age. As such it is the most precious symbol of our endurance as a race. According to this nostalgic reading, gothic is not to be looked upon as a method of building but, instead, as an expression of the Past, or as a metaphor for the accord between man and his History and the Landscape in which he has lived and suffered. Ruskin endows gothic with profoundly contemplative values by associating Architecture with the vast backward and abysm of Time.

His most picturesque reading of gothic is the "Lamp of Memory" chapter in *Seven Lamps,* where he repeats that the glory of gothic is its Age "and in that deep sense of voicefulness, of stern watching, of mysterious sympathy, nay, even of approval or condemnation, which we feel in walls that have long been washed by the passing waves of humanity." Marx said that the middle classes had destroyed all idyllic values by their constant revolutionizing of production. Ruskin is seeking such idyllic values in gothic: "For indeed, the greatest glory of a building is not in its stones, nor in its gold . . . it is in that golden stain of time, that we are to look for the real light, and color, and preciousness of architecture; and it is not until a building has assumed this character, till it has been . . . hallowed by the deeds of men, till its walls have been witnesses of suffering, and its pillars rise out of the shadows of death, that its existence, more lasting as it is than that of the natural objects of the world around it, can be gifted with even so much as these possess, of language and of life."

This view of gothic looks forward to Henry Adams' valedictory words to the Virgin and Chartres, after the pilgrimage he made to seek some refuge from the "great gallery of machines" in which he had lived:

> For seven hundred years Chartres has seen pilgrims, coming and going more or less like us, and will perhaps see them for another seven hundred years; but we shall see it no more, and can safely leave the Virgin in her majesty, with her three great prophets on either hand, as calm and confident in their own

> strength and in God's providence as they were when Saint Louis was born, but looking down from a deserted heaven, into an empty church, on a dead faith.

It also looks back to Alison, who had written that the associations of gothic are sublime "in proportion to their Antiquity, or the extent of their Duration." Alison believed that "the Gothic castle is still more sublime than all; because, besides the desolation of Time, it seems to have withstood the assaults of War." Ruin, then, is a symbol of History; it ceases to be a pleasure for the eye alone as it was for the fashionable seekers of picturesque like William Gilpin, who held:

> It is not every man who can build a house, that can execute a ruin. To give the stone its mouldering appearance—to make the widening chink run naturally through all the joints—to mutilate the ornaments—to peel the facing from the internal structure—to show how correspondent parts have once united, though now the chasm runs wide between them—and to scatter heaps of ruin around with negligence and ease; are great efforts of art.

Ruskin will have none of this quaint picturesque "sought in ruin and supposed to consist of decay." At the same time he will not have any restoration, for it is "impossible to raise the dead," and the "spirit which is given only by the hand and eye of the workman, never can be recalled." Only History can yield authentic architectural values: "I think a building cannot be considered as in its prime until four or five centuries have passed over it." True picturesqueness appears in ruins only "when by resemblance or association, they remind us of objects on which a true and essential sublimity exists, as of rocks or mountains, or stormy clouds or waves," a landscape in which man has possessed his History.

Having reached a nearly existential theory of gothic, Ruskin claims for mediaeval architecture the noblest values of association. His famous chapter on "The Nature of Gothic" in *Stones of Venice* proves that Ruskin takes architecture as a psychological symbol. He here defines gothic not by its external forms but by its "various mental characters" and the "fellowship there is between it and our Northern hearts." Since "Mental Expression" is more important than "Material Form," gothic for Ruskin becomes a kind of expressionist art, a phrasing of "characteristic or moral elements"—savageness, changefulness, naturalism, grotesqueness, rigidity, redundance. Gothic expresses the soul of its builders, and is a sign of "mountain brotherhood between the cathedral and the Alp." A racist reading is not far off. Ruskin's gothic is not an architecture but a "soul." Psychological landscape, psychological architecture: these are some final versions of picturesque, which turns out to be, at last, with the aid of the associational values of History and Locale, a form of symbolism or expressionism. At the close of the eighteenth century William Gilpin in his *Essays* was preaching an ethic of Time:

> There is still a *higher character* in landscape, than what arises from *uniformity of objects*—and that is the power of furnishing images *analogous to the various feelings, and sensations of the mind.* If the landscape painter can call up such representations, . . . where would be the harm of saying, that landscape, like history paintings, hath its ethics!
>
> (*Three Essays*)

Gilpin, like Ruskin, feels that "the stains of weather, the incrustations of moss" are imprints of a Memory "animated by a metaphorical or historical meaning"—a Memory falling like a shadow over gothic ruins.

IV

LUMINISM

Ruskin speaks of "the golden stain of time" as "the real light and color" of gothic. Inspired as it was by Claude's paintings, the picturesque eye was always sensitive to melodious color and light. To repeat the note written by Richard Payne Knight in the second edition of *Landscape:* "The picturesque is merely that kind of beauty which belongs exclusively to the sense of vision; or to the imagination, guided by that sense. It must always be remembered . . . that the eye, unassisted, perceives nothing but light variously graduated and modified." We might be reading the words of one of the impressionists. But Knight was speaking for a whole group of writers who insisted that picturesqueness is due to harmony of color and light, not to "roughness and sudden variation" or "irregularity." Uvedale Price explained the attraction Claude had for the eighteenth century:

> The pictures of Claude are brilliant in a high degree; but that brilliancy is so diffused over the whole of them . . . so mellowed

13 GUARDI (FRANCESCO):
Treasure Seekers (or *Caprice with Ruins on the Seashore*)

and subdued by the almost visible atmosphere which pervades every part, and unites them all together . . . the whole is splendor, the whole is repose; every thing lighted up, every thing in sweetest harmony . . .

One of the most charming effects of sunshine, is its giving to objects, not merely light, but that mellow golden hue, so beautiful in itself, and which, when diffused, as in a fine evening,

> over the whole landscape, creates that rich union and harmony so enchanting in nature and in Claude . . .
>
> (*Essays on the Picturesque*)

Similarly, in his essay on *Prints* William Gilpin looks for that "master-tint, which, like the key-tone in music, prevails over the whole piece." In landscape there should appear "the peculiar tints of seasons; of morning and evening; the light azure of a summer sky; the sultry glow of noon; the bluish or purple tinge, which the mountain assumes, as it recedes, or approaches; the grey moss upon the ruin . . ."

The Claudesque shimmer of yellow and azure tones comes and goes in eighteenth-century topographical poems, in the atmospheric harmony of the English garden with its blue vistas, in the twilit fantasies of the *genre pittoresque,* and in the fugitive gracious light falling over Guardi's Venice [13], or in Fragonard's smouldering shadows. In ways Addison did not foresee, the sight becomes a language of the imagination. Reacting against the "brown tree" convention, Constable [14] painted "under the sun" and found that "light and shade never stand still." Then he broke up his texture prismatically, almost like the impressionists, and his "unfinished" scenes have the glitter of dew and spring rain—"Constable's snow," it was called. Once his pigments were refracted into a silvery mirror-like idiom, he found, too, that "there are no lines in nature" but only gleams of light and planes of color—the planes that Cézanne was later to reorganize into cubist structures.

While Constable was giving landscape a new emerald accent, Turner and Ruskin were intensifying Claude's serene light into a fierce incandescence or an interior illumination. Turner's flaring color has the texture of passion, a romantic extravagance; and when Ruskin looks at storm clouds driving over La Riccia he feels in their radiance an emotive pace, a symbol of his own compulsion:

> I cannot call it color, it was conflagration. Purple, and crimson, and scarlet, like the curtains of God's tabernacle, the rejoicing trees sank into the valley in showers of light, every separate leaf quivering with buoyant and burning life . . . Far up into the reeesses of the valley, the green vistas arched like

Courtesy of the Widener Collection, National Gallery of Art, Washington, D.C.

14 CONSTABLE: *Wivenhoe Park*

> the hollows of mighty waves of some crystalline sea, with the arbutus flowers dashed along their flanks for foam, and silver flakes of orange spray tossed into the air around them, breaking over the gray walls of rock into a thousand separate stars. . . .
>
> (*Modern Painters,* Part II, sec. ii, chap. 2)

This is not landscape; it is vision, brightening the world by delight and worship. So Turner kindled the Alps in his water colors until ravines and snow peaks are burned away to symbols, luminous vapors that are triumphs over mere geological mass. Turner's is the light that never was on sea or land, heightening the romantic palette to an expressionist art that did not find its technical formula until Van Gogh wrote his signature large and searing over the landscape at Arles. This romantic coloring projected into nature originates in Claude's golden sunshine, but it is sublime in a way the first picturesque painters and poets would not have grasped. Ruskin writes a passage on the region of the rain-cloud to ask whether Claude could have given us Turner's meridian light:

> And then wait yet for one hour, until the east again becomes purple, and the heaving mountains, rolling against it in darkness, like waves of a wild sea, are drowned one by one in the glory of its burning: watch the white glaciers blaze in their winding paths about the mountains, like mighty serpents with scales of fire: watch the columnar peaks of solitary snow, kindling downwards, chasm by chasm, each in itself a new morning; their long avalanches cast down in keen streams brighter than the lightning, sending each his tribute of driven snow, like altar-smoke, up to the heaven; the rose-light of their silent domes flushing the heaven about them and above them, piercing with purer light through its purple lines of lifted cloud, casting a new glory on every wreath as it passes by, until the whole heaven, one scarlet canopy, is interwoven with a roof of waving flame, and tossing, vault beyond vault. . . .
>
> (*Modern Painters,* Part II, sec. iii, chap. 4)

Or, at an earlier hour, when the morning light has melted the hills and the sky, "like a wild, bright, impossible dream," casts its luster into the blue of the lake below, Ruskin again asks, "Has Claude given this?" Or has Claude seen the mists that hang steaming over torn cliffs, bathed in waving curtains of rain while the sun falls like a "red hot ball" dyeing all the air?

No: not exactly. For Claude gave only the classic tones of a fading baroque. But Shelley—who used color as flamingly as Delacroix or Ruskin or Turner—has a splendor that transforms the eighteenth-century picturesque to psychic language. The colors playing over Shelley's "Lines Written Among the Euganean Hills" are a symbolic dimension, and the sight becomes an instrument of an imagination as imperious as Van Gogh's. Shelley traces the manic-depressive course of his feelings as he lies above the burning Venetian lagoons, reading into their changing hues the cycle of his ecstasy and despair:

> Lo! the sun upsprings behind,
> Broad, red, radiant, half-reclined
> On the level quivering line
> Of the waters crystalline;
> And before that chasm of light,
> As within a furnace bright,
> Column, tower, and dome, and spire,
> Shine like obelisks of fire. . . .
> Noon descends around me now:
> 'Tis the noon of autumn's glow,
> When a soft and purple mist
> Like a vaporous amethyst,
> Or an air-dissolved star
> Mingling light and fragrance, far
> From the curved horizon's bound
> To the point of heaven's profound,
> Fills the overflowing sky. . . .

For Shelley and Turner the glare of noon and the blue dusk are keyed to psychic tumult and calm.

Turner's imagery is still unexplained. From about 1805 to 1810 he works in a flat, water-colorish medium with the subdued tones of English topographical painting, using fragile whites and grays and greens to block out scenes like his *Walton Reach* and *Washing Sheep* [15]. Then he inflames these neutral colors to a romantic glory, penetrating his Petworth series with a sunlight that is more explosive than the impressionist spec-

15 TURNER: *Washing Sheep*

16 TURNER: *Sunrise with Sea Monster*

trum. In this luminous phase Turner's composition shows two recurring patterns—a furious whorl of light or color, as in *Sunrise with Sea Monster* [16] or *Steamer in a Snowstorm* [17]; or else a gash of torrential light down the center with vague shapes surrounding, as in *Slave Ship, Yacht Approaching the Coast,* or *Venice: After the Ball.* The abyss of light in *Tapping the Furnace* is entirely unreadable from a literary point of view—a woman calmly sitting before huge, dim cogged wheels while two workmen are shrouded on the left in a great burst of scarlet and yellow, surrounded by a fiery halo, with a phoenix-like creature living at the heart of the tumult of color. The great red waves pulsing through *Petworth: Interior,* a yellow undertow at the left and green rhythms at the right, prove that Turner leaped from a tradition of the aquarelle to an art that is possessed.

As soon as this color lost its emotive charge, as it did later in Whistler's compositions in gray and suppressed blue, it was capable of being a more abstract language, a motif in itself, freeing painting from both nature and the passionate romantic involvement of the painter with his own work—which now became art for the sake of art. Baudelaire found that color is an

Reproduced by courtesy of The National Gallery, London

17 TURNER: *Steamer in a Snowstorm*

"abstraction," having its own laws of "harmony, melody, and counterpoint." Though Turner belongs with the romantics, his work illustrates the thesis Baudelaire held in his *Salon of 1846,* when he decided that "form and color are one" and that the painter must know the "counterpoint" to be able to "produce a harmony of twenty different reds." If there is melody, says Baudelaire, the work "already has meaning" apart from its subject—and "Melody is unity within color, or over-all color. Melody calls for a cadence." Gauguin saw that he could treat color as a "byzantine" decorative design. Turner, however, leads more directly to Kandinsky's abstract color than to Gauguin's, since Kandinsky is a romantic when he treats color as a notation for "pure" rhythms moving within the consciousness of the painter. Kandinsky's color is a psychic graph. Intervening between Turner and Gauguin or Kandinsky, the impressionists used color to record optical effects, to capture a certain quality of atmosphere, to gain an almost scientific retinal accuracy like the experimenters who diffracted light into its various hues. Strictly speaking, impressionism does not belong to the history we have been sketching, though it, also, like Turner's luminism, is an art committed to the moment, to time, to what is transitory. Impressionism catches the fleeting appearances of things outside, rather than the fleeting emotions passing like gusts over the romantic temperament. Shelley tried to escape from the outside world, from time, and the torment of his changing feeling by means of his platonism—but failed. His brightest visions are like seizures, when the whole world flares up with the light of the mind.

Nor is Ruskin an impressionist, but, instead, one of the early expressionists, as he proves when he looks at La Riccia under a violet sky. Ruskin belongs with Shelley and Turner, who was, for him, an incomparable master of the picturesque because Turner had "a range of feeling which no other painter can equal." Turner conveys, Ruskin says, "the truth of impression," which is "the far higher and deeper truth of mental vision," more valuable than any factual accuracy ("the truth of form"). Ruskin found his symbols where Turner and Shelley did—clouds, Alps, and water. They are symbols that translate the picturesque, with its roughness, broken light, and genial feel-

Courtesy, Museum of Fine Arts, Boston

18 TURNER: *Slave Ship*

ings, to romantic art. As Ruskin stands beside the Fall at Schaffhausen (which Turner painted) he feels in the vaulting cataract—sweeping from its crystal dome into hollows where the foam shatters into chrysoprase bursting on the wind and filling the air with thunder—a "sympathy with the wild water." He calls Turner's *Slave Ship* [18] the noblest marine ever painted. Using an amazing phrase, Ruskin says that Turner's sea is "an entirely imperative dream," purple and flashing in the angry sun:

> . . . the torn and streaming rain-clouds are moving in scarlet lines to lose themselves in the hollow of the night. The whole surface of the sea . . . is divided into two ridges of enormous swell . . . , a low broad heaving of the whole ocean, like the lifting of its bosom by deep-drawn breath after the torture of the storm. Between these two ridges the fire of the sunset falls along the trough of the sea, dyeing it with an awful but glorious light, the intense and lurid splendor which burns like gold, and bathes like blood. Along this fiery path and valley, the tossing waves . . . lift themselves in dark, indefinite, fantastic forms,

each casting a faint and ghastly shadow behind it along the illumined foam.

(*Modern Painters,* Part II, sec. v, chap. 3)

This is like the imperative dream world through which Shelley was driven when Alastor, the avenging spirit of the poet, perished beneath "the dim and horned moon hung low," languishing in a wilderness of tangled swamps and icy crags, an almost surrealist realm beyond the Caucasus:

With fierce gusts and precipitating force,
Through the white ridges of the chafed sea,
The waves arose. Higher and higher still
Their fierce necks writhed beneath the tempest's scourge
Like serpents struggling in a vulture's grasp. . . .
Stair above stair the eddying waters rose,
Circling immeasurably fast, and laved
With alternating dash the gnarled roots
Of mighty trees that stretched their giant arms
In darkness over it. I' the midst was left,
Reflecting yet distorting every cloud,
A pool of treacherous and tremendous calm.

Like Turner, Shelley is *voyant.* He too visits scenes where there is psychic thunder.

"Now observe," Ruskin notes, "this impression on the mind never results from a mere piece of scenery which can be included within the limits of the picture. It depends on the temper into which the mind has been brought, both by all the landscape round, and by what has been seen previously in the course of the day." This "Turnerian picturesque"—a new topography, Ruskin calls it—turns associationist psychology into an almost Freudian mechanism. Turner is a painter of visions—"dream-vision," Ruskin says: "for in a dream there is just this kind of confused remembrance of the forms of things which we have seen long ago, associated by new and strange laws." Ruskin described Turner's *Slave Ship* as being an "involuntary remembrance."

The strange laws of dream-remembrance—more compelling than either the ornamental caprices of the *genre pittoresque* or the picturesque pleasures of eighteenth-century reverie—operate with Freudian power in Shelley's "Vision of the Sea," a poetical fragment where the fantasy of Coleridge's "Ancient Mariner" is raised to illumination as manic as Rimbaud's "Bateau Ivre" or Lautréamont's "Chants de Maldoror." It is the analogue to Turner's mad sea in *The Slave Ship:*

> 'Tis the terror of tempest. The rags of the sail
> Are flickering in ribbons within the fierce gale:
> From the stark night of vapors the dim rain is driven . . .
> While the surf, like a chaos of stars, like a rout
> Of death-flames, like whirlpools of fire-flowing iron,
> With splendor and terror the black ship environ,
> Or like sulphur-flakes hurled from a mine of pale fire
> In fountains spout o'er it. In many a spire
> The pyramid-billows with white points of brine
> In the cope of the lightning inconstantly shine,
> As piercing the sky from the floor of the sea. . .
> The wrecks of the tempest, like vapours of gold,
> Are consuming in sunrise. . .
> One tiger is mingled in ghastly affray
> With a sea-snake. . .
> A blue shark is hanging within the blue ocean,
> The fin-winged tomb of the victor. . .

Hazlitt said that the romantic imagination "represents objects, not as they are in themselves, but as they are moulded by other thoughts and feelings, into an infinite variety of shapes and combinations of power" under the force of passion. Shelley's seascape, and Turner's, have the full charge of feeling that was generated in the associationist psychology and released in the tempest of romantic imagination roaring through verse—and through music—until it reached the insane pitch of Lautréamont's enraged sea boiling white with the carnal pleasure of sharks. Shelley, Turner, Ducasse—and Wagner—can excite reverie to hysteria.

These red Atlantic tumults are spiritual storms: the storm that swept through Turner's *Slave Ship,* where, as Ruskin says, the masts are written against the sky in blood, in the fearful hue of anger. Turner's sea is a burst of symbolic color. It is a prevision of Rimbaud's "plunge into the gulph." It is a flight toward invisible splendors, a poetic absolute, an omen of an art in which associations take the form of hallucination.

V

CORRESPONDENCES

Rimbaud said that his poetry required a prodigious disordering of all the senses. He wrote to Paul Demeny in 1871 that "Inventions of the unknown demand new forms." The statement reminds us that romanticism and symbolism relied upon a psychology rather than a style—a psychology which in their case amounted to an aesthetic, evolved from association and reverie and bringing, at the end of the nineteenth century, an art of suggestion that was, in the always-quoted phrase of Maurice Denis, *la déformation subjective de la nature.* Things were taken as symbols for what could not be stated. Denis and Redon and the symbolist painters wished, like Mallarmé, to enter *le monde ambigu de l'indéterminé.* Somewhat inconsistently they also believed that a picture is a plane surface covered with colors in a certain order. At the same time Pater and Proust were finding that a work of literature must be judged by "the quality of the language." This new awareness that painting and literature are first of all designs was to lead back from an aesthetic of suggestion to a formal sense of style under the auspices of Japanese prints and Art Nouveau. Feelings were not enough: there must also be pattern, contour, a motif worked out.

This return to style will be examined in the next chapter. Here we are dealing with the attempt to create art from "a state of soul" (*un état d'âme*), the last phase of a picturesque-romantic attitude persisting like a ground swell through the whole nineteenth century in painting and literature: in Delacroix, in Shelley, in Baudelaire, in Mallarmé and Odilon Redon. Hegel gives authority to this aesthetic when he describes "The Romantic in General":

> The external phenomenon is no longer able to express this inward life . . . and is forced to point back by suggestion to the spiritual content, the soul and its emotions, as the truly essential medium. Precisely for the same reason romantic art allows externality to go its own way freely. . . . Such a content as this, however, carries at the same time with it the result that as purely exterior matter, its worth is of no validity and insignificant; it only receives its genuine worth when the soul has made itself a home in it, and is taken to express not merely the ideal, but spiritual inwardness (*das Innerliche, die Innigkeit*).
>
> (*Philosophy of Fine Art,* Second Part, subsection iii)

Or as Carlyle put it in his essay on the Poet, the artist has a sense of "infinitude in him; communicates an Unendlichkeit"—"A kind of inarticulate unfathomable speech, which leads us to the edge of the Infinite, and lets us for moments gaze into that!" The poet is a *Seer* who "discloses the inner harmony of things." Aurier the symbolist seeks "that transcendent emotion, making the soul tremble before the fugitive drama of abstractions." Romantic-symbolist art thus is a kind of sorcery evoking what is unutterable. In 1893 Mallarmé wrote an essay on Magic which runs:

> To evoke the unmentioned object in a deliberate shadow, by allusive, never direct, words, that all amount equally to expressions of silence, is to attempt something that comes close to an act of creation: this act of creation achieves plausibility within the limits of the idea that the sorcerer of literature exclusively

> exploits, until he succeeds in bringing forth the semblance of an illusion. The verse is conceived as an incantation.
>
> (*National Observer,* January 28, 1893)

For want of a better term we might designate this mystical undercurrent as proto-expressionism—*proto*-expressionism because expressionism did not find its technique until Gauguin and Van Gogh gave it their legible designs. In fauvism the subjectivity of romanticism and symbolism becomes articulate. Van Gogh brings the passion of Delacroix and the subjective deformation of nature to a formal resolution.

Symbolist painters and poets were notoriously given to theories they failed to demonstrate in their own work. It has been said that there is no such thing as symbolism, but only symbolist poets and painters. Valéry himself has testified that the symbolists were held together "by something not yet visible."[11] He concludes that symbolism was not a school though there were long theoretical discussions among painters and poets inspired by a "negation"—a revolt against a "majority." They accomplished "a sort of revolution in the realm of values": not really in art, but in sentiment, which Valéry calls a "quasi-mystical type of aesthetic feeling" arising from a "psychophysiology," a study of sensibility, sounds, and rhythms. Whatever one makes of this, the record of the symbolist movement—if it was such—cannot be clearly written. Yet it must be examined, for it was a decisive turn in the history of modern styles. Like symbolist art itself, the course of symbolism can only be suggested, and its descent from the romantics, "those first seers," implied rather than diagrammed. Baudelaire foreshadows Mallarmé, who was a last romantic and a decadent—and influenced by Hugo, of all people.[12]

Instinctively Baudelaire saw Delacroix as a painter who "dominates the model as the creator dominates his creation." Baudelaire's man of imagination, embodied in Delacroix, is always in rebellion against nature because "it is useless and tedious to represent what *exists,* since nothing that exists, satisfies." (One thinks of Nietzsche's axiom that no artist tolerates actuality.) Baudelaire led the attack on realists—those "parasites of the object"—who kept looking outside for what "was only to be found within." He hated Daguerre, for photography and art are not the same thing, as he spent his life pointing out. If art is the enemy of photography, Nature is only an "excitant," a dictionary for use of the Imagination, which must "digest and transform":

> In the beginning of the world it created analogy and metaphor. It decomposes all creation, and with the raw materials accumulated and disposed in accordance with rules whose origins one cannot find save in the furthest depths of the soul, it creates a new world. . . .
>
> . . . The whole visible universe is but a storehouse of images and signs to which the imagination will give a relative place and value; it is a sort of pasture which the imagination must digest and transform.
>
> (*Salon of 1859*)

A work of art "inhabits its own proper atmosphere," which the so-called realists cannot create, for they try to live in a world where they do not truly exist: "in other words, the universe without man." The romantic, however, says, "I want to illuminate things with my mind, and to project their reflection upon other minds."

Doubtless Baudelaire read into Delacroix some of his own satanism. Yet there is an affinity between the art of the two, and between their temperaments, for Delacroix wrote in his *Journal* (27 February, 1824): "The things that are most real to me are the illusions which I create with my painting. Everything else is a quicksand." He feels in himself "some black depth that must be appeased. Unless I am writhing like a serpent in the coils of a pythoness, I am cold." Delacroix projects these writhings into his painting: "My picture is beginning to develop a rhythm, a powerful spiral momentum. . . . That silent power that speaks at first only to the eyes and then seizes and captivates every faculty of the soul!" Like Baudelaire he despises realism and seeks "mystery":

> . . . The figures and objects in the picture, which to one part of your intelligence seem to be the actual things themselves, are like a solid bridge to support your imagination as it probes

> the deep, mysterious emotions, of which these forms are, so to speak, *the hieroglyph,* but a hieroglyph far more eloquent than any cold representation, the mere equivalent of a printed symbol. . . . What I have been saying about the *power of painting* now becomes clear. If it has to record but a single moment it is capable of concentrating the *effect* of that moment. . . .
>
> (*Journal,* 20 October, 1853)

How truly romanticism is a quality of experience [13] rather than a style is indicated by Delacroix's various manners, which can absorb the realism he despised; so can Baudelaire's poems—"Une Charogne," for example. Delacroix's nude study of Mlle. Rose shows how when he left Guérin's studio he commanded a grim accuracy that makes the looser realism of Courbet look impulsive. Certain passages in *The Execution of Marino Faliero* might have been painted by Delaroche: the precise figure of the executioner, the hard white marble stairway, the headless body in the foreground; then the eye blurs and some of the background figures, the vaguely drooping banners, the shadowed persons in the foreground, might appear in Manet or even Tintoretto. The same incoherence of vision appears in *The Death of Sardanapalus* with its voluminous but empty background and the firm, lithe bodies of the nude women, those radiant images that easily do what Baudelaire wished to do in his verse: *transformer volupté en connaissance.* His portrait of George Sand dissolves flesh into the obscurities of Carrière and Henner; the ghostly shorthand in *Portrait of Paganini* might be by Daumier; the *Entombment* is like a sullen Rubens, an unearthly night amid which flames out a rebellious scarlet; and the *Sultan of Morocco* appears in a space as flat as Manet found when he began to simplify his color. The technique shifts; the temperament of the painter seems to be split; the eye cannot be fixed, and seems to have no coherent view of the world. Always, as with that other schizoid romantic temperament, Byron, there is the unquiet self, the unruly high spirit, the impulsive touch that adapts every technique to its own wilful expression, a stormy power that causes Childe Harold to feel himself in the lightning that flashes over the Alps. If neither Byron nor Delacroix had a style, they share Baudelaire's restlessness.

To think of them as romantic or realistic is to conceal the nature of the revolution in values taking place in science, also, at the same time: it is the desire to experiment, to prove everything by immediate evidence in either the laboratory or the heart. That is why the romantics were continually changing not only their methods but their findings, alternating between rapture and cynicism, aspiration and despair, the heights and the depths. The meaning of both romanticism and realism is to be read in the graph of a temperament. The romantic in his quest of personal evidence uses his own kind of realism, trying to get his own angle on experience, his own vision of an absolute; and since his feelings cannot be fixed, he is always forced to make new appraisals as his responses change. He has nothing to trust beyond this unstable experience. In his essay on "The Painter of Modern Life" Baudelaire says: "Modernity—it is the transitory, the fugitive, the contingent: half of art, the other half of which is the eternal, the unchanging." The hope of reaching the Eternal in the Momentary.

The history of the nineteenth-century arts is a course of experiments combined with a loss of absolutes—what Malraux calls *la monnaie de l'absolu,* the small change left after finalities have broken down. Yet the romantic, like the realist, was always driven to seek absolutes: hence romantic platonism with its visions of eternal Beauty, and the realistic belief in the iron laws of the universe—scientific, economic, geographic, racist. The changeless "natural" law of Malthus, Ricardo, and Huxley is only the obverse of Shelley's blinding vision of "the eternal, the infinite, and the one" and Mallarmé's icy realm of Beauty at heights Imagination can hardly scale. Taine and Buckle seek the absolute in laws of matter, milieu, and history; Baudelaire and Gautier seek the absolute in Art. The difference between romantic and realist empiricism is simply that the romantic turned toward the world inside where he could dwell more intently on the Immutable.

The age was deeply empirical; both the scientist and artist were always trying to test middle-class notions. Baudelaire and Flaubert were prosecuted; Darwin and Huxley made their way against the same group of prosecutors. The romantic, the realist, and often the scientist were all in revolt against *the official.*

Mallarmé wrote in 1891: "Is it possible to write poetry without reference to time-honored precepts? Poets have answered this question affirmatively, and I believe that they are right . . . today's poetry is, in the main, the result of the poet's boredom with official verse."[14] Zola was as abhorrent as Baudelaire since he represented, no less than the symbolists, a revision of values. Nor it is by chance that Zola's great documented novel *Germinal* opens by being a record of the iron laws of economics working themselves out in France's black country, the Voreux, and ends underground in scenes that are entirely symbolic in their nightmarish tone—the blind white horse Bataille plunging madly through the hellish depths of an industrial world in a melodrama that should be illustrated by Daumier. Is the art of Daumier romantic or realistic, visionary or topical? Is not the fantastic art of Gustave Doré and John Martin a version of the industrial waste land? Martin's mezzotint of *Satan Presiding at the Infernal Council* (1825 -27) is like some gaslighted foundry, the extravaganza of a machine age translated into scriptural legend. In romanticism or realism the century did not gain a style but, instead, provoked artists to reject the official, the usual, in every way they knew. The artist was an artist because of his temperament, not because of his style. The romantic and the symbolist—and often the realist, too—took a strange "Voyage," as Baudelaire wrote:

> Mais les vrais voyageurs sont ceux-là seuls qui partent
> Pour partir; coeurs légers, semblables aux ballons,
> De leur fatalité jamais ils ne s'écartent,
> Et, sans savoir pourquoi, disent toujours: Allons!

"Like balloons"—Baudelaire draws his very image from technology. The "voyagers" are those who, with Mallarmé, dare to give *un sens plus pur aux mots de la tribu,* finding a new language, new rhythms, setting their course over the horizon.

Turner's imperative dream and the long imaginative voyages taken by Shelley and Mallarmé are ventures into the invisible realms of spirit where all reality is subjective and so fleeting that, as Shelley complained, the poetic mind in creation is like a fading coal breathed into only transitory brightness. Baudelaire wrote of the poet-*voyant:*

> Ceux-là dont les désirs ont la forme des nues,
> Et qui rêvent, ainsi qu'un conscrit le canon,
> De vastes voluptés, changeantes, inconnues,
> Et dont l'esprit humain n'a jamais su le nom!
> ("*Le Voyage*")

Mallarmé told his friend Cazalis that he must "find isolation in the unknown regions of Revery." Romantic-symbolist art creates its forms by a subjective logic that derives from associationist psychology; and its flight from the world of things is also a quest of infinite beauties revealed only on "the heights of ecstasy." "What I am trying to say is so intimate, so veiled, so vague," Mallarmé says to Cazalis, "that I am afraid I have been too precise in places." Often there comes the desperate dream, like Shelley's vision of Prometheus—the spirit of man—pinnacled dim in the intense inane, or like Baudelaire's terrifying "Voyage à Cythère." Zola's vision of the underworld beneath the industrial black country is no less desperate. The romantics consciously sought the absolute, the shadow of some splendor which, as Shelley writes, floats though unseen among us, coming like the memory of music fled, and dearer for its mystery. The romantic absolute is the old eighteenth-century reverie changed into an illumination. Mallarmé thought of poetry as a form of Contemplation, "the image emanating from the reveries which things arouse in us." Reverie is raised to transcendental power, inspired, often, by Swedenborg and the German philosophers who followed Kant beyond the world of logic, time, and causality.

Shelley exclaimed that poetry "arrests the vanishing apparitions which haunt the interluminations of life," and in many ways the higher flights of German idealism accord with the "other-worldly" art of Shelley and the symbolists. In his *Critique of Judgment* Immanuel Kant had pointed out that sublimity is not found in any sensuous form, but is a revelation appearing when "the mind has been incited to go beyond the senses." Kant's absolute beauty does not exist in the material world; it denotes nothing in the object "but is a feeling which the subject has by itself and in the way it is affected by the images" of things. Therefore, Kant remarks, sense impressions never give us the truth about things, which can be known "only as they affect us": "Whatever they are in themselves remains unknown." If we are to reach beauty in its absolute form, we must transcend the experience of the senses and the ordinary "categories" of the mind, leaving the "seen" to know the "unseen." Already romanticism is heading toward the belief of Maurice Denis and the synthetist painters that art is a "subjective deformation of nature"—"L'art au lieu d'être la *copie* devenait la *déformation subjective* de la nature."

A turn from associationist psychology to romantic-symbolist subjectivity came in Schopenhauer, who took art to be one means of quenching the torment of the will but at the same time implied that art is also an expression of the will—the unconscious will at that. After Schopenhauer has said that art delivers us from the endless striving that drives us from goal to goal, from pain to pain, he writes a note on how we associate ideas, pointing out that our conscious thoughts are only like the surface of water and that the deeper currents of our being are all moved by the will, "the secret of our inner being, what sets in activity the association of thought itself." To these deeper unconscious impulses coursing beneath the clear surface of the mind, art must address itself: "We are only perfectly satisfied by the impression of a work of art when it leaves something which, with all our thinking about it, we cannot bring down to the distinctness of a conception." Or, as Baudelaire said, we must have from art some sense of "the expansion of things infinite," with echoes of some dim unity, a recognition to be made only in the shadows of our being.

This notion was taken up by Jouffroy in Lecture XXV of his popular collection of discourses known as *Cours d'Esthétique*, where he says that the beauty of art is an invisible beauty so inexpressible as to be nearly formless: "So the invisible can certainly by itself move us esthetically; and precisely in the invisible, the depth, resides the only true cause of esthetic feelings." In his thirty-second Lecture he goes on:

> There is the beauty of the invisible, which touches us by its own power. It is not changing; it exists in its own right. . . . A quality permanent and fundamental of the object from which it ema-

> nates, the beauty of the invisible is always inherent in it and cannot be alienated from it; it remains intrinsic. Thus this invisible beauty is the only beauty which one can, without being irresponsible, call beautiful. Consequently among all the sources of disinterested pleasure there is one alone that of itself is genuinely and positively beautiful—namely, the invisible.

In such a passage Jouffroy anticipates Mallarmé's conviction that all actuality is an illusion from which art must create "the purity of a dream"—while the object itself vanishes. The "music" of Shelley's and Baudelaire's poetry becomes a nearly inaudible tone. The "purity" of non-objective painting is only a final surrender of the object, "dematerialized," in Kandinsky's phrase, until "it represents no object of reality but in itself is a fully abstract being"—a "vibration in the soul."

The patriarch of this romantic-symbolist aesthetic is Hegel, with his turn to *Innigkeit* and the "music that forms the center of the romantic arts." The inwardness of Hegel's artist is an Absolute: "we have spoken of art as proceeding from the Absolute Idea, and have even assigned as its end the sensuous representation of the Absolute itself." Hegel's "concrete universal" proved to be a point of no return for the artist, as Mallarmé was to find in a generation of symbolist painters who protested, "Nous renoncions au réel." Reverie finally led the artist to "refuse objectivity." Novalis summarized when he wrote, "For all that is visible rests on an invisible foundation."

Paradoxically one must note that Novalis is only saying what one of the most devoted positivists of the century, Herbert Spencer, also said in his *First Principles* (1862) about the ultimate mystery in which science ends. What, he asks, are Space and Time, which in themselves are unthinkable: "Great magnitudes, great durations, great numbers, are none of them actually conceived, but are all of them conceived more or less symbolically." Or how can we understand rationally "the connexion between Force and Matter"? Spencer's conclusion is that the most indispensable scientific concepts are, like religious faith, beyond comprehension—"Of necessity, therefore, explanation must eventually bring us down to the inexplicable. The deepest truth which we can get at, must be unaccountable."

The Absolutes behind science "pass all understanding," and "Matter, in its ultimate nature, is as absolutely incomprehensible as Space and Time." As John Henry Newman put it, *Omnia exeunt in mysterium.* Carlyle exhorts us to "Pierce through the Time-element, glance into the Eternal."

If Schopenhauer is a turning point in romantic thought, Shelley's *Defence of Poetry* (1821) is the margin at which reverie passes over to symbolism. Almost every one of the notions later held by Baudelaire and Mallarmé is to be found in Shelley's essay, which accepts the world as Idea: "All things exist as they are perceived: at least in relation to the percipient." We might be reading Schopenhauer, who opens *The World as Will and Idea* (1819) by saying that the world is only my idea of the world, only an object in relation to the subject. Shelley believed the poetic imagination to be the instrument by which we discover final value, the "true and beautiful" in an absolute "indestructible order": "A poet participates in the eternal, the infinite, and the one; as far as relates to his conceptions, time and place and number are not." This participation comes by means of language, the "hieroglyphic of thoughts," "for language is arbitrarily produced by the imagination and has relation to thoughts alone." One recalls how Mallarmé insisted that poetry is made with words. For Shelley, too, words are "vitally metaphorical"; and the rhythm of words is enchantment:

> But poetry in a more restricted sense expresses those arrangements of language, and especially metrical language, which are created by that imperial faculty, whose throne is curtained within the invisible nature of man. And this springs from the nature itself of language, which is a more direct representation of the actions and passions of our internal being. . . .

So Shelley is led to a notion of analogy and correspondence, since the poet's words "unveil the permanent analogy of things by images . . . being the echo of the eternal music." The imagination finds the essential "similitudes of things." The associationist psychology had sought the affinities between our moods and the world outside, laying the groundwork for Shelley's sense of harmony between things and the self, a kind of "horizontal symbolism." Baudelaire found that nature is a "forest of symbols" capable of speaking to us in confused phrases suggesting a deeper unity, which Wordsworth had also felt behind the common face of things; and he uses Shelley's very echo image to intimate how these similitudes dimly agree:

> Comme de *longs échos* qui de loin se confondent
> Dans une ténébreuse et profonde unité,
> Vaste comme la nuit et comme la clarté,
> Les parfums, les couleurs et les sons se répondent.
> (*"Correspondances"*)

Baudelaire found in Delacroix a notion of harmony—an "arrangement of colors, lights, and shadows"—that led him to his "horizontal" correspondences between sense impressions. This horizontal correspondence became "vertical" or "ascensional" when Baudelaire adapted from Swedenborg and other occultists, and from Poe, the belief that the visible world has a counterpart in the invisible or celestial world.[15] Shelley reached this ascensional correspondence by platonism, perhaps, rather than by occultism; one of the persisting metaphors in his verse is the flight bearing the poet into the "light of thought," the heights from which he showers his rain of melody. Shelley's delight is sometimes shrill. Baudelaire centered his harmonies in the interior world of the soul, modulating them with prudence and self-possession. In *Les Paradis Artificiels* he explains that things outside "transform themselves, and at last they enter into the soul; or indeed you enter into them," and soar into "the azure of skies immensely expanded." There is a double correspondence: between sounds, perfumes, and colors, and between the natural and supernatural. The ascensional correspondences are an act of the "constructive imagination," as Baudelaire calls it, and expand the associationist psychology to symbolism. Mallarmé refined Baudelaire's ascensional correspondences to "constellations," fading reflections of a poet's vision resembling an unutterable dream.

The symbolist correspondences did not gain full philosophic support until Henri Bergson, at the opening of the twentieth century, proposed that states of consciousness permeate one another in the deeper life of the self, which endures at a level of unconscious memory. This submerged self exists in "duration" rather than time. Beyond the rational life where reason arranges things in a succession and in syllogisms, there is another life, pure quality and intensity, when experience fuses itself in intuitions that can only be symbolized or suggested. At these depths the self, as in a dream, passes insensibly from one state to another and is aware, inarticulately, of the echoes between experiences that resemble the symbolist sense of correspondence. In art, Bergson says, we have this "virtual" experience, rejecting quantity and objects. In Bergson's opinion "the feeling of the beautiful is no specific feeling, but every feeling experienced by us will assume an aesthetic character provided it has been *suggested,* and not *caused.*" Bergson discards associationist psychology as mechanistic, and substitutes intuitions enabling us to touch reality through symbols.

Both Shelley and Baudelaire are lifted to a transcendent sense of affinities inaccessible to everyday perception; and these affinities are shadows of absolutes, making the poet, Shelley says, inhabit "a world to which the familiar world is a chaos." It was Baudelaire's world, too:

> Vers le Ciel, où son oeil voit un trône splendide,
> Le Poète serein lève ses bras pieux,
> Et les vastes éclairs de son esprit lucide
> Lui dérobent l'aspect des peuples furieux. . . .
>
> ("*Bénédiction*")

In these exalted moments the poet dreams of *horizons bleuâtres* and plunges "au fond de l'Inconnu pour trouver du *nouveau.*" At Shelley's heights poetic vision is autonomous, coloring thoughts with its own radiance and "composing from them, as from elements, other thoughts, each containing within itself the principle of its own integrity." The poetic vision strips the world of its usual appearance: "it subdues to union under its light yoke all irreconcilable things," lifting the veil from hidden truth, revealing "the inmost naked beauty of the meaning never exposed." It redeems us from "time and place" by music, the harmony of deep analogies—"not melody alone, but harmony, . . . an internal adjustment of the sounds or motions thus excited to the impressions which excite them."

Like Verlaine, Shelley thinks of poetry as music first of all, since "the rest is literature."

> Sounds as well as thoughts have relation both between each other and towards that which they represent, and a perception of the order of those relations has always been found connected with a perception of the order of the relations of thoughts. Hence the language of poets has ever affected a certain uniform and harmonious recurrence of sound, without which it were not poetry.
>
> (*A Defence of Poetry*)

Baudelaire exclaims, "La musique souvent me prend comme une mer," and Mallarmé finds the "splendid freedom" of his new poetry—purged of "tribal words"—in the "sense of musical structure" that comes when he is able to listen to "his own particular and inward arabesque of sound," supremely difficult to transcribe. All this seems like Paul Valéry, who speaks of his own verse as beginning in a pure rhythm in himself; and Mallarmé in 1891 wrote Valéry, "The perfect poem we dream of can be suggested by Music itself." The music of poetry reveals to Shelley, Baudelaire, and Mallarmé a mysterious "Paysage" with *les grands ciels qui font rêver d'éternité.* Baudelaire's bohemian *paradis artificiel* is not quite Shelley's platonic realm; but for both poets "man is an instrument over which a series of external and internal impressions are driven, like the alternations of an ever-changing wind over an Aeolian lyre, which move it by their motion to ever-changing melody."

Both think of the poet as a nightingale sitting in darkness, singing music that rises from pain: "Sorrow, terror, anguish, despair itself, are often the chosen expressions of an approximation to the highest good." Both poets know the "shadow of pleasure which exists in pain." *Les Fleurs du Mal* has the "melancholy which is inseparable from the sweetest melody." This romantic music with demonic overtones is the voice of spirits destroyed, like Alastor, by their own visions.

Baudelaire asked: "What is pure art according to our modern notion?" He answered: "To create a suggestive magic embracing at the same instant both object and subject, the outside world and the artist himself." Mallarmé's symbolism, more precarious, would redeem poetry completely from time and place, nullifying the outside world by the Word which suggests *la notion pure.* This magic Word is a hieroglyph; his art is hermetic: "Toute chose sacrée . . . s'enveloppe de mystère." Mallarmé was afflicted by a *hantise de l'éternel,* enchanted by the Word that cannot be spoken, the silence of the Dream "where all objects vanish," the Azure in its terrible vacancy, for which there is no image. Mallarmé purifies symbolism to the point where the only absolute poem is the poem that cannot be written: it can only be thought. He accepts the extreme of Shelley's principle that "when composition begins, inspiration is already on the decline, and the most glorious poetry that has ever been communicated to the world is probably a feeble shadow of the original conceptions of the poet." The supreme poem, then, is silence; only the unheard melody is perfect, as Keats once knew.

Baudelaire attempts to translate life to art by "ascending"— "It is Imagination that first taught man the moral meaning of color, of contour, of sound and of scent," and the "dream" of the artist is a "composition" transforming nature, setting another horizon, giving a sensation of newness by its atmosphere. The deeper correspondences are felt in the "tone" of this atmosphere, and Baudelaire seems to have the same idea as Gauguin when he writes, "Obviously a particular tone is allotted to whichever part of a picture is to become the key and to govern the others." So Baudelaire invites us to take his "Voyage" to another world:

> Là, tout n'est qu'ordre et beauté,
> Luxe, calme, et volupté.

Baudelaire despised Vernet, "whose pictures have nothing to do with painting" because they were manufactured ("to the sound of pistol shots") rather than dreamed. Shelley dreamed. Delacroix dreamed, too, in his Rembrandtesque paintings like *Roger and Angelica,* where the world is vaporized as it is in Shelley's *Prometheus Unbound:*

Beneath is a wide plain of billowy mist,
As a lake paving in the morning sky,
With azure waves which burst in silver light,
Some Indian vale. Behold it, rolling on
Under the curdling winds, and islanding
The peak whereon we stand, midway, around,
Encinctured by the dark and blooming forests,
Dim twilight lawns, and stream-illumined caves,
And wind-enchanted shapes of wandering mist.

Baudelaire writes that Delacroix's paintings are faithful equivalents of the dreams that begot them, brought into being like another world: "Just as a dream inhabits its own proper atmosphere, so a conception which has become a composition needs to move within a colored setting peculiar to itself." Like Shelley or Baudelaire, Delacroix used nature only as a "dictionary," *une pure excitation.* Delacroix noted in his *Journal,* "The finest works of art are those that express the pure fantasy of the artist." Turner and Delacroix both seek a pure rhythm and color, a language of "romantic abstraction" like "the memory of music fled." Baudelaire required this purification when he wrote (long before Valéry) "the art of the colorist has an affinity with mathematics and music." He finds that most landscape painters are liars precisely because they do not lie. Shelley also thought of poetry as an abstract composition—as "arrangements of language, and especially metrical language" created by "that imperial faculty whose throne is curtained within the invisible nature of man." Color, words, sounds, rhythms were used as notations for the absolute even before romantic art changed to symbolism.

After Shelley and Turner, Delacroix and Baudelaire, the music was more faintly scored—in Mallarmé and Verlaine, who devoted himself to a verse where *l'Indécis au Précis se joint:*

Car nous voulons la Nuance encor,
Pas la Couleur, rien que la nuance!
Oh! la nuance seule fiance
Le rêve au rêve et la flûte au cor.
(*"Art Poétique"*)

The reaction against the marble art of Gautier and the Parnassians was the dreamed music of Verlaine. The symbolist rhythm appears in its most abstract design in Mallarmé's constellation of images, a constellation being a poem, which can be arranged on the page in typographical contours, a stylization close to Nabi and synthetist painting and to Art Nouveau. However, Mallarmé does not belong to Art Nouveau but to a last phase of an art so subjective and interior that nothing can be stated; it can only be evoked.

It is an art best represented by Odilon Redon's *The Thought* [19]. The worn features, the passively closed lids, the lifeless hair, the gently turned neck and shoulder speak of dreams that cannot be recovered. The image nearly dissolves in a vague light glancing across the pallid cheek, and shimmering like a glassy mere from one of Poe's tales. Redon's images are fragments—the ghastly cyclops-head, the single eye, the lonely flowers blooming in twilight pastel tones. The object is "truncated"—*l'objet coupé*. Redon's is an art of the *irréel*—wraithlike centaurs leaping across a dream-landscape. Redon is alien, an artist suited to the climate of Gérard de Nerval's *Sylvie:*

> We were then living in a strange period, such as usually succeeds revolutions or the decline of great reigns. . . . The only refuge left to us was the poet's ivory tower, which we climbed, ever higher, to isolate ourselves from the mob. Led by our masters to those high places, we breathed at last the pure air of solitude, we drank oblivion in the legendary golden cup, and we got drunk on poetry and love. Love, however, of vague forms, of blue and rosy hues, of metaphysical phantoms!

In his *Confidences d'Artiste* Redon explains that he rejected Courbet and naturalism in favor of a "representation of imaginary forms that haunted me," mysteries of "shadows and lines mentally conceived." Huysmans said he was like a spectral Goya, and Redon, who found that charcoal and pastel suited his vision better than oils, called his own art an exciting form of music, freer, with a logic of its own—a logic of strange associations felt *dans le monde ambigu de l'indéterminé.* His journals often speak of his wish to convey a sense of *l'équivoque, images dans images, formes qui vont être.* Remy de Gourmont called Redon's work a sort of metaphor. Almost like Valéry, who was intimate

Courtesy of Gemeente Musea, Amsterdam

19 REDON: *The Thought* (aquarelle)

with the symbolist group, Redon wants his images to have "the prestige of thought." This art, "expressif, suggestif, indéterminé," has its "irradiations"—"la lumière de la spiritualité" with "vast perspectives open to the improvisation of the dream." It is an art that should illustrate the sonnet "Dilection" written by Albert Samain:

> J'adore l'indécis, les sons, les couleurs frêles,
> Tout ce qui tremble, ondule, et frissonne, et chatoie,
> Les cheveux et les yeux, les feuilles, la soie,
> Et la spiritualité des formes grêles. . . .

The spirituality of frail forms: Redon said that his paintings allude rather than state.

Arthur Symons made the mistake of saying that Redon is a French Blake; but he is not like Blake, who has a steel precision, a litheness and muscularity, a rebellion quite unlike the morbid passivity of Redon, an artist able to disturb without stimulating. Maurice Denis was nearer the truth when he called Redon "our Mallarmé." For like Mallarmé this painter tried to enter the world of Night, where forms are evoked or transposed and approach definition without being defined. The atmosphere in which Redon's centaur-creatures exist is the atmosphere of Mallarmé's Faun, the half-consciousness of the dream. Redon himself puts it well in a remark on his own work:

> Suggestive art is like an irradiation of things in a dream, where a kind of thought also takes place. . . . This suggestive art is fulfilled in the provocative art of music most freely and radiantly; but it is also my own by a strange combining of diverse elements reconciled, forms transposed or changed without any resemblance to contingencies, nevertheless having a logic. . . . These forms specify nothing. They lead us, as music does, to the world of the uncertain and indefinite.
>
> (*À Soi-Même*)

Like Mallarmé's Herodias, he awaits *une chose inconnue.* Like Maeterlinck he prefers indirection. In Maeterlinck's theatre there are puppets, not men, since art always uses a "detour" and all realism falsifies. Every play should be symbolic, and "the symbol does not tolerate the presence of man." Instead, it affords only spectral forms whose mission is to suggest the revelation of a "secret beauty."

Mallarmé, who explains his intentions better than most of his critics, starts from the premise that "whatever is sacred must be clothed in mystery."[16] Art is orphic. He refuses to present anything directly as the Parnassians did, but instead will only imply, for the ideal poem only evokes objects, if they appear at all:

> We renounce that erroneous aesthetic . . . which would have the poet fill the delicate pages of his book with the actual and palpable wood of trees, rather than with the forest's shuddering or the silent scattering of thunder through the foliage. A few well chosen sounds blown heavenward on the trumpet of true majesty will suffice to conjure up the architecture of the ideal. . . . In literature, allusion is sufficient: essences are distilled and then embodied in Idea. . . . This is the ideal I would call Transposition. . . .
>
> (*Crisis in Poetry*)

"Structure is something else," he adds, a remark much to the point, for the evocative art of Redon and Mallarmé and the symbolists is really lacking a formal structure, depending as it does upon reverie, dream, or private illumination. Mallarmé's structure is a constellation of images astronomically distant, nearly invisible to the naked eye. Redon attempts to give us the affects of the dream, its atmosphere, its twilight forms. These are indeed only notations for a composition the reader or viewer must complete for himself.

Mallarmé did speak a new language; or, perhaps, tempered the old romantic language of feeling to its last music: "I am inventing a new language," he writes about his *Hérodiade*, "which must arise from a completely new poetics and which I can define briefly as follows: Describe not the object itself, but the effect it produces." The romantics had tried to do this and gave us the first subjective deformation of nature. Eventually Mallarmé tried to get along entirely without the object when his art approached the values of Night, *Néant*—Nothingness, the white blank page that represented best the poem in all its impossible purity. He is haunted by poems that cannot get written, or perhaps even imagined; for as he confessed to Cazalis, "When I had polished my poetry down to this depth, I came upon twin abysses which drove me mad. The first was Nothingness." He explains again: "My work was created only by elimination." The transcendence was most complete when the world of objects was entirely cancelled out, and only "pure" consciousness remained, intensely, as a configuration in the self—what Valéry later seems to have meant by referring to a "pure" secret rhythm. At this exalted level of abstraction poetry becomes a Word that cannot be spoken or heard. Like Shelley's Alastor, the poet is now destroyed by the very vision of the absolute, which is the supreme frustration of romantic-symbolist art. Mallarmé re-enacts in solitude Shelley's romantic agony, writing to Cazalis in 1866 and 1867:

> These last months have been terrifying. My Thought has thought itself through and reached a Pure Idea. . . . Eternity Itself is the least pure of all the regions where the Mind can wander—that Mind which is the abiding hermit of its own purity and untouched now even by the reflection of Time. . . .
>
> . . . My mind is moving in the midst of the Eternal and has felt Its waves, if I may so speak of the Immovable. . . .
>
> . . . Yes, I am travelling, but in unknown lands; and if I have fled from the fierce heat of reality and taken pleasure in cold imagery, it is because, for a month now, I have been on the purest glaciers of Esthetics; because, after I had found Nothingness, I found Beauty. You can't imagine the lucid heights that I have dared to climb.

So the object vanishes and *Le Rien est la Vérité.* As a result of this final vaporization of art, Nothing becomes symbolic of All, and the Sonnet in *yx*—with its cryptic value *ptyx*—represents the irreducible Unknown, *la notion pure, la disparition vibratoire* into which the music of poetry shimmers off: "évoquer petit à petit un objet pour montrer un état d'âme, ou, inversement, choisir un objet et en dégager un état d'âme, par une série de déchiffrements"—this is the end of poetry. The poem is an Act of Thought in which the world is emptied and nothing takes place except a Constellation as magic as the first act of creation. But in Mallarmé the Word is not made flesh—"nothing will have happened except a constellation." Or if the poem is not an Act of Thought, it is Aspiration, a last romantic flight to the infinite, signified by a naked intellectuality that accepts Absence, Winter, and the empty mirror as a release from Time, Space, Insensitivity, and all the dangers of living that are implied in the term Hazard. Ironically, the perfect poem, the pure Act of Thought, the disembodied Vision can never destroy Chance—the actualities that can be dealt with only in prose. Thus *Un Coup de Dés Jamais N'Abolira le Hasard.* The ultimate poem can, then, be neither written nor even thought: the *reductio ad absurdum* of Shelley's vision of the poet achieving Eternity, creating another order of reality.

In the course of meeting his defeat Mallarmé was able to feel intimations of what is ineffable. His music is for the mind as well as the ear, and his poetics are purified far beyond what the most daring romantic would have hoped. "L'Azur" lifts itself to an olympian vision that Shelley, with his hysteric temperament, did not attain:

> De l'éternel azur la sereine ironie
> Accable, belle indolemment comme les fleurs,
> Le poète impuissant qui maudit son génie
> A travers un désert stérile de Douleurs.

The autumn mists, a monotone making the scene livid, seem to show that the heavens are dead. But despair ends in belief:

> *Je suis hanté.* L'azur! L'azur! L'azur! L'azur!

From his blue and sterile solitude the poet can transcend the waste land the nineteenth century already had made. There is also a despair that the excitable and voluble Shelley never felt so bitterly as Mallarmé, doomed to silence and impotence:

> . . . la clarté déserte de ma lampe
> Sur le vide papier que la blancheur défend . . .

—a sterility more afflicting to the artist than the parched rocks of Eliot's landscape. The unheard melodies of the Urn that teased Keats out of thought have become unendurable for Mallarmé, a *poète maudit.* Rimbaud had, at least, like Shelley, the release of his hallucinations. For Mallarmé there was only an impossible Quiet.

It was in 1895 that Maurice Denis called Redon the Mallarmé of the symbolist painters. These painters were known by many names according to the changes that took place in the brief history of a movement that was not really a movement at all, and not really symbolist either, but a reaction against a wholly subjective art. First they were called *cloisonnistes,* then synthetists or Nabis, then neo-traditionalists, then *idéistes*, and finally symbolists or *déformateurs.* The group found its theories in Sérusier and Denis, and its chief painter in Gauguin. Eventually it found its poets in the imagists and neo-traditionalists, but only belatedly. The symbolist-synthetist band of painters was incoherent; but it did bring a reaction toward a formal style. The turn came in Maurice Denis' statement in his *Theories:* "One must remember that a painting before being a cavalry horse, a nude woman, or any sort of anecdote, is essentially a plane surface covered with colors arranged in a certain design."

"En un certain ordre assemblées"—art is first of all design. It was an axiom of neo-traditionalism, which had poetic expression in the "romanist" painters following Denis, and in T. S. Eliot as well. The sense of design reappears in Van Gogh and the *fauves* as well as in Gauguin. It takes monumental form in Cézanne, whose proto-cubist painting is "built." As soon as painting was taken as a way of *arranging* colors or lines, it ceased to be a mode of feeling, much less ephemeral feeling that cannot be imaged. The Nabis knew that art is a *representation* of feeling—by a certain kind of *techné.* Denis has turned back to the old critical question of how to treat, or represent, or design what the artist wishes to suggest. He is, curiously, only rephrasing what John Ruskin wrote in *Stones of Venice*—wrote and then forgot while he went on to search for the spirit of gothic and the associations clustering around it picturesquely: "We are to remember," Ruskin says, "that the arrangement of colours and lines is an art analogous to the composition of music, and entirely independent of the representation of facts. Good colouring does not necessarily convey the image of anything but itself. It consists in certain proportions and arrangements of rays of light. . . ." Gauguin, the greatest of the symbolist painters, discovered this and led Van Gogh, he says, to work in pure tone: "He painted yellow suns on a yellow surface, etc., learned the orchestration of pure tone by all the derivatives of this tone. Then in the landscape all the usual medley, the subjects of still life, a former necessity, was replaced by great harmonies of solid colors suggesting the total harmony of the picture, the literary or explanatory part, whatever you like to call it, taking a back seat in consequence." Painting is not reverie or suggestion only. It is not treating a certain subject. It is a construction, a design. What Ruskin said, would be true of byzantine art. It would, ironically, be true of Whistler, whom he called a charlatan. In any event these statements by Ruskin and Gauguin were signs that the arts were turning from picturesque, romantic, or symbolist feeling to a reformulation of style.

Part Three

NEO-MANNERISM

I

STYLE, STYLIZATION, AND BLOCKAGE

The purpose of Maurice Denis and the neo-traditionalists like the Nabis was to free nineteenth-century art, especially religious art, of fakes and stereotypes—*truquage* and the *poncif.* The intention was understandable, for the painting, architecture, and poetry of the century were littered with elegance that was often artistic junk. The junk had accumulated by 1847 when Couture's *Romans of the Decadence,* filled with official effects, academic nudes, and institutional statues, was given highest honors. It has been properly called an assortment of antique debris. The same debris was on view at the Crystal Palace in 1851, where industrial products of a machine age were encrusted with filagree that overspread the legs of chairs, brackets for gaslights, handles of scissors. Tennyson's *Idylls* were filled with poetic debris too, mostly gothic, and salvaged from the picturesque mediaevalism of romantic poems like Keats's "Eve of Saint Agnes." When he was not being an official bard, Tennyson knew well enough how to write another sort of verse:

. . . the more he looked at her,
The less he liked her; and his ways were harsh;
But Dora bore them meekly. Then before
The month was out he left his father's house,
And hired himself to work within the fields;
And half in love, half spite, he woo'd and wed
A laborer's daughter, Mary Morrison.

(*"Dora"*)

This is the plain language used by George Crabbe, by Wordsworth at times, and again by Robert Frost after Ezra Pound remarked (it is said) to his friend Eliot that poetry ought to be as well written as prose. It is the strong poetry of Corot in his Italian phase, or of Courbet in his simplest statement. In the novel the debris had been piling up since Scott and Hugo put together their own type of cumbersome mediaeval machines. Meanwhile architecture was getting along by "cultural patchwork." Art historians usually classify this sort of *poncif* as historicism. The historical debris was ruthlessly cleared away after mid-century by impressionists and post-impressionists, who by their revolts made possible cubism, that most fertile and authentic of modern styles. In spite of its accumulated junk the nineteenth century was an age of experiment in the arts, and the experimenters all had one purpose in mind: to find a style instead of trying to get along with parodies of styles.

The experiments of the impressionists were incomplete, for although they brought into painting a new atmosphere, their composition often remained conventional; it was left for the fauvists and the cubists, closely related, to develop a new formality in structure. Yet the impressionists accepted, unlike other painters of their day, the implications of scientific vision, exact observation, spectrum analysis, the camera-angle, and the techniques that brought positivism into modern life. The cubists were the principal heirs of the impressionists, and the great importance of cubism has been indicated by Francastel, who says, "Cubism is an authentically pictorial mode of representing what happened to artists in an epoch when the sum of man's attitudes was oriented to new conditions of life issuing directly from technique, but indirectly from all the scientific, aesthetic, philosophic, and literary speculation of preceding

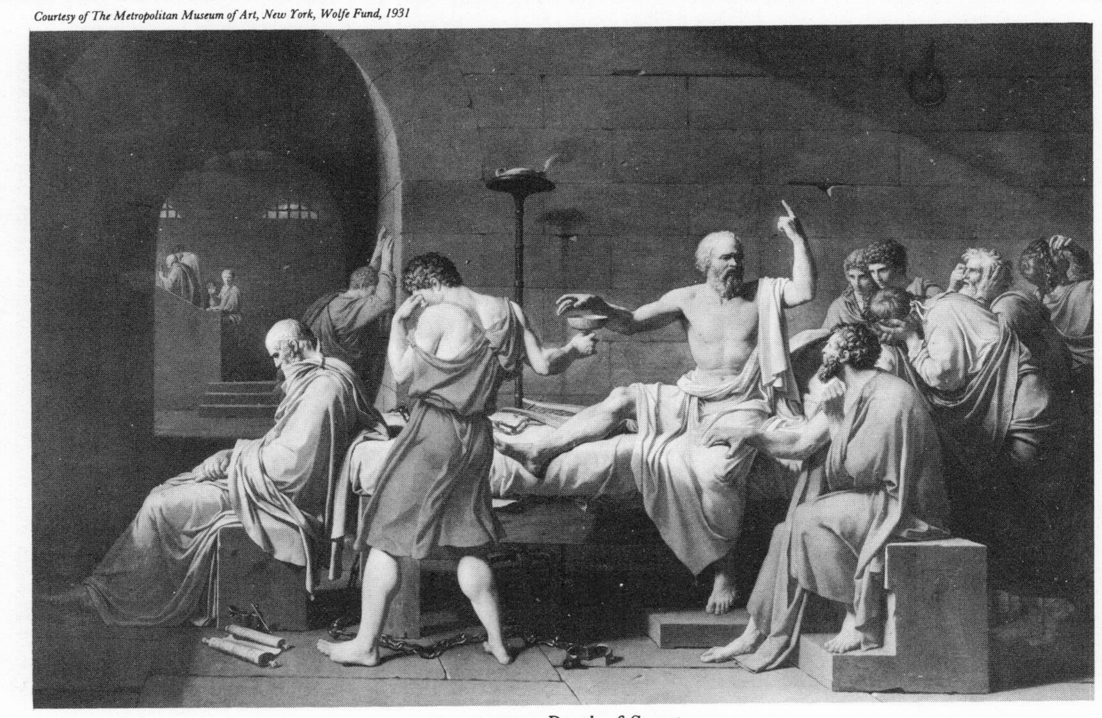

20 DAVID: *Death of Socrates*

generations."[1] That is why it is a style, not a parody of a style.

The dominating force in this new world was science, which had not only altered the entire economic order but put at man's disposal the technology of the machine. T. S. Eliot got the point when he said that the internal-combustion engine changed our way of life. He implied what Rubashov says in Koestler's novel: that Europe has not yet digested the consequences of the steam engine. The nineteenth century refused to assimilate its technology to its arts—the official artist, especially, sterilized art by alienating it from its day. Even a modern like Flaubert complains: "To return to the antique has been done already. To return to the Middle Ages has also been done already. Only the present remains. But the present offers shaky ground." Instead of accepting the machine and the new scientific world-view as a basis for artistic representation, the nineteenth-century artist attempted to conciliate new techniques with past forms. Francastel uses the convenient term *blockage* to indicate what happened when the painter or architect tried to compromise between art and technology. For the most part nineteenth-century stylizations are phases of the adaptation of new techniques to representation; and the adaptations were not always successful—at least not until the close of the century, which brought, even in its practice of art for art, a new coherence into design, a functionalism that was soon to be absorbed into the more imperious forces working themselves out through fauvism and cubism.

In other words the nineteenth-century arts show a conflict between perception and representation. The perception was often new. But the representation was often a concession to past styles. That is, the century often produced stylizations, but not a style. One thinks of Jacques Louis David, whose *Death of Marat* is severely recorded with the neutral eye of a journalist, but whose *Sabine Women* was an artifact intended "to paint ancient customs with such exactitude that the Greeks and the Romans, seeing my work, would not have found me foreign to their way of living." The journalist tries to see with the eye of Poussin and the Academy, and achieves only a stucco composition [20]. David never found his style. Nor did nineteenth-century architects desperately trying to adapt cast-iron pillars to gothic filagree; although their warehouses and docks and railway bridges, simply because they were utilitarian, shunned *truquage.* In spite of Viollet-le-Duc's studious accuracy, the great twin-spired cathedral at Moulins is a cold and gaudy stylization—not convincingly gothic.

The distinction between style and stylization is needed since the nineteenth century nourished two types of artists Focillon calls the pasticheur and the virtuoso:[2] the one diluting past styles or techniques, the other abandoning himself to his own originality, seeking effect for the sake of effect. Both can stylize; but neither can properly be said to have a style. Rather, each has a manner. Focillon was referring to minor painters; and it is true, as he says, that pastiche and virtuosity do tend to appear together in the wake of major artists. Yet the notion of pastiche and virtuosity has wider relevance to the many competing mannerisms in nineteenth-century painting, architecture, and literature. Pastiche is seen nearly everywhere—not only in Sargent and Watts and Tennyson, in his composite "Keatsian" beauty, but even in the pseudo-idyls of Corot. The virtuoso is more important. Byron, like most flagrant romantics, was virtuoso in his flair for the gesture which makes life an art. Dickens, like Balzac, is virtuoso in his enormous zest for a striking situation; and Forain would be a suitable illustrator for both novelists. Carlyle's fire-eyed germanic language is both pastiche and virtuosity, a titanic mannerism. Browning's harsh poetic shorthand and his spasmodic accent are virtuoso. Degas makes a virtuoso attack on the humdrum subject, and Constantin Guys has something of the dandy, who Baudelaire said was the typical hero of the age. He has his *air,* which is often a nineteenth-century surrogate for a style, as in Poe's case. The melodrama inherent in all the arts is a sign of manner and virtuosity: Emma Bovary's white hand scattering the torn letter from the window of the cab as she is borne to her adultery with Léon has the quality of the "fit and striking incident" that falsifies rather than represents the dreariness of middle-class existence.

But we need not make catalogs. It is clear that a considerable number of these artists transcended the pastiche and virtuosity, often performing technical experiments that had to be made even if the experiments were not brought to their final stages.

Nor is it hard to name those who tried these legitimate experiments. We could begin with Delacroix or Turner, and this time include Ingres along with the bleaker Corot of Italian scenes; and add Constable with his broken pigments, and Manet with his colored shadows and flat composition, and Monet with his refracted light, or Degas, who isolated his figures in a space that has some of the modern sense of the void, the pathos that Picasso feels so intimately in his blue period. These painters belong with Flaubert, with Zola, with the nightmarish Dickens who is almost a surrealist, a Daumier of the novel; they belong with Stendhal, too, and the experimental guttural Browning, each having his own dramatic vision. There is the overbearing virtuosity of Wagner. If the century lacked *a* style, it was not without extravagant talent—doubtless genius at times.

The pasticheur and virtuoso appear at critical periods in the history of the arts. What would the renaissance be without them? Without Uccello and Leonardo and Michelangelo? In many plays Shakespeare was a pasticheur—in *Measure for Measure,* for example, or *Cymbeline,* or perhaps *Hamlet*? He did not have *a* style either, but showed every sign of virtuosity. *Troilus and Cressida* is a virtuoso performance, and *Lear,* and doubtless *The Tempest,* not to mention *Hamlet* again. This uncertainty and fluctuation in Shakespeare will indicate that there is no particular merit, in itself, in an artist's having *a* style. It is simply a matter of history that certain periods do reach a coherent style —romanesque or gothic, probably, or rococo certainly; whereas in other periods, like the renaissance, changes occur so rapidly that new techniques shift the prevailing view of reality before many artists are able to cope with them. This is one reason why Western art, at least, always needs an *avant-garde,* especially in societies where technological revolutions are happening and where a middle class looks upon the arts as one more product to be standardized for sale in a mass market. Under such conditions it is difficult for an artist to be contemporary, since a genuinely contemporary art may not be saleable in a mass market, which seeks a conventional product. Yet technological revolutions (which are actually the "permanent revolution" always being carried on by the middle class) are always accompanied by a corresponding "permanent revolution" in the arts being carried on by the *avant-garde.* Pastiche and virtuosity are not necessarily damaging. Malraux has pointed out that every major artist begins by first accepting, then rejecting, the prevailing conventions in the arts. So there is nothing essentially injurious in the nineteenth-century loss of a style. The very "manners" we have been sketching are witness of an *avant-garde,* or experiments that must be made.

Indeed, the establishment of a style brings its own danger that the style becomes official, institutional—classic. Just as the mediaeval guilds became a vested interest against which the early academies of the renaissance reacted, so the renaissance academies themselves became a vested interest against which the romantics rebelled. Pevsner has summarized the situation by saying that the art of the nineteenth century "can only be adequately interpreted in terms of a continual tension between the official and the intimate." The last classic style before the nineteenth century was Poussinesque baroque, which, particularly in France, had ossified into an academism of a very tyrannical sort, against which every important artist of the century reacted by performing his own experiment. Feuerbach mentioned "something peculiar, damp, and mouldy which I should like to describe as academic air." More sarcastically Whistler said, "Whom the gods wish to make ridiculous, they made Academicians."

The significant history of the nineteenth-century arts was written in the *salon des refusés* and in the legal actions against Baudelaire's *Fleurs du Mal* and Flaubert's *Madame Bovary.* By the same token we may ask whether the eventual appearance of cubism, the archetypal modern style that summarized and concluded many of the major experiments of anti-academic art, has not, during the twentieth century, led to a new academism: what Lewis Mumford has called "academic functionalism," which now accepts streamlining as a style. There is, then, nothing necessarily charismatic about a style, and in particular a classic style.

II

THE NEO-MANNERIST CONDITION

The more significant point is that a great deal of nineteenth-century art—especially experimental art—is mannered or manneristic. The term mannerism cannot perhaps be adequately defined; yet in the development of styles mannerism is a phase that appears as a constant in the history of European art and literature, occurring whenever a so-called classic art disintegrates or is revised.[3] There appears a mannerist moment in the hellenistic art that produced Tanagra figurines and the Greek romances; there was a mannerist moment even in romanesque art before gothic emerged as a style; then, at the close of gothic, mannerism recurred in various guises during the *détente* or ogival period. Again after the height of a renaissance style, when proportions and perspective had been carefully formulated into a coherent system, mannerism appeared in the later sixteenth century—often as a kind of throwback to late-mediaeval art with its distortions and hypersensitivities. In somewhat other guises mannerism rephrases itself in the nineteenth century too, after the loss of a style in the eighteenth century. It is an aspect of pastiche and virtuosity.

However, if we are to apply the term mannerism to the arts of the nineteenth century, we must not do so in too confined a sense, and must consider any such mannerism as a symptom of unrest and experiment, not as a legitimate style. Mannerism is always experimental, and the nineteenth century is a period of experiment, like the later renaissance, the age that produced Parmigianino, Bronzino, Tintoretto, and El Greco, all of whom were mannerist. These painters had an artistic heritage to reject, and each rejected or revised it in his own way. From this point of view mannerism is negative, since it springs from denial. Nevertheless there is also a negation of negation, for in the course of rejecting artistic conventions the mannerists make a great many discoveries. One of the first symptoms of a mannerist reaction is a disturbed quality that appeared in Michelangelo's tormented figures, then, later, in Tintoretto's "white writing" and Greco's wraithlike saints. The Florentine mannerists like Pontormo sought some strange psychological effects by their arbitrary designs and perversions of classic figures. Often the mannerists turned from the outside world to a very subjective view of reality, a *disegno interno.* Mannerism is a highly personal art, testing reality by temperament.

Often it is hard to make a distinction between mannerist art and art that is merely mannered—that is, fashionable or precious. The truly mannerist art of the sixteenth century was symptom of a "time of troubles," the doubt and inquietude attending the rise of Protestantism, cruel religious wars, the Inquisition, the new science, and the malaise of European minds after the freshest energies of the renaissance had spent themselves. Then some of the younger painters began to experiment with the classic ideals of renaissance art, exploring new kinds of space, using watery color, twisting figures unnaturally, putting realism to shocking uses, setting things under a spotlight glare, seeing portrait figures from queer angles, and in general adding "strangeness to beauty." The phrase is Pater's, and Pater was far more attracted to mannerist than to renaissance style, as his reading of *Mona Lisa* reveals.

The true mannerist is over-intellectual—for Hamlet is a mannerist hero—and clever or risky, as the deliberately unorthodox work of Parmigianino shows in its defiance of perspective and its abnormal proportions. Renaissance mannerists had a consuming interest in aesthetic theory, sometimes painting compositions only to see how far an accepted canon could be altered. Mannerist beauty is usually very sophisticated, a kind of dandyism in painting, resorting to what is unnatural, strained, over-cultivated. Some mannerist work is merely stylish—the nudes contrived in the French school of Fontainebleau, for instance. Such beauty is synthetic—abstract, eclectic, painstakingly designed, like Flaubert's style in *Salammbô.* Vasari, a spokesman for mannerists who were fascinated by theories about art, says that a "fine manner" comes from copying "the most beautiful objects, and of afterwards combining the most perfect, whether the hand, head, torso, or leg, and joining them together to make one figure invested with every beauty." Mannerism is derivative and original, self-consciously willing to manipulate forms to gain its own highly individual accent. It nourishes pasticheurs and virtuosos who are merely mannered along with artists who are titans like Michelangelo; and above all there is a mannerist climate congenial to disturbed artists like El Greco. Mannerism is a result of different attempts to stylize, and is one symptom of the loss of a style, a revolt against a prevailing style, or a reformulating of style. It is prone to technical ingenuities, deliberate deviations, and every kind of unexpected emotional attack. John Donne is the great mannerist poet who uses most of these tactics.

When we think of the *disegno interno* of renaissance mannerism we are reminded that at the close of the eighteenth century the late-baroque canon of academic art broke down under the new psychology of David Hume, Burke, and Hogarth, who assume that beauty arises not from proportion but from a subjective impression or a sensibility that may be stimulated by the feelings one associates with an object. "Beauty," says Hume, "is no quality of things in themselves: It exists merely in the mind which contemplates them." There is no fixed standard of taste —only, at best, an agreement in sentiments. The old geometry of beauty was "overthrown from the bottom" by this eighteenth-century revolution in aesthetics, as it had been in the earlier mannerist period[4]; and there is something in common between the *disegno interno* of Italian mannerism and the private ideas in symbolist art and poetry.

Recently a number of continental art critics have traced how the arts of the nineteenth century repeat an earlier cycle in the arts from classic to mannerist to baroque to rococo.[5] The parallels between this earlier cycle and phases of nineteenth-century arts can readily be drawn, and soon we shall suggest some. But first it must be urged that these repetitions do not occur systematically. Too many developments in the nineteenth century are concurrent, and the industrial age is different from the culture of the renaissance and late-renaissance. Often we cannot clearly distinguish a nineteenth-century baroque from impressionism or early expressionism, and the phases, if they do repeat themselves, do not occur in a normal sequence. Without, then, insisting upon the exactness with which any such cycle recurs, it is enough to claim that the nineteenth century, having lost a style, produced many eclectic and experimental forms of an art that can conveniently be called mannered or manneristic, or stylizations that amount to neo-mannerism. Even neo-baroque and neo-rococo forms of art are symptoms of a neo-mannerist seeking for style.

The extraordinary self-consciousness of nineteenth-century arts expressed itself in aesthetic theories, which always flourish in manneristic periods—theories about realism, impressionism, symbolism, beauty, art. There has probably never been another age so vocally and in so many ways dedicated to Nature and at the same time so insistent upon the art-view of life and the cultivation of art for art's sake. As Flaubert said, "One must always be conscious of style." The nearly obsessive dedication to style led to the synthetic beauties of decadence, ingenious in stylizations. Yet all this artifice made a style possible. The decadent movement with its affected and over-cultivated devotion to art-for-art finally redeemed the nineteenth century from its mania for Nature, its fascination with the anecdote, and—after Art Nouveau—led to a new style. The very fine manner of the decadents brought an awareness of design; and the consciousness of the *motif* for its own sake became the basis of a composition that surrendered Nature and the striking episode. Flaubert the realist wrote to Louise Colet, "Art will be something halfway between algebra and music," and to Mademoiselle Leroyer de Chantpie, "The time has come to give it, by a pitiless method, the precision of the physical sciences. But the principal difficulty for me is still the style, the indefinable Beauty resulting from the actual conception." This care for style, together with a sense of malaise, the rejection of outworn official canons, and the need to experiment and theorize, means that much of nineteenth-century art is in a mannerist condition, or is at least prevailingly manneristic.

In a narrower sense some nineteenth-century painting does resemble the painting by earlier mannerists. Clearly there is a similarity between Ingres with his svelte line, his neutral tints, slick realism, and unnatural frigidity, and the chill, elegant mannerism of Parmigianino's madonnas. Or perhaps Ingres is a new Cranach? The presence of Ingres' *Madame Rivière* is as artificial and cruel as the figures in Bronzino, who also congealed his sitters. Ingres' odalisques [21] have the same unpleasant transparency we see in Parmigianino's bloodless Virgins, who yet remain voluptuous. The sinuosity of Ingres' figures is further perverted in drawings and paintings by Fuseli, who is a reincarnation of Spranger, painter of nudes for the court at Prague about 1600. Blake seems to have extracted from Michelangelo's muscular figures their serpentine distortion, making them more mannered than the nudes drawn by Pollaiuolo.

Could anything be, technically, more mannerist than Manet's *Dead Toreador* with its projected foreshortening, opalescent light, and strong psychological accent? These tricks had all been used by Tintoretto and by Rembrandt in his mannerist phase. One type of mannerist figure was the Sprecher, standing with his back to us gesticulating inward toward the events happening in angular mannerist space. El Greco used the Sprecher in his *Burial of Count Orgaz,* and Degas puts this figure to modern uses. Manet gives us a modern version of the reflected and reversed figure, with action implied rather than stated; and Degas' camera-trick of catching musicians in an orchestra pit against the glare of proscenium lights and off center is a variant reading of the reversed or psychological perspective Rembrandt used in *Syndics of the Cloth Guild.* The scribble in which Daumier shows Don Quixote riding into a phantasmal landscape is, again, another variation on Tintoretto's *Saint George Slaying the Dragon* or his San Rocco paintings, where *Saint Mary of Egypt* is outlined in "white writing" that empties the figure of flesh and leaves the landscape a flickering twilit rhythm of palms and

Louvre, Archives Photographiques, Paris

21 INGRES: *Odalisque Couchée*

rocks. How much of Greco's flaming line is repeated in Van Gogh. And how the nervous decorative line in Beardsley resembles the aesthetic line of Botticelli.

One can draw every sort of parallel in the handling of space and color. Degas' empty space, asymmetrical, and his angular approach, his raised horizon giving fantastic steepness to his scene, his casual grouping of figures and strong diagonal tensions all repeat the composition of Tintoretto, who broke up the harmonious space of renaissance painting and left his figures—highly mobile—suspended as if in a vacuum. The theatrical pose in Toulouse-Lautrec's posters is said to have been inspired by Japanese prints; but the mannerists had already used many of Lautrec's techniques of distortion and projection of figures against the frame. Parmigianino did his self-portrait as seen in a bull's eye mirror, his hand enlarged and thrown into the space where we are, just as Lautrec has the deformed image of La Goulue strolling out of poster-space into the Moulin Rouge. The mannerists often "bled" their scenes by crowding the foreground and slashing obliquely into the perspective, just as Degas slashes into a row of ballet girls poised over the footlights. At the very heart of impressionism is Bazille's *Lady in a Park* with its imbalance and luminous space recalling the radiant asymmetry of the Flemish little masters. Bazille's *Artist's Family on a Terrace* has the cold, full color we see in Vermeer or Terborch. Seurat calculates his intervals with the psychological tact that appeared in Rembrandt's *Syndics.* The unfinished off-center naturalism of Degas' *Vicomte Lepic and his Daughters,* glimpsed as they stroll along a Paris street, has the mannerist artifice that pulled Tintoretto's persons up spiral stairways or scattered them intimately downstage. The contrived naturalness of the impressionists, their note of impromptu in studio scenes, is a mannerist attack.

Even Prud'hon's classic mythologies with *Vengeance and Justice Pursuing Crime* are enveloped in melodramatic blackness that seems to be a lengthened shadow of seventeenth-century tenebrists like Caravaggio, who immersed Christ's figure in the same gloom except for the startling hand that appears like an anatomical fragment. The expressionism in Prud'hon and Goya is a rephrasing of the mannerist expressionism that comes like an upheaval in the early Caravaggio. Courbet's realism in *Re-*

turn from the Conference repeats the brutality of Caravaggio's devotional paintings, which shocked the Church, as did Courbet.

It would be easy to continue the parallels, extending them to baroque, late-baroque, and rococo. It may be that the great "machines" painted by David are a form of classic art—a heritage of late-baroque—and that the reaction against them caused the mannerism not only of the artists we have named but also many others like Puvis de Chavannes and Canova. Then there would be a nineteenth-century neo-baroque, which probably would include Delacroix, whose debt to Rubens is so deep, and Rude and Rodin, who modernize—or romanticize—Michelangelo's titanic statuary; and maybe even Renoir, with his monumental and thoughtless plenitude, again like Rubens'. There would be a rococo phase, which would not be hard to find in Constantin Guys, Beardsley, and perhaps Degas' statues, or in some of the impressionists or proto-impressionists like Bonington (who is very congenial to the spirit and technique of eighteenth-century Venetian painters like Guardi), Boudin, or even Monet, Sisley, and Bonnard. But this game is not worth the trouble. The recurrences are not to this degree exact—at least not until we come to Art Nouveau, which does indeed appear to be a kind of resurrection of rococo theory and design.

The immediate business is to see that the nineteenth-century arts are often mannered or manneristic in the sense that has been previously implied: there are a great many stylizations, and there is an intense and pervasive awareness of style itself, a form of self-consciousness that brings with it what has been well called "the savor of the artificial." It is a self-consciousness that reveals itself not only in aestheticism but also in the constant revivals of past styles, the historicism and eagerness to draw at will upon the "museum without walls." Antiquarianism was inherent in the romantic movement, which from a certain view was an attempt to recover some usable style from the past: notably from gothic or grecian, inspiring pseudo-mediaeval and plaster-classic art like the ballad and painting by Jacques Louis David. T. S. Eliot and Malraux rightly point out that we *know* so much more than past writers and painters; the nineteenth century developed the historical method, and the painter and writer were always finding their way lighted by "the lamp of memory" so that their "style" became a mode of archaeology.

The antiquarianism of the "gothic" eighteenth century was translated into the aesthetic of nineteenth-century mediaevalism by Chateaubriand, who wrote sentimentally of ritual and *les mystères chrétiens: des cloches, du vêtement des prêtres, des chants et des prières, de la messe, des solennités de l'église.* This gothicism was picturesque, representing a nostalgia and a revolt from the Manchester-values of industry. It was also manneristic, for it resembled the learned eclecticism recommended by Vasari to gain a "fine manner" by "copying the most beautiful objects" from earlier painters and reaching a style by synthesis. Victorian mediaevalism was studied and highly self-conscious, and the "poetic beauty" synthesized by Keats in his "mediaeval" passages was adopted as a mannerism in Tennyson, whose *Idylls* are an aesthetic rephrasing of Malory:

> Then saw they how there hove a dusky barge
> Dark as a funeral scarf from stem to stern,
> Beneath them; and descending they were ware
> That all the decks were dense with stately forms
> Black-stoled, black-hooded, like a dream—by these
> Three queens with crowns of gold—and from them rose
> A cry that shivered to the tingling stars. . . .

The Camden Society of 1839 and the whole brotherhood of Ecclesiologists with their prim dogmas and their concern to build with the "true gothic" of the fourteenth century (!) were neo-mannerists of the sort who caused Gautier to exclaim in despair: "Again the middle ages, always the middle ages! Who will deliver me from the middle ages, the middle ages that are not mediaeval? The middle ages of cardboard and terra cotta—mediaeval in nothing but name." These mannerists forced Pugin and Viollet-le-Duc to reject putty and cast-iron gothic in favor of a more authentic and better-grounded archaeology.

This self-conscious mediaevalism culminated in the pre-Raphaelite Brotherhood and its collateral groups on the Continent like the Nazarenes, the Nabis, and the neo-traditionalists at Beuron. In France the sentimental mediaevalism of Chateaubriand at last produced the mannerisms of Huysmans, who went to Chartres to find beauty and who in *Là-Bas* investigated all the profanities of the Black Mass. His hero Des Esseintes takes the highest of aesthetic lines by withdrawing entirely from his century and living in his "mediaeval" castle, cultivating a taste for the byzantine art of Gustave Moreau. The rituals of Rossetti's Blessed Damozel and his Dantesque sonnets in *The House of Life* are mannerisms that take more glaring form in paintings by Boecklin; and by mid-century Puvis de Chavannes is using fresco-like archaisms in a pale art that heralds the Nabis. Ruskin saw all Europe as a gothic museum.

There is no need to follow the history of neo-mediaevalism and other antiquarianisms to prove they are an aspect of the aesthetic movement, which fed its exquisite sense of the artificial on the museum, bringing into nineteenth-century art a manneristic notion of style even while there was lacking any legitimate style. Arnold was greatly concerned about style—"a peculiar recasting and heightening" of language. It was to be sought, he hoped, in Homer, or in the magic Celtic phrase. The artist or poet could not work without having an aesthetic sense of art-history such as Vasari had. Ingres consciously went back to Raphael to find his frozen manner. When Manet painted *Olympia* he was referring to Giorgione's *Sleeping Venus* or Titian's *Venus of Urbino;* when he painted *Le Déjeuner sur l'Herbe* he was quoting Giorgione's *Concert Champêtre* or Marcantonio's engraving of a lost Raphael. This is a mannerist form of wit. Gauguin is said to have advised a friend to avoid the Greeks but always to have before him "the Persians, the Cambodians, and a little of the Egyptians." The first mannerists were derivative and knowing in much the same way. We shall not pause to ask what use Whistler and Van Gogh made of the Japanese print. T. S. Eliot has remarked that "we dwell with satisfaction upon the poet's difference from his predecessors." Indeed; but the museum-perspective that came with the nineteenth-century historical view meant an inescapable eclecticism, a mannerist sense that beauty is an artifact.

Taking Beauty as a value in itself is characteristic of the mannerist effort to find a style. It is strong in the Parnassians, expressing itself in Gautier's verses on Art:

Oui, l'oeuvre sort plus belle
D'un forme au travail
Rebelle,
Vers, marbre, onyx, émail. . . .

Lutte avec le carrare,
Avec le paros dur
Et rare,
Gardiens du contour pur;

Emprunte à Syracuse
Son bronze où fermement
S'accuse
Le trait fier et charmant. . . .

Sculpte, lime, cisèle;
Que ton rêve flottant
Se scelle
Dans le bloc résistant!

("*L'Art*")

In *Mademoiselle de Maupin* (1835) Gautier proved that he was one of the guardians of synthetic Beauty—

> Beauty, the only thing which cannot be acquired, for all time beyond the reach of those who have not possessed it from the beginning; ephemeral and fragile flower which grows without being sown, pure gift of Heaven, O Beauty! . . . Though I ask for nothing but beauty, I must have it at a pitch of perfection such as I shall probably never find. Here and there I have seen, in a few women, parts that were wonderful . . . and the rest I left out of account.

We might be reading one of the pages of Vasari or another early mannerist who tried to abstract from Nature an Idea of Beauty existing independently of any object: "an idea and form in the intellect" Federigo Zuccaro called it in 1607. Gautier says that this obsessive sense of the beautiful has numbed him to bourgeois morality and made him sympathize with Caligula, who murdered the ugly. He prepares the way for Oscar Wilde, for George Moore, and that other belated aesthete André Gide, whose immoralism is a form of mannerism. The hero of Gautier's novel has the mannered sensibility of Pater's Florian Deleal and all those idyllic young men who cultivated stained-glass attitudes and neo-pagan pleasures.

Gautier's hero is a type of dandy, the central figure in the mannerist-aesthetic tradition, which makes art a substitute for life. As Baudelaire knows, dandyism is an effort to seek distinction, and the dandy is a fellow who "has no other profession but that of elegance." He has a "serious devotion to the frivolous" and is the heir of Sheridan, Brummell, and Byron, as well as the fictional character of Lovelace and the eighteenth-century fop. "Dandyism is the last gleam of heroism in times of decadence." The dandy aspires to indifference, but is not indifferent to cutting a figure. In an essay on "The Heroism of Modern Life" Baudelaire remarks that a great tradition has been lost and a new one not yet found; at this crisis the dandy appears, a figure from the studio, we might say, playing his insolent part in the pageant of society that floats just above "the underworld of a great city." The dandy is an elegant bohemian. Disraeli is the dandy of British politics and handles everything with an *air*.

The need of the artificial at the heart of nineteenth-century experience is symbolized by the heroes in Stendhal—poseurs who have many psychological mannerisms. Although they are more than dandies, these figures have a large strain of the dandy in them. They must live with flair; this is part of their sense of drama, of illusion. Julien Sorel and other Stendhalian adventurers behave in a contrived, over-responsive way. Perhaps they owe something to the volatile heroes of Laurence Sterne. Julien stands halfway between Hamlet and J. Alfred Prufrock, who also show a psychological dandyism. The key to Julien's behavior is the "continuous attention with which he watched his own slightest actions," making his whole existence a stratagem.

Realism in Stendhal is as artificial as the realism in Constantin Guys' fashionable sketches. In that great chapter on "An Evening in the Country" Julien contrives to "force the moment to its crisis" by taking Mme. de Rênal's hand; and as test of his ability to do his duty to himself focuses all his being on a dandiacal gesture—"At the precise moment when ten o'clock strikes, I shall carry out the intention which, all day long, I have been promising myself I would fulfil this evening, or I shall go up to my own room and blow my brains out." (One thinks of the mannered performance of Gide's Lafcadio, who is serious only about achieving his duty to himself, like Julien. Lafacdio—and Michel—are mannerist figures who have been transplanted by Gide from the nineteenth into the twentieth century, scions of the aesthetic movement devoted to Beauty.) This pitch of stylization is due to Julien's fine perception that the middle classes have muddled everything, blurred all values, obscured logic and feeling by their stupidity: "This age is destined to bring everything to confusion." So Julien must "abandon all prudence" and somehow act decisively, in *style.* It is not true that Stendhal's fiction is a "mirror carried along a high road" reflecting everything accurately. If it is a mirror at all, it is a distorting mirror, sharply stylizing the image it catches. Julien's life is an affectation, a *formality.* It may be that Stendhal is the most important mannerist of the century.

Baudelaire has this strong sense of style. "Strictly speaking, there is neither line nor color in nature," he writes. "It is man that creates line and color. They are twin abstractions." A sense of style and the artificial must have been what attracted Baudelaire to Poe, who defines poetry as "the rhythmical creation of Beauty" and abstracts the emotions to a *motif.* Accepting the poem "written solely for the poem's sake," Poe asks that "we must be simple, precise, terse" and devote verse to a "contemplation of Beauty." It is abstract music, of pure contour. No more preposterous critical document has ever appeared than Poe's "Philosophy of Composition," arguing that the writing of a poem should proceed "step by step to its completion with the precision and rigid consequence of a mathematical problem." The Italian mannerists had this notion of Beauty as an Idea or Design in the mind. Poe says that a poem must be intense and brief to gain a unity of effect. His account of writing "The Raven," even if it be untruthful, shows the manneristic need to *contrive.* "It has always appeared to me that a close circumscription of space is absolutely necessary to the effect of insulated incident:—it has the force of a frame to a picture." Poems like "City in the Sea" isolate their images from what is natural. Stories like "Masque of the Red Death" are a visual pattern carefully worked up apart from reality. The color is abstract in Baudelaire's sense of the word. Poe's insulated designs are related, through Baudelaire, to the art of symbolists and decadents, whose music is another stylization in a century without a style.

III

THE IMPRESSIONIST EXPERIMENT

The symbolists are often linked with the impressionists. In its first intentions, however, impressionism is a different sort of stylization, although it, also, lays foundations of fauvism and cubism. If symbolism is the axis of nineteenth-century poetry, impressionism is the most important and inconsistent movement in nineteenth-century painting—if, indeed, it is a movement at all; for the closer it is seen, the more it appears to be only a historical circumstance that a number of painters met and exchanged views in certain quarters of Paris, or at Argenteuil, during the 1870's and 1880's. Monet met Boudin at Havre in 1858 (the sea left its mark on impressionism), but Corot, Rousseau, Daubigny, and Diaz had already gained a "virgin impression of nature" in the forest at Barbizon. In the 1850's also, Japanese prints with their "cut" edges gave some unconventional notions of space. In 1863 Manet exhibited his *Déjeuner sur l'Herbe,* and three years later Monet painted *Femmes au Jardin* in the open air. The first impressionist show was held, significantly, at the shop of Nadar the photographer, in 1874. The high years of the enterprise were the 1870's, the Argenteuil period. The last show came in 1886. It is true that many of the so-called impressionist painters often used the same brushwork and color and subjects; yet they differed from each other in almost every other way.

If Manet is an impressionist, what are we to call Renoir? If Renoir is an impressionist, where shall we place Degas? What are we to think of Cézanne, who is—and is not—to be identified with the group? Does Bazille really belong? Should we include someone like Paul Guigou, who has a strange similarity to Renoir and Van Gogh? To confuse matters worse, impressionism changes almost imperceptibly into pointillism and post-impressionism, which, in turn, becomes cubist and is closely related to fauvism in color and form. Then too, the boundaries between impressionism and symbolism are often indistinguishable, especially in Monet. Sometimes we see Manet adopting Degas' technique, or Renoir adopting Monet's; or Renoir and Monet painting the same Duck Pond in 1873, or Renoir performing volcanic feats like Van Gogh. From Monet's methods Bonnard develops a technique that approaches Matisse. Monet, who lived until 1926, was always receptive to different methods. In 1866 he tries his own *Déjeuner sur l'Herbe.* In 1882 his still life with plates, tarts, and a carafe has Van Gogh's distortion; and his basket of red and green apples has Cézanne's solidity. He can render a houseboat on a river with Renoir's heavy hand, or he washes a garden scene with Whistler's lavender. In 1888 appears a vase of flowers that is nearly tachist in brushwork. Earlier, some of his park scenes have Bazille's naïveté; there is a bleak *Church at Verneuil* that could be mistaken for a Utrillo; his *Road at Chailly* might be by a Barbizon painter; his marines resemble Manet's studies.

These interactions must shake our confidence in any single definition of impressionism, which is rightly called multiple. No matter what one says of the impressionists, it is never entirely trustworthy. They have no method—only methods. Like the symbolists they are first of all independents, revolting against the salons. And like symbolism, impressionism leads toward subjective interpretations.

Impressionism is a wide range of experiments, though few were carried to conclusions in the nineteenth century. Above all impressionism is an area of conflict between vision and design, between perception and representation, since the visual experience was new and the composition was not. Roger Fry has pointed out that there were really two modes of impressionism: the impressionism that exploited an oblique angle of vision, as in Degas; and the impressionism that was a study of atmospheric effects, as in Monet. The impressionists made a great many compromises between these two modes of vision, conciliations so serviceable, in spite of their inconsistencies, that from Degas' unexpected angle eventually came the art of Lautrec and the expressonist technique of abstract distortion in Van Gogh; and from Monet's atmosphere eventually came pointillism and divisionism, serving as a bridge to tachism and neo-plastic painting. Impressionism also shares with pre-Raphaelitism the intention to return to nature, and links the early naturalism of Courbet with the classic return to nature in Cézanne. Insofar, also, as it was a kind of naturalism, it was an aspect of the science that was atomizing the world into an imponderable substance, pulverizing things into molecules that resemble the vibrant *foule des touches* in Seurat.

How are we to reconcile these competing techniques into a movement? Without denying the contradictions innate in impressionism, or the tentative form of its experiments, we can say that the impressionists, diverse as they were, brought to the evolution of modern style a new sense of atmosphere and, consequently, a new sense of space, a new sense of time, a new sense of the motif apart from mere anecdote or illustration.[6] Let us grant that impressionism is a number of stylizations rather than a style; it remains true that these painters belong with Baudelaire in his effort to transform *volupté* to *connaissance.* To transvalue sensation to perception, to translate optical notations to painting—this was the victory of the impressionists, revolting against academic decrees, developing each in his own way, having a new *consciousness* of technique, without which there is no recovery of style.

Bazille hits the authentic note of early impressionism in 1866 when he tells his parents, "I am trying to paint as well as I can a subject as simple as possible. The subject doesn't matter so long as I am doing something interesting as painting." Writing retrospectively in 1891, Albert Aurier makes a remark that says nearly everything:

> Impressionism is and must be only a kind of realism, a realism refined, spiritualized, and amateur, but always realism. This aim admitted, it is another imitation of matter, no longer perhaps in its accustomed form but as a form seen, a color seen, a translation of sensation with all its impromptu of immediate notation, with all the distortions of a quick subjective synthesis.
> (*Mercure de France*)

Exactly. The impressionist notations slide from the naturalistic and scientific toward subjective poetry, causing an ambiguity inherent in painters like Monet. By 1880 Charles Ephrussi had pointed out that the impressionists took painting out of the studio, stripped it of conventions (not, however, "*all* conventions," as Ephrussi wrote), put it face to face with nature, tried to catch the honest sensation, however strange it might seem, bathed in an atmosphere and light always changing; they found a harmony within fleeting tones; they treated with disdain every accepted legality. The impressionists tried to see nature as a milieu, not as a mere background; and most of their revolutionary effects followed. One of the most revolutionary was to free painting from the tyranny of the anecdote, since their interest was not in the subject, as Bazille noted, but in the handling. Georges Rivière insisted in 1877: "To treat a subject for its tones, not for itself—that is what distinguishes impressionists from other painters."

In the course of breaking down the atmosphere by light, color, brushwork, each painter found his own *facture,* or changing *factures.* Renoir's restaurant or forest scenes sometimes refract sunlight into blotches; but when he paints the rocky, sear Provençal landscape with its tormented pines and ravines, he can also erupt into Van Gogh's rhythms. In these scenes he thins down his languid color to a blond, penetrating grey that glares barrenly with the heat of a southern sky. By their brushwork the impressionists belong to the history of painting, in contrast to the nineteenth-century history of illustration. The difference, roughly, between nineteenth-century illustrators and painters was the difference between those who drew, then colored, and those who colored. The illustrators did not paint; they perverted painting into colored drawing. None of the great painters except Ingres thought of drawing as primary. In contrast to illustrators like Meissonier, Rossetti, and the pre-Raphaelites, the authentic painters worked only from brush and pigment: Constable, Turner, Delacroix, Monet, Degas, Cézanne, and—Bazille apart—nearly all the impressionists and post-impressionists.

Obviously the impressionists—minus Degas—have in common their study of color and light outdoors. Yet if we judge by the celebrated *Déjeuner sur l'Herbe* we must question whether Manet did go outdoors. Here is a highly conventional composition with a nude from the renaissance quoted *out of context.* The light and poses are from the studio, and there is no enveloping atmosphere. The foliage is academic, the shadows are dirty, and the stream and grass are daubed. Except for the nude, and the spilled fruit and blue dress in the left foreground, the touch and vision are uncertain; and the nude, the fruit, and the dress are from the studio. The most damning note is the little redbreast flying overhead—an outrageous studio item. The simple color and the flat, open treatment in a few broad planes may be due to the Japanese print; but there is no pervasive quality of light. One almost suspects that this painting had a mere *succès de scandale,* that its "impressionism" consists chiefly in its defiant naturalism—Manet's anachronistic nude. The *Olympia,* an impudent version of the renaissance Venus, has the same harsh anachronism. The sheet is luridly and solidly handled, and the figure of the nude is actually *drawn* by the hard light on her flesh; but again this illumination seems to be the chill northern light of the studio. The decorative—nearly Japanese—simplification is due to Manet's usual device of presenting his figure strongly against a flimsy background, a device also used in paintings like *The Street Singer* and *The Fifer Boy.* The truly impressionist atmosphere appears in works like *Bar at the Folies Bergère,* or in the casual glimpse of ordinary life he offers us in *The Railroad.* The deviations in impressionism are underscored in Manet, especially its close alliance with the realism that intended to devalue "big" subjects. Manet's still lifes and his portraits—his close study of *Zola,* for example—have the reliability of Dutch masters. In spite of his naturalism few painters are more derivative than Manet, who is forever quoting someone—Goya (in *The Balcony*), Velázquez (in *Dead Toreador*), Hals (in *Bon Bock*), or Giorgione, or Titian, or his fellow impressionists. Yet there is the novelty of *Blonde With Nude Bust,* looking ahead to Matisse.

Inconsistent as he may be, Manet had a care for composition Monet lacked. One of the fallibilities of plein-air impressionism was a weak sense of design. While Monet was most undeniably outdoors in his *Basin at Argenteuil,* his suffused color caused him to neglect everything else; and his extremely loose, if not slovenly, horizontals and verticals must be overlooked if one is to take pleasure in such canvases. Sometimes Monet is so heedless of space that he wedges a flimsy red rectangle of poppies into the green hollow of a concave bank without creating any sense whatever of the poppies' being embraced by the curve of the hill.

Degas has the strongest sense of design of any of the impressionists (unless we wish to include Cézanne in the group). Affected by either the Japanese print, or photography by Nadar, or both, Degas frankly brought impressionism back into the studio: "You know what I think of painters who work in the open," he said: "If I were the government I would have a company of police watching out for men who paint landscapes from nature." Degas told Mallarmé, "Art is deceit. An artist is only an artist at certain hours through an effort of the will; objects possess the same appearance for everyone; the study of nature is a convention." He dismissed nature and realism as vulgarities: "common, without character, without expression, lacking what is the beauty and the life of the ugly in nature and in art: *style.*" Here, in the midst of painters who were getting out of the atelier, is a dandy. Almost like Oscar Wilde he thought of nature as imitating art; for him painting was never a copy or a direct impression. He was always trying to free his designs "from nature's tyranny." "If then two or three natural accents can be added, obviously no harm is done. The air we see in the paintings of the old masters is never the air we breathe." His instinct for "arrangements" alienated him from the outdoor motifs of Monet and his predecessor Courbet. "No art was ever less spontaneous than mine," Degas said. "I am a colorist with line." His space is none the less atmospheric, for he saturates his vacuums with light and relates his figures by diffusing about them the pastel tones that make them poetic. He is the most consciously artful of the impressionists, making the remark that he liked only poseurs: "How do you expect me to give a man a figure if he doesn't know how to give himself one?" Degas' extremely sensitive address gives finesse to everything he touches, and his care for the right pose makes easy the transition from the impressionists to Toulouse-Lautrec.

Bazille and Pissarro may be the only other impressionists who brought this strong design to their sensations. Pissarro is perhaps more variable in technique than the others, at times using the blurred colors of Monet, then shifting toward the pointillism of Seurat or toward the graphic planes of Cézanne. In *Côte du Jallais* (1867) Pissarro shows how impressionist "touches" can solidify light and color into the volumes Cézanne built in his studies of Gardanne. Renoir constructs volumes too, but on quite different principles, modelling profusely in easy masses that remind us of Rubens' baroque flesh. Renoir's is an impressionism of the hand rather than of the eye; he translates ocular experience to a haptic color. When his brushwork lacks vigor, as it does in *La Balançoire,* where he tries (like Monet) to see only light and shadow, the surface is merely splotched or mottled, having a texture that resembles pulled feathers. When, however, Renoir trusts his own coarse touch, he strengthens the lyric transparencies of Monet to a robust, expressive over-statement, supplementing the thoughtless and forthright realism of Courbet. Renoir's structures are organic almost in the sense that Whitman's equally lush verse is organic; Renoir has the dense and hearty vernacular that Degas, the purist, detested. Yet we know how Degas admired Renoir: "he can do what he likes." If Degas, with his fastidious eye, is the dandy of impressionism, Renoir is the anti-dandy. By the same sort of illogicality Baudelaire admired Whitman.

On the whole it remains true that the impressionists "were

an eye." After all, Monet is at the center of the group with his talent for seeing the boulevards at twilight or the trains leaving Saint Lazare, harmonies of steam and steel. Monet raised the sketch, the *pochade* or *ébauche,* to the level of art. This aspect of impressionism is almost illustration. But impressionism is far more than illustration; it is a storm center of experimental pressures that were disturbing the climate of mid-century art. The extreme diversity of method and temperament among the group of the Batignolles goes to prove that impressionism was not a style but a mode of seeing anew, a revolution that was to change the whole course of painting. If Monet's impression of breathing locomotives was partly illustration, it was also a new perception of an age of steam and speed, a sense of the poetry inherent in a middle-class order based on the machine, commerce, and the suburbs. Monet was groping toward a means of bringing vision into relation with a style. These steaming engines released painting from the burden of the literary subject and, like Degas' view of ballet girls, found a new meaning in the commonplace. Monet's locomotives are not journalistic or photographic records; they are modulations sensitively keyed.

Francastel has stated that these quick impressions of things involve conceptions of space the romantics never discovered because they used the old scenographic scheme of composition.[7] The impressionists discovered that space is qualified by light and also, under the Japanese influence, that different fragments of space can be combined as the angle of vision shifts. Monet treats space as a function of color, and Degas fixes our attention in a new mobile focus. Both learned that the structure of the world is relative, that as the angle of vision shifts, details are displaced, that color is not confined to contour, and that three-dimensional space is not an absolute value but, instead, "polysensorial." The impressionists had no consistent theory of space, but they did find new ways of figuring space. The space in impressionist painting is not geometric but "apprehensive" for the reason that the object on which they fixed their attention created, they found, its own kind of space and existed in its own atmosphere. Following the impressionists, Van Gogh learned that pure color creates its own space with dimensions that cannot be confined in the old scenographic perspective.

Meanwhile Gauguin was flattening space into decorative fields by applying the line (the *cloison*) to the canvas, not to the object. Cézanne made the discovery that an object intently seen becomes autonomous—hence the imperious contour of his Montagne Sainte-Victoire, which again and again becomes for him the pole of new magnetic distortions of space. In short, impressionist figurations of space converge on the cubist experience of space, which is congenial to a scientific theory of relativity as well as to apprehensive space. The nineteenth century needed new notions of space in art; and impressionism, however incoherently, afforded some of these notions.

Monet's compositions are also musical and show how impressionism verged toward symbolism as well as cubism. The deep inconsistencies and far-reaching effects of impressionism appear best in Monet's prophetic versatility. *Femmes au Jardin* (1866–67), Monet's first major work, proves that impressionism rose as a form of naturalism. We are told that Monet took his theme from a photograph; yet the painting is an astonishingly accurate study of a human field of vision, having the bull's-eye focus of normal sight rather than the indiscriminate detail of the camera lens. The focus is on the parasol, the white skirt, and the flowers held by the woman seated in the center; the foreground leaves and grass are blurred as they are when the eye fixes on an object in the middle distance; the background foliage is indistinct. Already Monet is distorting space by apprehensive vision. This selective focus is unlike the literal total finish of pre-Raphaelite painters, who attempt the realism of the camera. Monet is, as usual, sensitive to light rather than color, and the white dress and flowers, the simple greens in sun and shadow, set the tone. The work is an extended *croquis* or *pochade,* deliberately unfinished, like the vignettes of the Goncourts.

This ocular realism culminated belatedly in the *Nymphéas* series, begun in the 1890's and taking final form in the two huge masterworks exhibited in 1909 and now spread on the oval walls of the Orangerie: the finale of impressionism and its most provocative single undertaking. Each room has four stretches of canvas, two long and two short, with apertures between the sections; and the two sequences, composed of separate canvases seamed together, trace the changing light and the reflection of clouds over water from dawn to dusk. In a sense the *Nymphéas* is a misuse of easel painting: a hesitant step toward returning from the easel to the wall, needing fresco, not oil—although fresco, too, would be unsuitable to these fusions of color. The seams caused Monet trouble; evidently he painted a kind of false seam here and there to hide the actual seams between units of canvas. The whole sequence, in spite of the repeated trunks of willow trees, has a very low level of structure; passages excerpted from either series could be taken as independent abstractions or tachist compositions. The color itself is nearly an abstraction, and there is a note of Art Nouveau in the subdued grey-blue tonality, quasi-Whistleresque—a frankly decorative texture. The flowers and trailing branches bring in a note of *japonaiserie.* There is no convincing deep space, for all relations are translated into surface light. The unity of the composition is atmospheric and temporal, and the illusion is, by implication, cinematic, one passage developing from another with the continuity of the film. Monet anticipates the technique of the non-objective cinema. Time, in the guise of gradually changing color, becomes a formula for space, since space here appears only as a passage from one vanishing tone to another along an oval surface not very different from the curved cineramic screen, or the curved space of galaxies. In fact, the impressionist atmospheric continuum here takes on galactic implications. Seemingly Monet tried to pull back toward conventional framing by using dark intervals; but the composition remains incorrigibly modern, and the recurring trunks betray the essentially cinematic mode of vision and space toward which he is working. Abstract painters are only projecting Monet's methods in the *Nymphéas* to their logical conclusions.

This feat was preceded by Monet's many *fin de siècle* "harmonies" [22] that evaporate water lilies, the pools in his garden, and the façade of Rouen cathedral into musical suggestions. An art that began in optical notations adds a psychological resonance and becomes nuanced into symbolism, *études* entirely dissolving matter in light and merely "whispering" as they transcend sensation. The façade of Rouen is a pure metaphor

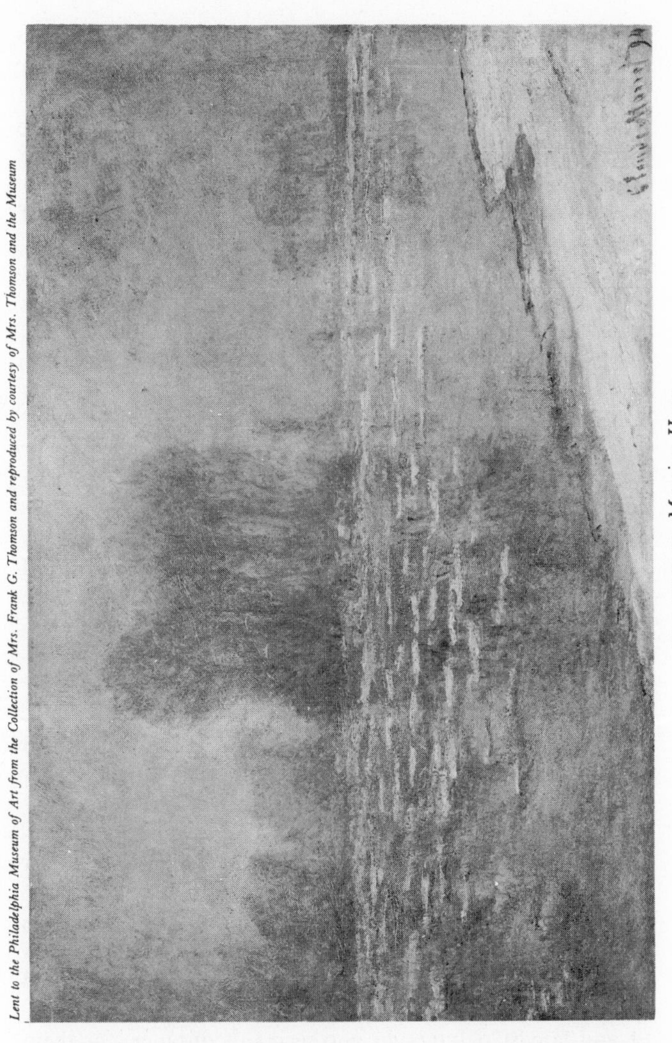

22 MONET: *Morning Haze*

Lent to the Philadelphia Museum of Art from the Collection of Mrs. Frank G. Thomson and reproduced by courtesy of Mrs. Thomson and the Museum

for values Monet tried to intimate in the very title of this series of paintings in 1894: *Harmonie blanche—effet du matin; Harmonie bleu; Harmonie bleu et or; Harmonie grise; Harmonie brune—effet du soir.* He is no longer concerned with the façade—only with the effect. Like Mallarmé he is presenting "non la chose, mais l'effet qu'elle produit." The shimmering pools in his garden are a form of equivalent to represent "something impossible, water with flowers that undulate in the sun's rays," volatilized by reverie as if they appeared in Mallarmé's prose-poem "Le Nénuphar Blanc," one of the *Divagations* implying the "presence" of a woman by means of the "whiteness" of a dream of her as the poet floats in his boat over a crystalline pond.

Monet's paintings done at Bordighera or Venice under full Mediterranean light lose their whispered meanings and show that when he was in the Midi some strain entered into his art, as was the case with Van Gogh's molten color. Impressionism was an authentically northern painting, born of a Barbizon milieu, of the beclouded coast of Normandy and the muted greys of Boudin and Jongkind, or of the uncertain weather at Argenteuil. Expressionism was fostered under the constant heightening of the Mediterranean sun. Monet's natural range is within the Flemish and Dutch scale, the neutrality of the Low Countries. In 1894 Signac complained that the South offered only a white light that devoured all local color. "Just because they are in the *midi* people expect to see reds, blues, greens, yellows. . . . It is on the contrary the North—Holland for example—that is *colored* (local colors), the South being *luminous.*"[8] The Argenteuil period is the core of impressionism. A bright, steady sun leads Monet to a different kind of painting, toward Renoir's southern *luxe* and agitation; for Renoir is the proto-fauvist, not Monet. Monet needs the haze of Gare Saint Lazare, foggy days along the Seine, which give him his atmosphere and keep him perfectly in key. Expressionist art is not plein air but an exasperation of what is seen.

Monet's symbolism arises from a need for *distance:* he removes his scene—or disengages it from his feelings—by his broken brushwork, so that the atmosphere appears only from afar, and gradually. That is why his symbolism "whispers." Expressionist and fauvist painters do not need this distance; for them everything is, almost painfully, present, as it is in Van Gogh's vision of the plains near Arles, or Vlaminck's red trees. Van Gogh lacks the neutral atmospheric continuum of Monet, whose attention is first of all on nature—what is outside—not on projecting his feelings. In spite of its symbolism, Monet's work has a climatic realism inherent in the northern tradition. The need for distance means that Monet cannot make his statement with emphasis or in great detail. He extracts the value he wants by modulating light and color, avoiding the over-definition of photography and the realism that was only a specification. Like the symbolist poets he creates an atmosphere in which things exist. The Goncourts took the wrong way to realism, Baudelaire the right, as Monet proves by his poetic distance. So impressionist realism in Monet is always sliding off toward symbolism, with increasingly refined harmonies. Monet felt appearances come and go in an envelope of light in which frail forms can, for an instant, be evoked. Then they vanish again, leaving only the tonality that is their being: almost a memory. Monet's music therefore resembles that of Debussy, who said he wanted to write a score "assez souple, assez heurtée pour s'adapter aux mouvements lyriques de l'âme, aux caprices de la rêverie." The music for *Pelléas and Mélisande* was intended to suggest "correspondances mysterieuses." The extreme mobility of Monet's art requires, like music, the time-dimension, and gives his representations a transitory, accidental character best conveyed by a technique of the incomplete, the *métier inachevé*.

Because Monet's later impressionism merges into symbolism it, too, is relevant to the philosophy of Henri Bergson, who was convinced of the inadequacy of the intellect to deal with the "fringe of intuition, vague and evanescent," surrounding every clear idea. Bergson believed that "we change without ceasing" in the endless flow of psychic life, which is a zone of experience inaccessible to reason, a faculty able to deal with sense and outward things but not what Wordsworth called "fallings from us, vanishings." Our deep selves, according to Bergson, are immersed in a kind of time he calls duration, not to be measured by hours or days, but felt as a memory. Our intuitions have a mobility because in the medium of duration they penetrate each other, enveloping our deep experiences like an atmosphere, a quality saturating the level of consciousness where perceptions melt into each other as they do in dreams. Our genuine life is lived, not thought; for we think in categories of the clock and calendar, but we exist in a milieu of duration which is a continual passage from one state of soul to another. Monet brings into the *Nymphéas* these mobilities and interpenetrations, translating the intervals of time into passages melting into each other like a quality of experience. Bergson finds a secret and abiding "correspondence" behind our perceptions and actions, which are fixed by logic in an immobility that denies the unceasing transformations in the hidden self. Intuition, not reason, is the instrument to reveal to us the "very inwardness of life" capable of being "enlarged" indefinitely by suggestions extending beyond, or around, space and time. Thus Bergson, along with Mallarmé and Monet, seeks *connaissance* beyond *volupté,* linking the art of the *Nymphéas* with Proust's research and with Thomas Mann, who explores the great modern augment of time, "the medium of life," manifesting itself in music or, more "oceanically," as a "heightening" of experience to enchantment. Almost like an echo of Shelley, certain pages of *Creative Evolution* seek an idealism that makes all true experience poetic: "Consciousness is the name for the rocket whose extinguished fragments fall back as matter." The things before us are always capable of recovering their ideality, and are always being prevented by the matter they bear.

"Physics is but logic spoiled," Bergson says, and like Monet he denies density and weight—the automatism of matter—to find reality in an atmospheric continuum that is at the same instant both mobility and eternity. If we suppress time and space, Bergson believes, things re-enter each other: "What was extended in space is contracted into pure Form. And past, present, and future shrink into a single moment, which is eternity." Out of the transitory emerges the eternal; out of the mutable appears the immutable; out of the vibration of light, changing hour by hour, a design or tonality abstracts itself. As Monet withdrew into his garden, he seems to have passed out of time into duration and to have reached a pantheistic serenity such as Wordsworth knew. He seems to have felt as "immediate data of consciousness" the transparencies Bergson found at the heart of human experience. His color, tranquillized into disembodied blues, greys, and whites, is a mystique. The symbolist poets, too, found that around every clear idea there is a fringe of recognition fading off into the unknown; and only the music of correspondence can suggest what cannot be named. The music of the *Nymphéas* has the symbolist overtones of Mallarmé's "melodious clarity" and resounds like the remembered sonata in Proust's novel.

Théodore Duret says that impressionist painting was done with an aim of creating directly from nature, getting the artist out into the open air to record the fugitive effects of changing light and time. Accordingly Monet loosened his composition in favor of surface appearances that make his painting an illusion changing with the hour. The illogicality is that after he had painted his frieze of water lilies as a continuous passage of changing tone, he had left nothing but "the uniform quality of the texture."[9] So this texture became an abstraction. Duret remarks about Monet's repetition of the same scene in changing atmospheres:

> To seize, in passing, the variations in aspect which the same scene assumes at different moments, and to fix them on the canvas with precision, is an extremely delicate operation. . . . Painting of this kind necessitates the pursuit of what are in effect abstractions. It is necessary to be able to disengage the fugitive motive from the unchanging groundwork and to do it with rapidity, for the different effects to be seized overlap one another, and if the eye does not arrest them as they pass, they flow into one another.
>
> (*Manet and the French Impressionists*)

The impressionists ventured to arrest an optical sensation as a fixed value; thus the atmosphere is more important than the scene, and objects in time and space must be translated to some other dimension, the essence of a sensation that can be symbolized only by a certain tonality harmonizing the experience.

A new time-sense and a new space-sense are thus inherent in the impressionist atmosphere, and, illogically, in its care to record the fugitive, impressionism faces toward abstract art, the notation of a feeling that escapes the tyranny of the senses and represents a *quality* of experience. The impressionist object exists in a new milieu, a special temper of light and air that penetrates and encloses the figures, which appear in time, but with a presence that is also eternal, extracted from the changing hour and light. This is one way of refusing the object, as the non-objective painters say. Monet's atmospheric continuum not only transvalues time and the object; it also brings into painting an existential dimension, a sense of immersion in the fugitive, the transient—which is the real. The medium of this proto-existential painting was the little touch, the *tache,* the module that proves itself eventually to be a unit from which can be built up structures of great complexity. This modular principle, which underlies the entire cubist movement and its study of changing relations in space, originates in the impressionist "division" and brings into art—along with atmospheric time—a new geometry, a new method of organizing structures from identical, replaceable parts, a technique that enables modern architecture to treat prefabricated units in functional ways. Impressionism, then, prepares the constructivist abstractions of the twentieth century. Cézanne ended impressionism by his logic of colored planes.

His planes were mobile, and his painting was cinematic. In its many forms impressionism was cinematic—not only in Monet's *Nymphéas* but, more generally, in the various ways painters like Bazille and Degas were indebted to the camera, or competed with photography. In the 1830's Daguerre replaced the "heliographic picture" by the diorama, then the daguerreotype. Thence came the camera and, eventually, the cinema, the primary technique of the twentieth century. The cinema employs the camera artistically, endowing photography with *connaissance.* Perhaps the most symbolic change in the arts during the last century is the shift from camera to cinema. What had been only an instrument for reportage became a medium that expressed the time-sense and the space-sense toward which the whole nineteenth century was drifting. The cinema adds a fourth dimension: space cannot be represented apart from time and motion. It brings into art the existential time-field, the field of human experience, releasing us from the mechanism of associationist psychology, which treated time and space as separable; it is the art that approaches Bergson's notion of consciousness as a continual transforming of experience. Entirely visual, the cinema creates illusions of mass, motion, light, and distance on a plane surface, utilizing the angle shot, the fade-out, the double (montage) image, the mobile, distorted, or plural perspective, the cutback.

Although it is hard to say how the impressionists were affected by the camera, we know that Nadar was one of their close friends and that Bazille seems to have composed his *Réunion de Famille* (1867) as a "poetry of the daguerreotype." The carefully arrested figures on the terrace, evidently surprised by some visitor, have the static quality of the early photograph, when it was necessary for the sitter to hold a pose for a time. Like other painters of his day, Bazille documented his composition by the camera. We know also that the composition of Monet's *Femmes au Jardin* was suggested by a photograph of Bazille's cousins. Courbet seems to have used one of Nadar's photographs for the nude in his *Atelier du Peintre.* This naïve daguerreotype vision becomes nearly cinematic in Degas, who is "visual" in a different way from Monet. Degas specializes in the angle shot. In *L'Absinthe* (1876) he pulls his two figures to the right, catching them at an impromptu angle as they stare out of the composition in opposite directions. This is another kind of documentation. Two years later *The Café Singer* exploits the close-up, an instantaneous glimpse of an arm and a face in the glare of footlights—for Degas already has the contrived lighting of the movie set. Then in a long series of ballet girls rehearsing he opens up his central spaces, emptying the heart of his scene in great gulfs that dwarf the dancers gesticulating in the theatrical distance. Or he uses the *découpage* of the movie shot in *Ballerina and Lady with a Fan* (1885) [23], where the dancers are sliced off by the frame or by the profile of the woman holding the fan in the lower right foreground. (Here is an instance where the technique of the camera intersects the technique of the Japanese print.) There are also the twisting angular bodies of women drying after a bath, stepping into a tub, combing their hair—most of these figures being seen from a raised angle, distorting their forms and even the space in which they move. Degas' instantaneous impression of Vicomte Lepic and his daughters on a Paris street is perhaps the clearest evidence that impressionist painting knew cinematic methods long before the cinema.

Courtesy of the John G. Johnson Collection, Philadelphia Museum of Art

23 DEGAS: *Ballerina and Lady with a Fan*

Each of these cinematic tricks can be traced back to the Italian mannerists of the sixteenth and seventeenth centuries. They, too, used strong foreground framing to project their figures, and they were fond of diagonal or mobile perspective, the artifice of the close-up, asymmetrical or empty space, and the serpentine figure with its often ugly instability. The first mannerists also experimented with reversed perspective, like the reflections in Manet's *Bar at the Folies Bergère*. Tintoretto and

El Greco often passed their figures through a haunting light that evaporates them into transparencies reminding us of the pastel gaslight illusions in Degas' theatres. The flickering dimensions of the cinema were not new to painting; yet the impressionists were laying a groundwork for the revolutionary methods of "polyvisional" cubism. The cinematic tendencies in impressionist painting are only transformations of realism.

Finally, if impressionism technically is a forerunner of the cinema, it derives, technically, from the methods of the aquarelle, which used color as a value in itself, apart from drawing, and which deliberately accepted the unfinished, the sketch, the *inachevé.* Because of this affiliation with water color or gouache, impressionism is a reaction against photographic realism with its complete finish. Then too, the impressionists adapted to oil the "touch" that was already used by English topographical water colorists of the late eighteenth century. Three of the major pre-impressionist painters—Constable, Corot, and Turner—have the water-color touch, and accept the unfinished.

The "strong" Corot handles the landscape at Volterra as if he were Cézanne, in broad water-color brushwork—a grey-green architecture on a grey-green hill reduced to a few planes. In the "unfinished" version of his *Bridge at Narni* the brushwork is even looser, resembling Claude Lorrain's water colors and gaining Claude's effects—namely, that a play of light enters the washed surface, giving support to the classic space that is built from the merest splashes of low color. The same steady architectural light falls over Corot's view of Saint-Lô. It is a northern light of a sustaining quality that is felt in still lifes by Chardin, tempered to the air of France, England, and the Low Countries. For Chardin, too, resembles Cézanne.

It is the grey poetic light that pervades Constable's *Weymouth Bay* and *Wivenhoe Park* or any of his water-colorish unfinished pictures. The first and strongest version of *Salisbury Cathedral* is a small study in dull green and broken brushwork, totally unlike the finished work that is nearly calendar art. Constable's water-color touch in *Cornfield With Figures,* so thinly and quickly handled that the canvas shows through the pigment, gives a vibrant light the impressionists never improved. The subdued

24 CONSTABLE: *River Stour Near Flatford Mill—Afternoon*

tone of Crome and David Cox and other British water colorists never strains the medium and keeps the whole composition in key—a feat Constable achieves in one of his most Cézanne-like visions, the *River Stour Near Flatford Mill: Afternoon* (1827) [24]. The very title shows how he competes with impressionist painting, not alone in broken brushwork and a logic of tone, but also in an impressionist sensitivity to the hour, the light that is the signature of time. Corot strikes this chord of the moment in his Constable-like *Palace of the Popes, Avignon,* a work that has none of the southern glare but, instead, the brown-and-green water-color tone that serves as substructure and proves that he has the tempered impressionist eye. Probably Constable's most impressive work is *Dale in Helmingham Park* [25]—a single tree trunk, diagonal, handled in so rough and free an impasto that the pigment seems to be blistered. This trunk is an ambiguous image: a completely honest, naïve impressionist notation—or else a monstrous apparition with dreamlike, if not surrealist, presence. It is evidence that impressionism is naturalistic in origins, and that Constable and

Corot can depend only on their eye, not needing any picturesque associations.

Turner's luminism was essentially different from the impressionist light and color in Constable and Corot, and different in brushwork also, since Turner did not handle his pigment in planes. Nevertheless his luminism derives from water color, a wash that he ignites to plangent harmonies. Only water color explains why Turner, like Constable and Corot, so suddenly and formidably appears early in the century. In his "unfinished" river scenes like *Walton Reach* Turner is very close to Constable and Corot, using ghostly greys, greens, whites that are nearly monochromatic and "Chinese." The crashing orchestrations follow: resplendent Alpine gouaches, the scarlet Petworth music, the bronze seascapes. Compared with Monet's *Gare Saint Lazare,* Turner's *Rain, Steam, and Speed* shows how the English painter by-passed impressionism on his flight to symbolist dreams. Impressionism eventually absorbed Turner's

Reproduced by courtesy of The National Gallery, London

25 CONSTABLE: *Dale in Helmingham Park*

luminism—along with Monet's later harmonies—as it moved toward symbolism and expressionism.

In literature impressionism took forms that have aptly been called pan-impressionism, since distinctions between impressionism, symbolism, and decadence—difficult to make in painting—are at times invisible in the novel and poetry. Impressionism appeared in unlikely places, and the sense of enveloping atmosphere affected novelists like Zola, who was thoroughly conversant with the painting of his day. He called *Une Page d'Amour* (1877) *une oeuvre demi-teinte;* and Mallarmé admired this rather mechanical fiction as an "uninterrupted poem." Certainly it is not uninterruptedly poetic, but there is no denying that Zola uses a double texture—the insensitive psychology of the love affair between Hélène and Henri, and the panoramas of the City spread out in passages like some hazy impressionist canvas: Paris seen under lurid sunsets, shimmering dawns, or sullen thunderstorms after which the sun breaks out in drifting light. With her changing moods Hélène watches the great vague spectacle from her window, brooding as the slate-blue roofs are touched with flaming gold by the "victorious sun," or as the pale spring twilight draws a film of shadow over the dome of the Pantheon and the boulevards fading out in violet mist. The scene always harmonizes with her reverie as she "yields to the fatality of passion." Monet saw Paris as a "composition," the way Hélène does:

> But the sky had altered. The sun, sinking toward the slopes of Meudon, had parted the last clouds and shone out resplendent. The heavens were aflame with glory. On the far horizon the landslide of chalky boulders that lay across Charenton and Choisy-le-Roi had become a mass of carmine blocks edged with shining lacquer; the flotilla of small clouds swimming slowly in the blue over Paris put out crimson sails; while the film of white silk hung above Montmartre seemed all of a sudden to be a net of gold mesh ready to catch the stars as they appeared. The city lay outspread under this blazing vault, yellow, streaked with long shadows. Below, on the huge square, cabs and omnibuses intermingled in a haze of orange dust, while the dark swarm of passers-by took on a paler glow, speckled with light. . . . Further on, vehicles and pedestrians

> disappeared from sight; only the glinting lamps of a file of carriages passing over some distant bridge could be dimly discerned. To the left the tall chimneys of the Manutention, upright and rose-tinged, puffed out big whirls of delicate flesh-colored smoke; while on the other side of the river the fine elms on the Quai d'Orsay formed a dark mass, pierced by shafts of brightness. . . .

Like the impressionists Zola paints in breadth, dissolving the whole City in melting tones that absorb the mechanical features of his composition.

These impressionistic effects are perhaps closer to symbolism in writers like Pater or Proust. If the atmosphere of Monet's *Nymphéas* is an abstraction, Pater could be said to have the same half-symbolist value in many passages where sensations of hour and place are translated into an aesthetic dimension, a formal design, a tonality with Monet-like modulations:

> So he yielded himself to these things, to be played upon by them like a musical instrument . . . the phases of the seasons and of the growing or waning day, down even to the shadowy changes wrought on bare wall or ceiling—the light cast up from the snow, bringing out their darkest angles; the brown light in the cloud which meant rain; that almost too austere clearness, in the protracted light of the lengthening day, before warm weather began, as if it lingered but to make a severer workday, with the school-books opened earlier and later; that beam of June sunshine, at last, as he lay awake before the time, a way of gold-dust across the darkness; all the humming, the freshness, the perfume of the garden seemed to lie upon it—and coming in one afternoon in September, along the red gravel walk, to look for a basket of yellow crab-apples left in the cool, old parlour, he remembered it the more, and how the colours struck upon him. . . .
>
> *(Child in the House)*

Like Monet, Pater deals with his sensations at a certain atmospheric distance, and begins the distillation of impressionist art that was finally completed in Proust's finer sort of memory. Meanwhile in painting the heavily loaded color of Delacroix was being refined into the cool melodies of Whistler's twilight.

The sense of atmospheric continuum affects the poetry of the day, too, which in certain cases tries to stay within a given register, like the tone-poem in music. In Henley's "London Voluntaries" the quality of the atmosphere is an abstract harmony extracted from a momentary light and color fixed in a dominant key or design. Using a "scherzando" movement, Henley sees London bathed in an "aery unsubstantial charm" recalling Monet's compositions based upon a quality in Venetian light and air:

> For earth and sky and air
> Are golden everywhere,
> And golden with a gold so suave and fine
> The looking on it lifts the heart like wine.
> Trafalgar Square
> (The fountains volleying golden glaze)
> Shines like an angel market. High aloft
> Over his couchant Lions, in a haze
> Shimmering and bland and soft,
> A dust of chrysoprase,
> Our Sailor takes the golden gaze
> Of the saluting sun, and flames superb. . . .
> Golden, all golden! In a golden glory,
> Long-lapsing down a golden coasted sky,
> The day not dies, but seems
> Dispersed in wafts and drifts of gold. . . .

"Shimmering and bland and soft"—the treatment is doubtless loose, though the golden tone disengages itself from the hour and the place, transcribing optical sensations into a thematic monochrome. In the same way Whistler's nocturnes stylize Shelley's romantic color into tone-poems, and the sense of atmospheric continuum passes from the impressionists into the aestheticism of Swinburne's diffuse music.

It is in the novel, however, that the sense of atmosphere takes on its larger artistic meaning, for Proust and Henry James learned how to envelop their scenes, their figures, their action in a certain climate—James called it "weather," a quality of light —which is a psychological as well as a narrative ambience, penetrating the very language. At times it is nearly an abstraction. There is the cool white moment in James's *Beast in the Jungle* when Marcher sees May Bartram in the waning spring twilight with a sadness "sharper than the grayest hours of autumn." The fireplace is empty and immaculate, as if it were never to have warmth again, and May's serene thin face looks like an artificial lily in the whiteness of the place, her white dress and faded green scarf giving her the silvery, virginal appearance of a figure seen under a glass bell. For Proust the Méséglise Way and the Guermantes Way volatilize themselves into an impression of states of consciousness, memories as disturbing as a dream.

The sense of atmospheric light and color, the tendency to volatilize impressions into music is strong in Tennyson, who was extremely sensitive to the play of light and shadow. He specialized in dim vistas that resemble Corot's pastorals rather than the impressionists; like Corot he is impressionistic rather than impressionist in the exact sense. His sensuousness is cloudy, like Corot's woodland idyls, of which Wilde said, "It is twilight always for the dancing nymphs whom Corot set free among the silver poplars of France. In eternal twilight they move, those frail diaphanous figures, whose tremulous white feet seem not to touch the dew-drenched grass they tread on." Tennyson's filmy vision in "Oenone" and the "Lotos-Eaters" reminds us of this Corot, not of Manet:

> A land of streams! Some, like a downward smoke,
> Slow-dropping veils of thinnest lawn, did go;
> And some thro' wavering lights and shadows broke,
> Rolling a slumbrous sheet of foam below.
> They saw the gleaming river seaward flow
> From the inner land; far off, three mountain-tops,
> Three silent pinnacles of aged snow,
> Stood sunset-flushed; and, dewed with showery drops,
> Up-clomb the shadowy pine above the woven copse.

Not only Corot: also the glittering dewy Barbizon landscapes by Daubigny and Rousseau; and the mistiness of half-symbolist painters like Carrière and Henner; or the somewhat evaporated artificialities of Nabi painters like Sérusier and Puvis. In any case Tennyson's milieu is twilight—the nocturne—and he often uses the crepuscular palette of the impressionists. There is something of the broken color and blurred line in Swinburne's verse, which resembles Monet's slacker melodies. Swinburne scored his metre in a music that often empties his verse of everything but an aural motif:

> The full streams feed on flower of rushes,
> Ripe grasses trammel a travelling foot,
> The faint fresh flame of the new year flushes
> From leaf to flower and flower to fruit;
> The fruit and the leaf are as gold and fire,
> And the oat is heard above the lyre,
> And the hoofed heel of a satyr crushes
> The chestnut husk at the chestnut root.

Both Swinburne and Tennyson repeat words, syllables, phrases until they might be said to use a "modular" technique, arranging and rearranging vowels and consonants as if they were units to be treated like the primary hues in divisionism.

Strangely enough the experiment most like impressionism may have been undertaken by Walt Whitman, that slipshod poet, garrulous to the very last, who seems akin to Courbet in his monumental and indiscriminate vulgarity, his commonplace enthusiasms which he elevated to heroic superfluities. Whitman did exactly what the French thought he did: he found a new language, simplified, and broke down the poetic medium to his barbaric yawp. He accepted reality like the impressionists, and looked to the world "outdoors" with a naïve eye as if he saw everything for the first time. He is the poet of "Continuities," as he calls them, who is able to take actualities as he finds them spread about him everywhere—feeling them all, like Renoir, giving himself to flesh and appetite, trying to assimilate them to poetry. In "Backward Glance" Whitman says that he abandoned conventional poetic themes, the myths and verse of the past, to accept the challenge of "modern science" and use it poetically, much as the later impressionists tried to assimilate Chevreul's theory to their palette and brushwork:

> Arthur vanish'd with all his knights, Merlin and Lancelot
> and Galahad all gone, dissolv'd utterly like an exhalation. . . .
> (*"Song of the Exposition"*)

Whitman has the impressionist indifference to the "literary," even while he is at times clumsily literary.

Like some of the impressionists Whitman has a new technique but a weak sense of design. "I round and finish little, if anything." He tries to make the *pochade* into art, as did Monet; only Monet succeeds much better. He finds that the ordinary is "miraculous"—"Every cubic inch of space is a miracle." He suffers from this expansiveness, like the impressionists, whose subjects were often banal, especially their landscapes. Whitman has the undisciplined impressionist sprawl, the attraction to "big" areas like the picnics and cosmic outdoor performances Monet tried, largely to prove all "big" subjects do not come from the studio. Whitman did not create a style; but he did reduce poetry to a primary vocabulary and purged it of academic properties, ventures congenial to impressionism.

Gauguin explained what happened between impressionism and the moderns when he said that the impressionists studied color "but kept the shackles of representation." That is why Gauguin broke with impressionism: "I obtain by arrangements of lines and colors, using as a pretext some subject borrowed from human life or nature, symphonies, harmonies that represent nothing absolutely *real* in the vulgar sense of the word; they express no idea directly but they should make one think as music does, without the aid of ideas or images, simply by the mysterious relationships existing between our brains and such arrangements of colors and lines." This statement marks the transition from the various impressionist experiments to post-impressionism, fauvism, and Art Nouveau—and thus to modern art. Gauguin was able to pass beyond impressionism because he wrenched nature into *cloisonnisme,* and in so doing became a leader among the Nabi painters, who accused the impressionists of lacking style.

The Nabis turned back toward the middle ages, and while impressionism was working itself out in France toward Gauguin, Cézanne, and a new style, there was occurring in England the pre-Raphaelite movement, which is also part of the larger international current setting toward Art Nouveau and the moderns.

IV

NAZARENES,

LYONNAIS,

AND PRE-RAPHAELITES

We cannot be much more decisive about the international pre-Raphaelite movement than about impressionism, since it appeared in differing forms but usually with similar traits and consequences, in Germany, in France, in England, and during most of the early and middle nineteenth century, or even later, when it merges imperceptibly into the Nabi-synthetist-symbolist developments and Art Nouveau. Whether it should be taken as another aspect of nineteenth-century photographic naturalism, as a special phase of historicism, as an archaeological mannerism, as a brand of aestheticism, or as a forerunner of Art Nouveau is debatable, for there are resemblances to all of these. Everywhere it is attended by neo-mediaeval revivals in religion, while at the same time it is another symptom of revolt against official art in the name of a return to nature. These traits indicate how easily it may be considered an early kind of neo-traditionalism or "romanism" that appeared in France among the Nabi painters. It has a passion for documentation, a scrupulous care for accuracy, which also links it with the daguerreotype and the camera. Thus it illustrates the truth of Delacroix's statement that "Realism is the grand expedient which innovators use to revive the interest of an indifferent public. . . . Suddenly a return to nature is proclaimed by a man who claims to be inspired."

Pre-Raphaelitism was always an art of the intellectuals, a rather stilted or even esoteric variant of an *avant-garde* painting and poetry. Because its roots were shallow, it never attained a coherent symbolism although most of the pre-Raphaelite painters and poets had an air of consecration and were devoted to symbolic effects and suggestions, giving their work a halo of implied meaning even if it is hard to say what these meanings are. Their affectations have an almost ritualistic tone. Everything is *posed;* and their most photographic details seem unnatural. The air of prearrangement and contrivance—one indelible mark of mannerism—hangs over their work; and they are fond of "pure" line and "pure" color—though their line is usually harsh and metallic, and their color is often insipid and liquid, or else sour. Their execution, in short, is cold or at times uncertain or timid, as if they were afraid reality would violate their precautions.

These precautions make the pre-Raphaelites significant as far as we are concerned with them: for although they used the anecdote, they treated it in a highly stylized way. In so doing they gradually shifted emphasis from the anecdote itself to the artificial design that eventually purified itself in Art Nouveau. Pre-Raphaelite painting and poetry began by being narrative or illustrative and ended by being frankly and consciously ornamental. The anecdotes—even the "symbolic" religious anecdotes—became vehicles for a liberated pattern. Like impressionism, pre-Raphaelitism often transcends the episode, the literary narrative, and tends to release the pose, the motif, the carefully worked-up detail, as an independent decorative surface. This loss of the anecdote was necessary before the arts of the century could reformalize themselves into a modern style. However negligible pre-Raphaelitism may be in itself, no matter how confused it may be in purpose or method, it is one further proof that decadence is a phase in the evolution of modern art. Rossetti's Blessed Damozel leaning from the gold bar of heaven with her three lilies, her white roses, her yellow hair, her deep still eyes, and his Dantesque maidens like Cecily, Magdalen, and Rosalys sitting circled with garlanded brows and flamelike robes—all this pseudo-mediaeval aestheticism is another stylization in a century without a style.

Nor can we dogmatically say who is pre-Raphaelite, Lyonnais, or Nazarene. In France, at least, the pre-Raphaelites trace back to the Empire style with its rigors and clarities, the statuemania that made the "classic" work of David and Guérin so frigid. The linear art of Flaxman owes something, also, to Perugino's own pre-Raphaelite mannerism and his pietistic affectations. However, Ingres is more obviously indebted to Perugino than is Flaxman, and Ingres' extremely pure line, his graphic detail, his enamelled formulas were a continual and powerful influence on the whole course of nineteenth-century stylization. Every sort of archaism can be found in Ingres: the silhouette of the Greek vase, the bland modelling of Roman marble, the suave figures of Pompeiian frescoes, the careful details in Florentine quattrocento painting. There is, besides, a strong note of mannerism, of Sodoma, of Bronzino, of Velázquez. Ingres' realism casts itself into sinuous designs. Or it exists in the strange—already decadent—climate of the harem and groups of odalisques, his vision of *Ruggiero Liberating Angelica,* or *The Source* with its overheated symbolism. In his painting of *The Martyrdom of Saint Symphorien* done for the cathedral at Autun in 1834, Ingres is a fully developed pre-Raphaelite painter (even if this work bears the mark of Raphael, not the earlier renaissance). The ritualistic gesture of the Saint, the archaeological details, the Puvis-like profile of Symphorien and his carven robes, the literary composition resemble the methods of Holman Hunt.

This stylization in Ingres affected a group known as the Lyonnais, a fellowship of neo-mediaeval painters centered at Lyons.[10] They seem also to have been inspired by Maurice Quay, one of David's pupils, who about 1800 adopted a "Phrygian" mode of religious painting in accord with his mystical theories of art. In 1842 Hyppolyte Flandrin, one of the Lyonnais, painted for the choir of Saint-Germain-des-Prés a

Christ's Entry into Jerusalem that is like a cameo in its pale artifice, its chiselled realism, its congealed action. These neo-Catholic stylizations influenced Puvis de Chavannes, then became a dogma in Maurice Denis and his disciples late in the century. Along with the Lyonnais, a group of German painters about 1810 took the same path to Rome toward the "primitive" art of the quattrocento. Led by Overbeck, who was devoted to Florentine madonnas, they moved to the Pincio, joined the Church, lived ascetically, and dedicated themselves to a painstaking craftsmanship. Overbeck admired Raphael, although he refused the renaissance paganism, and he studied Perugino. The Nazarenes wished to revive fresco; but they rendered everything with such minuteness that they were known as "atomists." Cornelius, one of the Nazarenes, taught Father Desiderius Lenz, who founded a neo-Catholic school of painting about 1860 at Beuron in the Black Forest; this monastic institution was in touch with the French neo-traditionalists through Dom Verkade, a Benedictine and one of the Nabis. There is an unbroken continuity from Ingres and Puvis through the pre-Raphaelites to Denis and the Nabis. The Continental symptoms of pre-Raphaelite art were so widespread that they appear even in Degas, whose *Misfortunes of the City of Orléans* attempted a mediaeval stylization: it looks like a bad imitation of Burne-Jones, though the awkward figures show Degas' interest in motion.

The Lyonnais and Nazarenes were sects within the great neo-mediaeval communion that persisted through the whole century and inspired not only Ruskin's neo-gothic theories but also the more archaeological studies of Welby Pugin and Viollet-le-Duc. In 1836 Pugin suggested that "the degraded state of the arts is purely owing to the absence of Catholic feeling" and to the calamity of Protestantism after the fifteenth century. "Where," he despairingly asks, "where was that inward unity of soul—where that faith that had anciently bound men together" and built the cathedrals where we can "feel the sublimity of Christian worship"? The meeting-house and the conventicle were made by men "who ponder between a mortgage, a railroad, or a chapel as the best investment of their money." Pugin had a legitimate complaint about "modern paltry taste," but he belongs to the quaint archives of Ecclesiology rather than to the history of pre-Raphaelitism. So also does Viollet-le-Duc, who was wise enough to see that neo-Catholicism would not suffice: "I cannot admit the propriety of imposing upon our own age any reproduction of antique or mediaeval forms of art." He was intelligent enough to understand that "A locomotive is beautiful," as a "true expression of brutal energy." Yet he admitted that "our art is sick." In all this he agrees with Henry Adams.

Ruskin belongs more properly to the pre-Raphaelite movement because he championed the British "Brotherhood" that united into a formal school for a brief span between, roughly, 1849 and 1857, with a membership and a program that soon disintegrated in many directions. The British version of pre-Raphaelitism is better known than the Continental versions largely because of Ruskin's tract of 1851, which, however, misinterprets the intention and work of the group by confusing pre-Raphaelite painting with painting by Turner. Ruskin does, nevertheless, stress the pre-Raphaelite "intentness of observation and facility of imitation"—their photographic eye, in short. Although Ruskin spent a good deal of money and trouble patronizing Rossetti, who was not the central figure in the Brotherhood, he implies in a passage in *Modern Painters* that Holman Hunt's work is more typical of the pre-Raphaelites. Characteristically Ruskin chooses Hunt's anecdotal religious painting *The Light of the World*—the figure of Christ, crowned with thorns, standing in the dark with a lighted lantern and knocking upon a closed door—as the supreme pre-Raphaelite canvas. The passage is worth repeating because it reveals how the pre-Raphaelite archaizing naturalism was put in the service of morality or religion:

> The perfect unison of expression, as the painter's main purpose, with the full and natural exertion of his pictorial power in the details of the work, is found only in the old pre-Raphaelite periods, and in the modern pre-Raphaelite school. In the works of Giotto, Angelico, Orcagna, John Bellini, and one or two more, these two conditions of high art are entirely fulfilled . . .; and in the modern pre-Raphaelite school they are fulfilled nearly to the uttermost. Hunt's *Light of the World* is, I believe,

the most perfect instance of expressional purpose with technical power, which the world has yet produced.

Ruskin is right in taking Hunt as a central figure amid British pre-Raphaelites, and we must turn to Hunt to discover the authentic pre-Raphaelite program in its confusions and defections. Hunt's two volumes on *Pre-Raphaelitism and the Pre-Raphaelite Brotherhood* prove that behind the manifestoes of the original group there was a sad indecision about purpose and technique. The first aim, in common with so many other movements in the century, was to return to nature, to document scenes almost photographically. Like the impressionists, the pre-Raphaelites seem to drift toward the scientific method. But inconsistent with this objectivity is a tendency to moralize—to choose melodramatic episodes like *The Awakened Conscience,* Hunt's painting in which a kept woman, suddenly hearing the voice of remorse, turns, with artless symbolism, from the embrace of her raffish lover, strumming on a piano, to a new life.

Along with this preference for a "noble subject" goes the pre-Raphaelite religious theme, usually an incident from the Bible, like John Everett Millais' *Christ in the House of His Parents,* a vaguely symbolic episode when the Child has cut his palm on a nail in his father's carpenter shop and stands, in the pose of the Crucified, holding up his left hand to the Virgin, who, like her husband, is lower-class British. Or the theme, as Ruskin's passage suggests, may be frankly allegorical, phrased, preferably, in pseudo-mediaeval guise or Arthurian iconography. Rossetti, especially, went in for chivalric themes that Tennyson also used with pre-Raphaelite effects in his *Idylls.* The legendary, the anecdotal, the symbolic-moral-religious note—all this represented in photographic accuracy and laboriously worked-up or "finished": that was essentially the pre-Raphaelite program. Rossetti's somewhat morbid sexual atmosphere was not necessarily pre-Raphaelite. Hunt says that the group was chiefly dedicated to "the unending study of Nature."

The pre-Raphaelite effort to "look at the world without eyelids" inspired a painting that was often merely illustration, like the incident William Dyce meticulously recorded in his *George Herbert at Bemerton,* where the trees, the fishing gear, the stone wall are as carefully finished as the flora in Millais' *Ophelia,* who sinks to her watery death under the photographic leaves of a willow, borne up for a moment by her billowing gown. Hunt made heroic efforts to document his paintings as accurately as the foregrounds in Tennyson's scenes are documented by the poet's myopic vision. This care to document relates the whole pre-Raphaelite Brotherhood in England to the documented novel, the careful realism in Flaubert, the case histories in the Goncourts' stories, or the astonishingly authentic record of Maupassant's *Une Vie.* The revolution in nineteenth-century style occurs precisely at the points where this painful documentation—this photographic accuracy—takes on a new artistic value, the value of the decorative, and thus produces a high pitch of stylization. The most literal illustration is translated to ornamental detail.

We can actually see this revolution occurring in Hunt, who was among the most plodding and anxiously literal of the pre-Raphaelites. He affirms that the Brotherhood intended to revolt against academism with its brownness, conventionality, and studio effects. The original membership—Hunt, Millais, the Rossetti brothers, Woolner, and Collinson—also rejected the antiquarianism and historicism of the Nazarenes, and wanted to see things with eyes wide open:

> We were challenging the whole profession with a daring innovation. . . . We were intending to stand or fall by the determination to cut away all conventions not endorsed by further appeal to unsophisticated Nature. German antiquarianism, which was Brown's last form of allegiance to Continental dogma, was one of the principal enemies which we originally committed ourselves to destroy.

When Hunt painted *The Eve of Saint Agnes* in 1847 he hung up a sprig of mistletoe and tested all his effects by lamplight. He tells how he worked from actuality:

> . . . seeing that there was a fig tree in the garden of Mr. Stephens' father at Lambeth, I had accepted an invitation to bring the canvas there, and had painted the tree direct upon it, its leaves and branches in full sunlight, with what was then un-

> precedented exactness. In the foreground I painted also a patch of grass with dandelion puffs and blossoms, and over one of these last a bumble-bee hovered . . . instead of the meaningless spread of whitey brown which usually served for the near ground, I represented gravelly variations and pebbles, all diverse tints and shapes as found in Nature.

Hunt went to every trouble to make a proper gilded lantern for his Christ to hold in *Light of the World,* which he painted outdoors, working between 9 P.M. and 5 A.M. standing in a little box to protect himself from chill:

> A lamp which I at first tried, proved to be too strong and blinding to allow me to distinguish the subtleties of hue of the moonlit scene, and I had to be satisfied with the illumination from a common candle.

When his friend Millais proposed painting a picture to show the door opened and the sinner repenting before Christ, Hunt strongly objected that since Millais worked faster than he, the scene of repentance would be done first and thus damage the meaning of Hunt's Christ standing at the closed door: the result of Christ's appeal would be presented before the appeal itself. Thus the pre-Raphaelites were led from art to life by their worried realism.

The *reductio ad absurdum* of the whole method was Hunt's painting of *Rienzi,* "the background not done either from conventional fancy or memory, but from Nature." He did not even make sketches but recorded "direct from the scene itself on to the canvas of the final picture." Even then he got into difficulty with the sword in his painting illustrating *The Two Gentlemen of Verona.* In spite of his protest against German antiquarianism, Hunt found himself involved in an exhausting controversy with his critics about whether Valentine and Proteus carried the right kind of swords: seemingly they were of Charles I make; and, worse, Silvia's gown was embroidered with a Louis XIV pattern! Hunt is at dire pains to make clear that when the picture was painted in 1850 he learned from authoritative sources about swords: "the spreading out of the hilt horizontally sometimes became the dominant feature . . . with the cross bar still represented by a then knobbed rod, or a hoop further up the handle." So he is really all right about the swords. He is less easy about Julia's gown, which he made from modern fabrics, to be sure; but he guarantees his critics that he embroidered the sleeves himself—and, finally, "the hat also I made myself." Or there is the endless account of Hunt's trials while painting *The Scapegoat* (1854–56) standing on the shore of the Dead Sea and betokening Christ's plight. He has to wait for the Day of Atonement so the background will be right; he leads the goat over the salt marsh to "scrutinize its manner of walking on the yielding crust." He struggles to find three suitable goats for models, since the wretched creatures die; he tethers them under the burning sun while he paints them hair by hair, as Rossetti painted his calf in *Found.*

Absurd as all this documentation was, Hunt was aware that the nineteenth century craved this sort of exactitude, which suited science, practicality, and pragmatism. "My contention," Hunt explains, "was that more exact truth was distinctly called for by the additional knowledge and longings of the modern mind." He was conscious, too, that this exactitude was almost analogous to the scientific method: "In agreeing to use the utmost elaboration in painting our first pictures, we never meant more than to insist that the practice was essential for training the eye and hand of the young artist." In this sense his work was a laboratory method.

Oddly he had not the least sympathy for the experiments taking place across the Channel, showing complete incomprehension of French painting, which he dismisses as an "injurious" Continental taste tinged with moral turpitude: "Wild revolt shows itself in the art of our day in the form of Impressionism." The "hideous canvases" of the Impressionists were for Hunt merely proof of "monstrous developments" among Parisian students, whose "coarse horse play" could produce only "chaotic form" having a "poisonous influence" on those who exhibited "sullied pigment plastered on offensively"—"a standing peril to art." Hunt never saw that the deeper peril to art was in the later work of Millais, who fell away from the

Brotherhood and became a wealthy popular painter. Millais told Hunt late in life, after he had painted *Bubbles* (used as advertising copy for Pears' Soap):

> I want proof that the people of my day enjoy my work, and how can I get this better than by finding people willing to give me money for my productions? . . . There is a fashion going now for little girls in mob caps. Well, I satisfy this while it continues; but immediately the demand shows signs of flagging, I am ready to take to some other fashion . . . or I shall do portraits or landscapes. . . . You take my advice, old boy, and just take the world as it is, and don't make it your business to rub people the wrong way.

We can believe Hunt, however, that fidelity to nature seemed revolutionary among the first pre-Raphaelites. At least this fidelity appears everywhere in their poetry. The foreground of Rossetti's sonnet "Silent Noon" is finished as carefully as a documented painting:

> Your hands lie open in the long fresh grass—
> The finger points look through like rosy blooms:
> Your eyes smile peace. The pasture gleams and glooms
> 'Neath billowing skies that scatter and amass.
> All round our nest, as far as the eye can pass,
> Are golden kingcup fields with silver edge
> Where the cow-parsley skirts the hawthorne-hedge.
> 'Tis visible silence, still as hour-glass,
> Deep in the sun-searched growths the dragon fly
> Hangs like a blue thread loosened from the sky. . . .

That dragon fly in the still bright landscape has the pre-Raphaelite realism. It is not exactly the realism of Flaubert or the Goncourts, who also were discovering actuality in their own way best explained in the journals of the brothers:

> There is left in our life nothing but one consuming interest—*the passion for the study of reality*. . . . We are like men for whom, following years of drawing from a wax model, the academy of

the living has suddenly been revealed—or rather, life itself, with its entrails still warm and its tripe still palpitating.

(May 22, 1865)

This observation is scientific by intent and prompted a "clinical study of love" in *Germinie Lacerteux.* The Goncourts have the neutrality of Maupassant. They insist, "About every painting that gives rise to a moral impression we may say, as a general truth, that it is a bad painting."

The British pre-Raphaelites were always moralizing, or symbolizing something, trying to graft evangelistic meanings on their accurate observation. They were fond of legendary and even ritualistic subjects. They wished to put their art in the service of "justice and truth," if not of faith. They kept in mind "the sublime interests of humanity," and they felt "indignation towards arrogant vice" along with "honest pity for the victims." In fact, they preached—sometimes melodramatically, rejecting the "materialistic school" and being rather sanctimonious in the process. Hunt confesses, "We were never realists." Above all they were attracted to religious themes, precisely the themes to encourage allegorical or ritual treatment. Hunt tells how he painted *Christ in the Carpenter Shop,* which had as its major title *The Shadow of Death:* the young Christ standing with arms outspread, his shadow symbolizing his pose on Golgotha and cast on the wall. The shadow of the Cross is seen only by Mary. Hunt was quite clear about his symbolism; his problem was to arrange things so that the shadow would be seen by Mary alone and yet allow him to manage all the particulars of the shop accurately. "I could not settle how to overcome the difficulties of arranging the details of my picture, until I had made it my business to visit many native carpenters at work, and had been over to Bethlehem, and searched out the traditional tools." In spite of his care and planning, the picture is unnatural. The painful documentation in pre-Raphaelite painting did not prevent the artificiality that is inherent in works like *Christ in the House of His Parents* and *The Scapegoat.* The concern for allegory or pseudo-symbolism meant that the synthetic was superimposed on the naturalistic.

Tennyson's early verse was often synthetic in the same way, its illustrative details and feudal designs making it a pre-Raphaelite "Palace of Art":

Full of great rooms and small the palace stood,
All various, each a perfect whole
From living Nature, fit for every mood
And change of my still soul.

(One thinks of that later decadent pseudo-gothic palace built for himself by Joris-Karl Huysmans' aesthetic hero Des Esseintes.)

For some were hung with arras green and blue,
Showing a gaudy summer-morn,
Where with puffed cheek the belted hunter blew
His wreathed bugle horn.

One seemed all dark and red—a tract of sand,
And someone pacing there alone,
Who paced forever in a glimmering land,
Lit with a low large moon.

(1832–42)

(One thinks too of the highly stylized settings in Poe's "Masque of the Red Death," which is ornamental symbolism.) These decorative patterns reappear in the *Idylls,* and in Rossetti's chivalric drawings and poems. They are striking in William Morris' wallpapers, tapestries, manuscript illumination, and ballads like "Winter Weather," a neo-gothic composition with strongly silhouetted figures and landscapes and brilliant detail: the tower grows black against the dawn; the red and blue knights are paired in exact symmetry; the banners, deep-blue and blood-red, droop straight down over the lances in the solemn weather. Tennyson's "Lady of Shalott" is a brocade in yellow and white (for already we are looking ahead to the yellow and white abstractions of the nineties and Beardsley).

Pre-Raphaelite artifice is brought to its manneristic phase in a poem like Rossetti's "Card Dealer," which might have been worked up by Poe:

Her fingers let them softly through,
Smooth polished silent things;
And each one as it falls reflects

In swift light-shadowings,
Blood-red and purple, green and blue,
The great eyes of her rings.

(1849)

Here again color and sound are almost entirely ornamental. Rossetti, who is not wholly typical of the British pre-Raphaelites, casts over these highly finished figures a strange light, an enchanted atmosphere that gives the composition a dreamlike unreality and remoteness:

In painting her I shrined her face
'Mid mystic trees, where light falls in
Hardly at all; a covert place
Where you might think to find a din
Of doubtful talk, and a live flame
Wandering, and many a shape whose name
Not itself knoweth, and old dew
And your own footsteps meeting you,
And all things going as they came.

A deep dim wood: and there she stands
As in that wood that day: for so
Was the still movement of her hands
And such the pure line's gracious flow.
And passing fair the type must seem,
Unknown the presence and the dream.
'Tis she: though of herself, alas!
Less than her shadow on the grass
Or than her image in the stream.

(*"The Portrait,"* 1847)

This air of contrivance is very marked in Rossetti, who stylized the female head, especially, in both drawing and poetry, into hushed, exotic, medusa-like features, sinuous and bruised; beauty has added the note of strangeness that also envelops Pater's vision of Mona Lisa smiling amid her blue mysterious rocks, her face shadowed by old sins of the flesh. These creatures of tainted charm breed fast among the decadents. Whether Rossetti was drawing Lizzie Siddal, Fanny Cornforth, or Jane Burden, he strained Hunt's photographic accuracies into the beguiled mask of the Fatal Woman whose glance is hyacinth light, whose pallor is belied by her passionate mouth, her cloying grace. The design is clear and wiry; the details are overwrought.

These Rossetti women are still. It has been said that Rossetti arrests time. He does, and by his design. His art shows how in the pre-Raphaelites there is usually a competition between vision and design, for the vision is naturalistic in its details, nevertheless artificial in its whole composition. Burne-Jones fixes his figures, like Rossetti (or Degas), in a pose. Hunt recognized this problem, but only obscurely, when he complained that "Our methods of work, however, had serious results on our output," for while each fine detail of a composition was being worked up "it was of vital importance to have all the surrounding parts of the design in sight." Therefore studies made separately of the parts "when transferred to the canvas proved to be irresponsive to the rest," so that all the parts had to be worked up at the same time. This is a quattrocento problem in painting, and in the renaissance caused a fussiness about detail that results in "decorative isolation." The task was to hold all the details in the same plane of interest. Since pre-Raphaelite painters did not trust the eye as Monet did, they over-executed their surfaces into a finish that could be held together only by a design superscribed over the details. The frozen quality in Ford Madox Brown's intensely realized painting of emigrants called *The Last of England,* with man and wife staring at the distant coast, is due to the competition—or conflict—between vision and design. The naturalism exists in the parts, not in the whole, which seems an artifact. The inconsistency was inherent in the daguerreotype also with its note of actuality and its carefully set poses. It is a difficulty Bazille met, and it reappears in Henry Alexander Bowler's pre-Raphaelite painting of *The Doubt* (1856), a camera-like glimpse of a woman fixed in bright sunlight in a graveyard; she leans on a headstone thinking about the inscription on it ("Can These Dry Bones Live?") while a butterfly dances about her. Their work suffers strain from this over-visibility.

Design often controls vision in pre-Raphaelite poems written to illustrate paintings and paintings done to illustrate poems.

The narrative in Morris' ballads like "Winter Weather" congeals into this sort of fixity, which emphasizes what Stevenson in his neo-romantic way called the fit and striking gesture. Morris' brutal incident is stylized into a ballet-movement. Or take Rossetti's still stanza from "The Blessed Damozel," a celestial daguerreotype:

> Circlewise sit they, with bound locks
> And foreheads garlanded;
> Into the fine cloth white like flame
> Weaving the golden thread. . . .

Tennyson's *Idylls* are filled with these pre-Raphaelite embroideries and contours, which he retraced from Keat's pseudo-mediaeval poems, a constant source of pre-Raphaelite ornamentation. In Morris' "Blue Closet" and "The Chapel in Lyoness" the design is formalized into an abstraction.

> Gold or gems she did not wear,
> But her yellow rippled hair,
> Like a veil hid Guendolen!
>
> 'Twixt the sunlight and the shade,
> My rough hands so strangely made,
> Folded golden Guendolen;
>
> Hands used to grip the sword-hilt hard,
> Framed her face, while on the sward
> Tears fell down from Guendolen.
>
> (1858)

This passage from "Rapunzel" is a composition with Puvis-like line and blond decorative color. Morris and Rossetti found what Maurice Denis found: that "colors, sounds, words have a miraculously expressive value quite aside from representation, quite aside from their literal meaning." Thus the ornamental field excerpted itself from narrative incidents.

George Moore said that for over a century painting was only a handmaiden to literature, and the painter a sort of librettist. It would be possible to arrange in a scale the steps by which pre-Raphaelite painting freed itself from the libretto. Millais' *Order of Release,* showing the returned soldier embracing his wife, is entirely literature. The mongrel dog fawning on the soldier has probably the most convincingly canine hair ever fixed on canvas; one has an irresistible impulse to stroke it. Then would come Collinson's *Empty Purse,* surely one of the ugliest pre-Raphaelite pictures with its bitter green background and pink ribbons. The Victorian maid has charitably spent everything and now stands beside a table with a handbill spelled out like a collage: "Saint Bride's Church, Bazaar, Useful and Fancy Articles—Patroness Lady Dorcas." This is literature too, with a note of social betterment. Then would come F. G. Stephens' *The Proposal*—a mediaevalish youth, looking rather like John Ruskin at a bad moment and clad in a kind of red leotard, earnestly wooing a girl in brown who has an air of being underprivileged: mediaevalism translated into the depressing features of the lower middle class. The anxious pre-Raphaelite symbolism would appear in Rossetti's *Ecce Ancilla Domini* (dated March, 1850) [26], a meagre composition in white and blue, with a red screen embroidered with lilies denoting purity and coldness. The Virgin, clearly a London type, crouches in the pallid dawn, her eyes (as George Moore noted) "deep pools of light" and her red hair "a symbol of the soul." For Moore this is a "spiritual drama." Rossetti has invented an aesthetic-synthetic gothic figure of "strange hybrid grace." It is the mode Burne-Jones adopted in 1880 for his *Golden Stair* [27] with its mannerist spiral and still sad figures—a pre-Raphaelitism qualified by decadence. Rossetti's color in *Ecce Ancilla,* and his silhouette-drawing, have a certain *japonaiserie* that reappears in Whistler's non-literary arrangements, "magical passages from gray to green, from green again to changing evanescent gray."

The impressionists intended to observe nature, but found that light and color detached themselves from the scene as a kind of syntax apart; in the same way the pre-Raphaelites found that their photographic and pseudo-mediaeval details were a separate grammar of ornament. Pre-Raphaelitism, like impressionism in its course from Monet to Seurat and post-impressionism, was a repudiation of wax models and studio mechanics. It turned to direct observation, exactitude, honesty—a naked vision that also inspired the little poem written as a creed

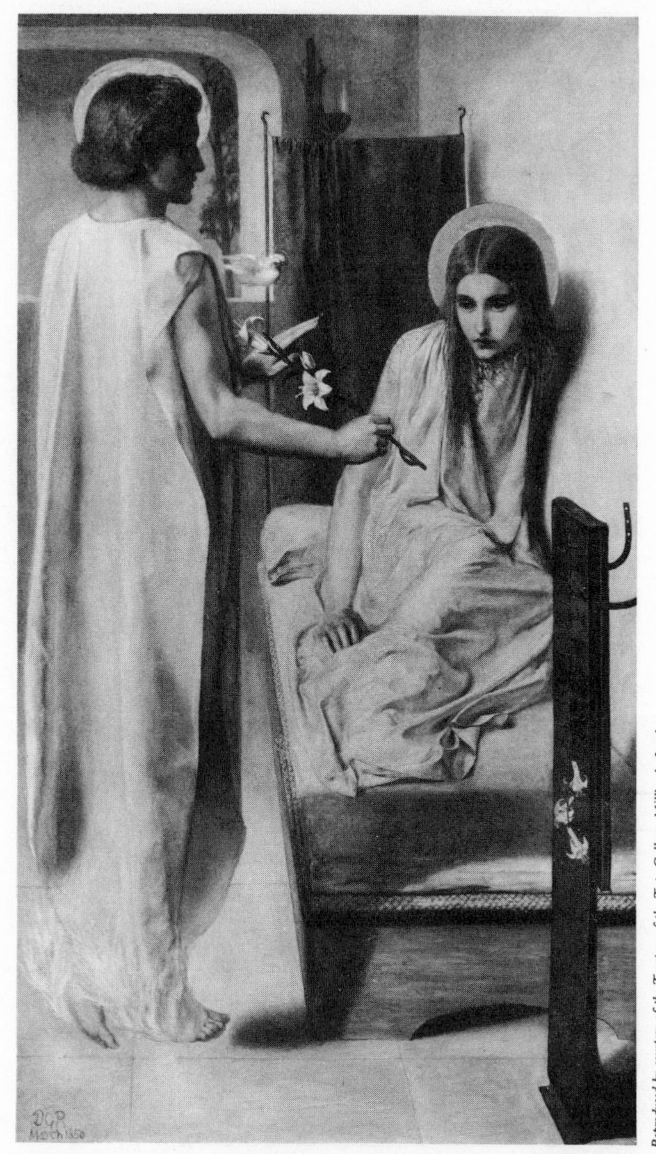

26 ROSSETTI: *Ecce Ancilla Domini*

27 BURNE-JONES: *The Golden Stair*

in the short-lived pre-Raphaelite magazine called *The Germ:*

> When whoso merely hath a little thought
> Will plainly think the thought which is in him,
> Not imaging another's bright or dim,
> Not mangling with new words what others taught . . .

then he is pre-Raphaelite. The Brotherhood in its moral earnestness relied on incidents and situations from common life, episodes like Rossetti's painting of the "fallen woman" in *Found* or his rather lurid poem "Jenny." When the illustrative details had been carefully worked up in each passage, the parts became greater than the whole, or at least incompatible with the whole; then they crystallized on the surface as decorative color and contour.

In spite of their different aims and methods pre-Raphaelites and impressionists were led toward two-dimensional illusions. Artistically the pre-Raphaelites were redeemed by their very artificialities. The loss of the anecdote was a crisis in the nineteenth-century arts; and the impressionists and pre-Raphaelites lost it at about the same time, when they relinquished nature for harmonies in color or surface design. Neither pre-Raphaelites nor impressionists had *a* style. Both stylized, and often in a mannered way. But both are precursors of Art Nouveau.

V

THE NABIS

AND ART NOUVEAU

The acceptance of artifice, then, in literature and painting is from one point of view decadent; but from another it is the new formalism toward which all the main streams of the time were flowing among pre-Raphaelites, impressionists, symbolists, realists like Gautier, and that amorphous group known as Nabis, synthetists, or neo-traditionalists. The symbolists admired the byzantine because it was a hieratic, ritualistic art subduing nature to style. The very term byzantine has a double reference: to either the highly stylized art of the Christian East, or else the late-century aestheticism of the decadents and neo-pagans. Behind both meanings there is an obeisance to style. And if style means anything at the close of the nineteenth century, it is the discovery of the *motif* by itself and for itself as the essence of art. This emphasis on abstract design links Nabi art and Art Nouveau, which had better be considered together as comparable indications of a new formalism—a formalism that enlisted the knowing sympathies of aesthetes as well as the

Courtesy of the Chester Dale Collection, National Gallery of Art, Washington, D.C.

28 GAUGUIN: *Fatata Te Miti*

rather pompous devotion of the neo-traditionalists who called themselves "romanists" and hoped to turn French literature and art back toward its native "greco-roman principle." Only the most arbitrary decisions can divide the Nabis from Art Nouveau, the byzantine from either.

The so-called Nabi painters stand at the crossroads where a good many of the mannerisms of nineteenth-century art intersect to lead toward a new sense of style. The group is more important for its interests and theories than for its painting, which was a makeshift of symbolism, Gauguin, Japanese stylization, mediaevalism in its many forms, and the neo-traditionalism that found its voice in the writings of Maurice Denis.[11] The composite nature of Nabi speculation and technique is indicated by their relations with Gauguin, who met Émile Bernard in Brittany in 1886 and who became through him conversant with the whole Nabi company, not only at Pont-Aven in 1888, and at Pouldu, but at the Café Voltaire in Paris after November, 1890. There Gauguin told the poet Charles Morice, "Primitive art proceeds from the mind and uses nature. So-called refined art proceeds from sensuality and serves nature.

Nature is the servant of the former and the mistress of the latter." Gauguin's painting [28] gave to primitivism a hieratic note because he treated color in closed lines or *cloisons* resembling the leading in mediaeval stained glass. Thence arose the technique of *cloisonnisme* or painting in well-defined areas of flat color, which enabled Gauguin to avoid "copying nature too much." As he said, "I have sacrificed everything for the benefit of style." Gauguin taught Sérusier to treat color as an abstraction, to paint "as blue as possible," and in 1888 he had written to his friend Schuffenecker the advice: "Don't copy nature too much. Art is an abstraction; derive this abstraction from nature while dreaming before it, but think more of creating than of the actual result." Then will appear "the *synthesis* of form and color derived from the observation of the dominant element only."

Here was a principle that appealed strongly to a gathering of independent painters, including Bernard, Sérusier, Denis [29], Seguin, and Filiger, patronized by Monsieur and Madame Ranson in Paris. At the Ransons' they studied Japanese prints and mediaeval stained glass while they were admiring Cézanne, Puvis de Chavannes, and Odilon Redon. Sérusier, their early theorist, was inspired not only by Gauguin but also, apparently, by the Egyptians, the Greeks, the Cambodians, the Chinese, and the Gothic. Cazalis brought to the group their "hebraizing" mystique—whence their name of Nabi (meaning "prophet"). Maurice Denis, a devout Catholic, seems to have caused the conversion of Verkade, who joined the neo-Catholic or neo-Nazarene artists working at Beuron, and so linked the Nabis with the Lyonnais of an earlier generation and with the Catholic art of Desvallières and Rouault in the present century. If the Nabis were not a school, they were united by an admiration for symbolism, tradition, Cézanne, Puvis, and Gauguin, and by a revolt against naturalism and impressionism. Denis notes in his *Journal* for 1898 that the impressionists made the mistake of working after the model and *d'après nature,* whereas painting should be symbolist and subjective (*toute émotion peut devenir un sujet de tableau*). The group also repudiated academism, although they obviously did not free themselves from their nostalgia for mediaeval art. Nabi painting was cerebral, Sérusier having proposed that style is a product of the mind.

Musée d'Art Moderne, Paris, Archives Photographiques

29 DENIS (MAURICE): *The Muses*

The Nabi program was at best incoherent. Albert Aurier made a somewhat desperate attempt to describe it in an article on Gauguin in 1891, saying it was Ideological (its sole purpose is to express the Idea), Symbolistic (it expresses the Idea through Forms), Synthetic (these Forms are Signs), Subjective (the object is considered not merely an object but as a Sign of an Idea), and Decorative (like the "primitive" art of Egyptians and Greeks). Maurice Denis in his *Théories* and *Nouvelles Théories* stresses the Nabi quest for style. One of the Nabi intentions was to "paint nudes one could not sleep with." Here the Nabis agree with symbolists like Mallarmé, who said that the poetic act is to see a number of motifs grouped in a pattern. Denis sympathetically added that "nature cannot for the artist be anything but a state of soul." He extended the symbolist theories about poetry to painting when he took painting to be "an expressive synthesis, the symbol of a sensation that becomes an eloquent transcription" or pictorial equivalent of an emotion. (There is something in common between the Nabi search for pictorial signs or equivalents and T. S. Eliot's later search for objective correlatives.) Rejecting the whole atmosphere of plein air, the Nabis proclaimed the *rupture du moi connaissant avec l'objet, c'est à dire avec la nature.*

Gauguin's primitivism notwithstanding, Nabi painting re-entered the studio. The very meaning of synthetism was to fuse nature and abstract ideas. Gauguin's *cloisonnisme* seemed to be a way to get such a fusion, and to break with *les bourgeois* too—for Nabi-synthetist art disdained *la collectivité.* Aurier says that painting is *une stylisation raisonnée.* Late in the century the Nabis revive the notion of Poe and Baudelaire that art is a rhythmical creation of Beauty. Gauguin talks like a symbolist or Nabi when he says, "The idea is the form of things outside those things." The non-naturalistic color of Gauguin and the Nabis is due to their treating painting as painting, since "all lyricism is allowed, and one ought to use metaphor like a poet." The Nabi equivalent or sign is a pictorial metaphor. There is a byzantine note in all this, a late-century obsession with style. Denis in fact is wholly in accord with Art Nouveau decorative contours, an atelier style, when he writes in his *Journal* in 1900 that a painter should depend upon "predominance of the silhouette, of the arabesque, of calligraphy, the linear interpretation of the model and drapery," making a "compromise between vegetal and geometric ornament" and seeking "beauty of profile." Denis admires the painting on vases, which is not sculptural.

In general Nabi painting had two main currents: one sending Sérusier, Denis, Verkade, Roussel, and Ranson toward the middle ages and Gauguin; the other sending Bonnard, Vuillard, Vallotton, and other intimists or early fauvists toward the

Japanese and Degas.[12] Both groups accept the arabesque, the silhouette, the decorative surface—the wall, in short. In 1890 Jean Verkade wanted, like Puvis, to decorate walls: "Des murs, des murs à décorer. . . . Il n'y a pas de tableau, il n'y a que décorations." The Nabis tried to replace solids by planes so that instead of nature there would be a synthetic pattern with "exact line defining the form." The Nabi ideal was the bleached over-bred painting by Puvis; but there was a strong note of Gauguin also in the half-mural composition of Denis, *Les Muses* (1893), which has, besides, the curves of Art Nouveau.

Sérusier in *A B C de la Peinture* shows how the nineteenth-century problem of recording sensation changed to a Nabi-synthetist problem of representation or *connaissance:* "To decorate a surface is to underscore correct proportions. If these are not correct, the figure is a mere dissimulation—a disguise, a deception, a lie." Nabi theory declares that a picture is "an object having its own laws" and that a great error is to oppose the idea of nature to the idea of style. Byzantine art captured the Nabi imagination exactly because, as Denis remarked, the perfection of its décor corresponds to a spiritual concept; it is a *rapport* between the painting and the mind rather than between the mind and nature. This rejection of objectivity caused synthetist paintings to be esoteric—for Denis confessed that Nabi mysticism was for the most part "a singular mélange of Plotinus, Edgar Poe, Baudelaire, and Schopenhauer, along with Mme. Blavatsky, Péladan, and the exhibits of the Rosicrucians." Often Nabi work was spiritless and debilitated, with the ineffectual artifices to be seen in Maeterlinck's theatre. Yet Nabi emphasis on abstract form led from symbolism to fauvism—by way of Gauguin; we can see the results in Van Gogh's arbitrary color.

Denis might have said that the whole group was seeking a canon. They were in sympathy with the "romanism" of Jean Moréas, who proposed to return to the "greco-latin" tradition —a *chaîne gallique*—that had been broken by romanticism and naturalism. Moréas thought that literature, especially, had been menaced "by too much fog." Their need for a tradition led the Nabis to a mediaevalism more hermetic than the pre-Raphaelite mediaevalism. Under Denis they headed toward a dogma that eventually became a form of neo-Catholicism, the principle that "painting is an essentially religious art" and that an impious century must return to the aesthetic of Fra Angelico—*qui seule est vraiment catholique,* Denis says in his *Journal.* This is more orthodox than the confused Ecclesiology in England. Denis urges outright, "Art must return to the cloister." He sees in the stained glass at Saint Pierre, Chartres, the hope for modern art. In 1903 Denis visited Beuron, where in the snow and damp, black monks passed along corridors hung with paintings derived from Giotto's works. In his warm, simple cell Verkade talked with Denis about painting, stressing the Nabi technique that seemed so Christian: "une bonne couleur, un bon dessein, de bonnes proportions. . . . La couleur est surtout utile pour la décoration, peu pour l'éxpression." The Beuron neo-mediaeval style descends from Ingres—"lines, lines, always lines"—and rejects Delacroix; and it adapts itself to the mural. The Catholic Church alone can guard this tradition. To the monks of Beuron "protestantism is a laicisation," as Denis writes. The effects on Rouault are well known. There are also echoes of the entire Nabi program in the neo-orthodoxies of T. S. Eliot, who may have accepted some of these notions through T. E. Hulme—of whom more presently.

In summary, Denis says the Nabis were "born of symbolism, also called synthetism, and wavered between mystic expression and decoration." Precisely because of this syncretism the Nabis were middlemen for new conceptions of art, conceptions that originated in Baudelaire and faced toward Cézanne, Yeats, Hulme, Eliot, and the moderns who have transcended romanticism, realism, and personality and brought into the foreground the major problem of representation. Denis shows how the Nabis faced toward this problem when he writes:

> The painter, according to Cézanne's phrase, ought not to try to reproduce nature but to represent it by equivalents—plastic equivalents. . . . "The aim in art being not any longer the direct and immediate reproduction of the object, all the elements of a pictorial language—lines, planes, shadows, lights, colors—become abstract elements that can be combined, rarefied, exaggerated, distorted according to their expressive power to attain that major end of the work: the projection of the idea, the dream, the mind."
>
> (*Nouvelles Théories*)

Their admiration for *la qualité décorative* brings the Nabis into the compass not only of symbolism but that much wider manifestation known as decadence or aestheticism, the extravagant attitudes of an Oscar Wilde, who said, "The first duty of life is to be as artificial as possible. What the second duty is, no one has discovered." It goes to show how much in the air the sense of "style" was that Wilde should have said, "All art is at once surface and symbol." Wilde accepted the synthetist notion that "Primarily a picture is a beautifully covered surface. It is primarily," he told art students in one of his lectures, "a purely decorative thing."

In his *Intentions* Wilde, who temperamentally had little in common with the Nabis, expands his thesis that "the more we study Art, the less we care for Nature. What Art really reveals to us is Nature's lack of design." This is precisely why Denis and the Nabis rejected the impressionists. Wilde also writes the axiom with which that byzantine artist, the young André Gide, began his early half-symbolist work: "It is through Art, and through Art only, that we can realize our perfection." Anticipating Gide's character Lafcadio, Wilde advances his opinion that "Life imitates Art far more than Art imitates Life."

> Life holds the mirror up to Art, and either reproduces some strange type imagined by painter or sculptor, or realizes in fact what has been dreamed in fiction. . . . Where, if not from the Impressionists, do we get those wonderful brown fogs that come creeping down our streets, blurring the gas lamps and changing the houses into monstrous shadows? . . . Nature . . . is our creation. It is in our brain that she quickens to life.
>
> *(Intentions)*

(Meanwhile Albert Aurier was writing in Paris that "The artist has above all the duty to avoid carefully that antinomy of all art: concrete truth, *trompe l'oeil,* so as not to give by his picture that fallacious impression of nature which would act on the spectator just like nature itself.") For Wilde, every artist is a successful liar, and "as a method, realism is a complete failure." (Gide later says, echoing, "The best passages of my novel are those wholly invented.")

Wilde represents a last phase of neo-mannerism with its acute consciousness of style. If we except Gide, he is the last dandy. Both are dedicated to the artificial, and are symptomatic of the art-view of life that finally emerged from the romanticism of the early years of the century. Pater, too, as an academic dandy attempts to discipline feeling to art, bringing to literature an overbred sense of his medium. He requires that a writer attend to the minutest details if he is "to deal scrupulously with his instrument"; he must heed a "vision within" and must "give the phrase, the sentence, the structural member, the entire composition, song, or essay, a similar unity with its subject and with itself:—a style is in the right way when it tends towards that." By this care for language Pater is led to a notion of style as an abstraction with a purity that had caused Flaubert to think "the idea only exists by virtue of its form." Such convictions open the way for Croce. At the close of the century there appears under the guise of decadence, aestheticism, and byzantine art a devotion to style as an absolute, an exercise in exploiting a medium formally. Neo-mannerism has crystallized itself in carefully discriminated designs.

The crystallization was not entirely "pure" in Nabi painting, or even in Nabi theory, because the Nabis did not accept the logic of the decorative without qualifications: they were distracted by their mystique. But there was another crystallization—brief, to be sure—in that form of decorative art known internationally under different names: in France it was called Art Nouveau; in Germany it was called Jugendstil or Sezession; it was nameless in Belgium but there produced a modern functional art and architecture with Victor Horta and Henry van de Velde; in England and Scotland it was an outgrowth of the arts-and-crafts movements and also of Whistler's Japanese manner.[13] Essentially it is, like rococo, a movement within the decorative arts. Indeed it can best be considered as a neo-rococo manifestation. Rococo, as we know, was not so much an architecture as a system of decoration used by architects. It is true that Art Nouveau produced some modern buildings with bare walls and a functional use of materials—for example, the White House in Chelsea (1877) designed for Whistler by E. W. Godwin—but essentially it was a development associated with architecture rather than an independent style. The "feminine" ironwork of Paris Metro stations survives as a relic of Art Nouveau.

Since it took so many forms internationally, Art Nouveau is not easily described, and the difficulty is greater because it is closely related to impressionism, aestheticism, synthetism, pre-Raphaelite arts-and-crafts movements, the Japanese fad, and fauvism; it also foreshadows the Bauhaus. Its origins are deep in the century. The Goncourt brothers always claimed priority in the Japanese vogue: "We were the first to introduce the taste for Chinese and Japanese objects," they said about 1868. More important, they saw the similarity between Japanese taste and the rococo revival, Jules de Goncourt stating, "The search after *reality* in literature, the resurrection of eighteenth-century art, the triumph of *japonisme*—are not these the three great literary and artistic movements of the second one-half of the nineteenth century?"

Also in 1868 appeared Owen Jones's *Grammar of Ornament* with its notion that decorative arts should all arise from architecture and that "beauty of form is produced by lines growing out one from the other in gradual undulations." Jones probably gives us the key: Art Nouveau is a "return to the significant motif," a liberation of seductive design based upon curvilinear decoration, an "organic" floral line that is called maidenhair. This melodious, rhythmic line was a revolt from the cluttered naturalism of nineteenth-century decoration and from Biedermeier, as well as a rejection of the picturesque details that had flowered in pseudo-gothicism and the abbey mode. Art Nouveau cleaned up the decorative junk by returning to a highly stylized line that is both floral and geometric. Thus the new ornamental motifs were, as in rococo, easily assimilated to the architectural fabric.

Art Nouveau was inspired by nature; but nature was formalized into rhythmic and repeated outlines appearing in graphic arts as well as in architecture. The Japanese taste suited this linear embroidery, as Aubrey Beardsley shows. Nor was the quattrocento line of Botticelli without its effect on this highly decorative and very composite distortion that pointed toward fauvism. In 1877 one could already see hung on the green and gold walls of Sir Coutts Lindsay's Grosvenor Gallery in London the various "greenery-yallery" ornamental "arrangements" painted by Japanesy young men like Whistler [30], Burne-Jones, or G. F. Watts, deriving vaguely from a belated pre-Raphaelitism, Hiroshige, and impressionism. By 1895 the new motifs came into the foreground when Sigfried Bing opened his Maison de l'Art Nouveau in Paris; and the Paris exhibition of 1900 marked a moment when Art Nouveau, having reached its height, was about to be absorbed into a genuinely modern style. Art Nouveau was a cultivated and short-lived mode of decoration, too slight, possibly, to survive in the face of an art like Cézanne's or the early skyscrapers.

Its importance, however, is far out of proportion to its brief history, not only because it liberated the motif but, more significantly, because it brought decoration back into functional relation with architecture. For architecture is the basic art in the sense that whenever other fine arts are disengaged from it they tend to lose their functional value—however brilliant may be their accomplishment. Architecture is a primary art simply because of the human condition.[14] It is the art with maximum presence, since a building surrounds us on all sides and has an ambience unavailable to painting or sculpture. There is an "existential" increment in building, for we actually move inside the space enclosed by walls: to enter a temple or a palace is to know the meaning of *Dasein.* Since prehistoric times the wall has been a natural support of painting, whether in the cave, the temple, the palace, or the tomb. Does this explain why fresco painting by its very technique has a certain monumentality, and why the byzantine ikon has its own hieratic stature, no matter how small in scale—because it is a fragment of the wall, detached? Does this explain why it is more difficult to create mythical painting on the easel than on the wall, where painting remained until relatively late in the renaissance? Sculpture and painting attained major styles during grecian, byzantine, romanesque, and mediaeval periods while they were auxiliary to architecture, integral with the wall or fabric. Stained glass was only painting fitted to architectural uses. With the invention of oil, the nature of painting changed; and it is noted that Van Eyck treated his major works as if they were enlarged miniatures or illustrations. Oil allows an inti-

30 WHISTLER: *Nocturne—Blue and Silver: Cremorne Lights*

macy and minuteness of touch impossible in fresco or other forms of mural painting. Accordingly the personality of the artist became significant during the renaissance after the medium of oil brought the easel picture, which made possible all sorts of experiments: it could be re-touched; it was detachable, movable, transferable from place to place; it was deprived of the context of painting destined for the wall. With oil painting came the studio, privacy of conception and creation, privacy of ownership. A painting was an object to be traded on the market or gathered in collections or museums, losing some of its most potent relation to life. After it was excluded from architectural space, painting changed its very nature; it had to develop its own illusion of "deep" space in the guise of vanishing-point perspective, a world apart, with three illusory dimensions not required by an architectural framework. Easel painting endowed the artist with a freedom hard not to abuse. The renaissance optical perspective may have perverted the methods and purposes inherent in painting and brought the *trompe l'oeil,* the literary anecdote, and the mistaken belief that painting is an autonomous art given to its own mystique of beauty.

Painting on the wall required a *métier;* and *métier*—a publicly practised craft—has been called the bond between the artist and society. Notoriously painting in the early nineteenth century had lost this sense of *métier,* not only because training in the official academies was a mere superficial imitation of the antique, but also because the painter found at his disposal synthetic pigments whose nature and use he did not know. In earlier generations a painter had to grind, as if by rite, the colors he used—colors derived from natural substances. His art was primarily craft. Notoriously, also, the modern painter has a "nostalgia for a *métier*," as Jean Cassou puts it. He has no *métier* but only an individual sensibility, which has meant the fragmentation of painting. "The painter has killed painting." (Eliot has made the same complaint about poetry and has sought an "impersonal" medium.) Renoir and Cézanne yearned for a *métier,* regretting lost craft secrets. Architecture, by contrast, never lost its *métier*—at least never so entirely as painting. This too may explain why modern architecture has been in a stronger position than modern painting, and also why the modern "crisis in the easel picture" has led modern painting to accept the wall again. The painter needed to return to the wall to revitalize his technique by contact with an art that never lost its *métier.* Many recent masters like Gromaire, Lurçat, Saint-Saens, Matisse, and Picasso have returned to tapestry, one of the minor arts where there is a *métier,* as there was in stained glass or fresco, and where there is a need for the wall. Rouault tried to adopt a stained-glass *métier.*

The loss of *métier* was another result of the easel. Early renaissance painting, like mediaeval painting, was auxiliary to the wall; it remained so, mostly, through the baroque period, when elaborate ceilings and altarpieces determined the form of an art that was still public, requiring certain methods, designs, subjects. During the renaissance, however, fresco often left the wall by implication even while it appeared on the wall. Botticelli and Luini both frescoed easel figures on the wall, and Michelangelo treated the Sixtine Chapel roof as if it were a congeries of easel paintings; his very architectural "framework" on the roof is a figment. To this extent he violated the premises of mural painting to create an illusion of sculptural figures floating on high. Indeed, the late-renaissance and baroque mythological ceiling is anti-architectural insofar as it is conceived in the space and volume of easel painting. It is worth noting that Uccello's great grim decorative *Battle* in the Louvre is, in spite of its renaissance perspective, a throwback: though acutely foreshortened, it denies easel space and calls out for the wall. The fall of the lances like heavy timber, the activity of the composition, and the absurd perspective do not, strangely enough, damage the mural quality of this painting, which is monumentally spread. It has an architectural gravity lacking to Velázquez' *Surrender of Breda,* which by contrast is conceived and painted from an easel viewpoint. For one thing, Uccello does not model his figures as Velázquez does; and there is no unifying atmospheric perspective. Uccello treats each truculent figure independently, as if he were working in mosaic, an art with a rigid *métier.* He keeps the byzantine note. The result is a dominating sense of space without any atmospheric ambience. Unexpectedly, too, it might be held that rococo was the last art with a *métier,* and this in spite of its fragility: not only because of the strong sense of craft used publicly by a poet like Pope, but also because rococo painting of the overdoor or panel adapted itself to architecture. After the decline of rococo there was only easel painting that produced academic machines or a private revolt by independents. In any case it would appear that so far as abstract painting today returns to the wall—that is, becomes decorative—it will recover the *métier* that tapestry and the minor arts never lost. Rococo was a minor art. As a style it is noteworthy chiefly because it existed as an aspect of architecture and was frankly decorative. After rococo, architecture on its own account disguised itself by pastiche, with damaging results on other arts that exist symbiotically with it.

What is true of painting is also true of sculpture, which had its great periods while—in the West, at least—it stood in close relation to an architectural framework. The divorce of sculpture from building or landscape caused some of the same problems that arose when painting was divorced from the wall; and the modern solution has been to set both in organic relations again to their primal matrix.

Maurice Denis notes in his *Journal* in 1904 that the new painting must be a renunciation, a simplification, accepting an *ordonnance architectonique*—"because architecture is the first and most ancient art" to which style must return. However synthetic Nabi theory may be, Denis understood the contribution made by Puvis de Chavannes, whose two series of paintings of the life of Sainte Geneviève in the Pantheon show that he intended to make these works a mural decoration. The colors—chiefly gray and blue, and unlike the gaudy hues of other Pantheon subjects by Laurens and Detaille—are adapted to the pale wall. Puvis depended on simple fresco rhythms suitable to a neutral plane, and he did not make the mistake of crowding his scenes. Consequently the Geneviève sequences, finished in 1877 and 1898, are broad and easy to read. The figures are held flat, spread thinly in horizontal space, harking back to Perugino. The shallow design is pre-Raphaelite, and the clean line derives from the Ingres manner. Apparent as the artifice may be, Puvis' melancholy, lonely figures do have a mural quietude.

Nevertheless Puvis is not so important in the Art Nouveau tradition as the severe theoretical work of Seurat, who appears exactly at the juncture of post-impressionism, or divisionism, with the decorative painting that again sought the wall. Under the pretence of a scientific theory of complementary colors

Seurat laboriously worked out compositions that are inherently mural, adapted to fresco, not oil. The *Grande Jatte* (1884–86) is one of the most earnest attempts in the century to discipline painting by a *métier,* and the somewhat hollow intellectualism of Seurat's design should not blind us to the significance of the nearly mosaic-like craft that caused him to take such pride in his painful execution of his surface. It is ironic that the stilted, wholly doctrinaire scene, which required a forethought necessary to fresco painting, should have been attempted in oil. Nor should the immobility of this arrangement or its pseudo-statuesque manner prevent its being taken as a variant of Art Nouveau, for Seurat brings into post-impressionism a strong sense of the ornamental surface. He approved, in fact, the principle of Signac, that kindred spirit, who wrote, "It seems that the first consideration of a painter who stands before the white canvas should be to decide what curves and arabesques should cut the surface. . . ." These curves and arabesques appear with great clarity in the foreground of *Le Cirque* (1890–91)—in the edge of the curtain held by the clown, in the lithe figure of the circus master, in the arabesque of the whip, in the delicate curve of the crop raised by the rider, and the cusp of the tumbling acrobat in the background. How readily the theatrical gestures in Degas lent themselves to Art Nouveau is better indicated by Seurat's *Le Chahut* (1889–90) with its springing curvilinear rhythms, the swirl of the skirts, the Japanese grace of the cello and the gas flares. Divisionism has taken on the firm organic line of Art Nouveau, and adapted itself to designs that urgently need the wall.

For Art Nouveau is not a style but a mode of decoration that makes possible a return to architecture. It is a neo-rococo form of ornamentation related to Whistler's Peacock Room [31, 32]. If Art Nouveau is "based wholly on one motive, a long sensitive curve," it is also a flat pattern—like the rococo swirl, which appears against the empty field of a panel. In Germany and Austria, particularly, Art Nouveau was *Flaechenkunst* and *Flaechenraum,* essentially a two-dimensional design developing in three-dimensional space, thanks to its architectural context. A great many ingenuities in Art Nouveau found expression in graphic arts and printing, or in carpets, drapes, or other tex-

Courtesy of the Smithsonian Institution, Freer Gallery of Art, Washington, D.C.

31, 32 WHISTLER: *The Peacock Room*
(oil color and gold on leather and wood)

Courtesy of the Smithsonian Institution, Freer Gallery of Art, Washington, D.C.

Courtesy of the Fogg Art Museum, Harvard University, Grenville L. Winthrop Bequest

33 BEARDSLEY: *The Peacock Skirt* (drawing for *Salome*)

tiles showing traits apparent in Beardsley [33] and Eckmann —"a flat pattern again, with long curves, gracefully entwined, and again full of the joy of tracing many consonant lines."

Blake and Rossetti had alike stressed the "pure line's gracious flow," a contour that flourishes in Beardsley's pseudo-Botticelliesque drawing. Art Nouveau often simplified itself to sinuous black-and-white lines, giving an effect that among the

Nabis was known as *cloisonnisme.* Gauguin flattened color and volume by enclosing them in *cernes,* outlines like stained-glass medallions. Mediating between symbolism, Art Nouveau, and fauvist abstraction, Gauguin favored "flat" stylization and withdrew from nature. "Everything must be sacrificed to pure color," he said, and the dreamlike surface of his Tahitian paintings unites Art Nouveau to the symbolism of Baudelaire and the Nabis: "I have tried to interpret my vision in an appropriate décor and with all the simplicity the medium permits." Gauguin's woodcuts are stylized Art Nouveau décor, a very expressive *Flaechenkunst.* They illustrate Oscar Wilde's thesis that "Art begins with abstract decoration, with purely imaginative and pleasurable work dealing with what is unreal and non-existent." One touch of nature may, Wilde supposes, make the whole world kin—but "two touches of nature will destroy any work of Art." To look at a thing is not the same as to see it: "One does not see anything until one sees its beauty." And beauty is an abstract pattern: "The more abstract, the more ideal an art is, the more it reveals to us the temper of its age." Whenever Art Nouveau used motifs from nature—as Guimard [34] used floral or tendril motifs for his Metro entries—these themes were stylized into "swirl and blob" rhythms.

The clean line is basic to Art Nouveau, the line in all its ornamental value, as we see it in mediaeval Celtic strapwork (for the Celtic twilight also brought to Art Nouveau a sense of style) or in Japanese prints and drawings by Hokusai or Hiroshige, who belong to the history of Art Nouveau as well as to impressionism. Van Gogh has a Japanese moment in 1888, his violent curves being a kind of parody of Art Nouveau; and Monet, Degas, Mary Cassatt, and most of the impressionists borrowed designs from the block-print. But distinctions between "Japanese young men," impressionists, and aesthetes are so uncertain that it may be well to adopt the phrase "pan-impressionism" to refer to the relation of Whistler, Lautrec, and Lafcadio Hearn to Art Nouveau.[15] Impressionism blends into symbolism in Gauguin and others, and both line and color become a nearly abstract ornamental scheme with vaguely emotional overtones. Wilde's poems are pan-impressionist:

34 GUIMARD (HECTOR): *Decorative Panel for Dining Room—Le Castel Béranger, 16 rue de la Fontaine, Paris, 1894–98*

The Thames nocturne of blue and gold
Changed to a harmony in gray;
A barge with ochre-coloured hay
Dropt from the wharf: and chill and cold

The yellow fog came creeping down
The bridges, till the houses' walls
Seemed changed to shadows. . . .
(*"Impression de Matin"*)

This has the subdued Art Nouveau colors: pastels were in vogue, and the 1890's brought a craze for yellow and white while Whistler did his blue-grey nocturnes. Whether color had Gauguin's wealth or Whistler's faded melody, it was abstract and decorative—even in the quaint vignettes of Kate Greenaway.

As early as 1850 the British decorators like Dyce, Hay, and Redgrave used flat patterns in wallpapers and carpets, agreeing with Christopher Dresser that roses should not be treated plastically in carpets, to be walked on:

> . . . the material of which an object is formed should be used in a manner consistent with its own nature, and in that particular way in which it can be most easily "worked". . . . Curves will be found to be beautiful just as they are subtle in character. . . .
>
> (Dresser: *Principles of Decorative Design,* 1873)

Owen Jones argued that "All ornament should be based upon a geometrical construction," and he used color geometrically according to the law of color-perspective that blue retires, yellow advances, and red is intermediate. Jones used only primary colors in small areas. German designers, also, were fond of geometric themes. Whether, then, they were pan-impressionist or geometric, color and line became abstract in Art Nouveau.

The great originality of Art Nouveau was to make decoration functional. About 1897 Eugène Grasset [35] lectured in Paris on the curvilinear as a form of pure decoration suited to practical use, saying:

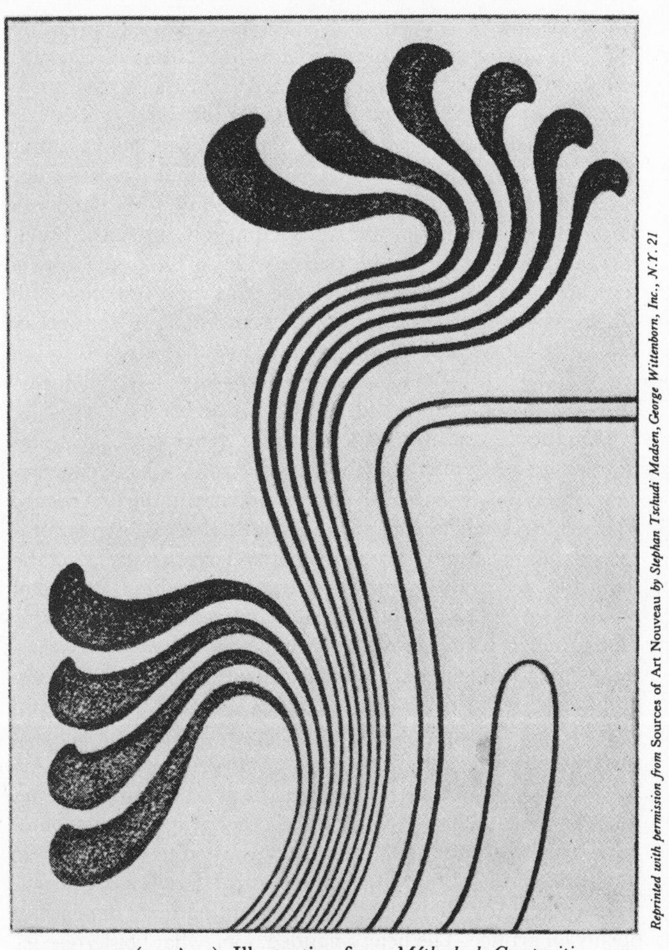

35 GRASSET (EUGÈNE): Illustration from *Méthode de Composition, 1905*

. . . the form of an object must be adapted to the use of the object, and not altered by ornamentation; and, secondly, . . . materials impose a limit on the form of an object, and this limit must not be exceeded by any *tour de force* whatsoever.

Although the "vermicelli and peacock" effects in Horta and Whistler are sometimes over-wrought into a sort of "decorative dandyism," Art Nouveau is a curious amalgam of aestheticism and functionalism, making the beautiful also organic.

The "melodious line" of Art Nouveau has the "abstract grace" of Pater's prose with its care for "latent figurative texture" and "architectural design" that requires an asceticism to avoid superfluities so that style acquires its euphony. Pater, it is said, used to correct his proofs with an eye to the flow of sentences and paragraphs down the page; and we know with what anxiety Mallarmé set up the typography of *Un Coup de Dés* as a "constellation." Such candid artifice also led to the use of many brittle poetic forms like the rondeau, the villanelle, and other designs exotic to English verse, at least.

Like rococo, Art Nouveau thrives in minor arts, and seems to restate the flourishes in rococo décor. Art Nouveau uses delicate asymmetries like the occult balance in the first rococo style with its tendrils, swirls, and acanthus fronds. The decorative designs of Gauguin, Beardsley, and Toorop alike reject the third dimension, along with shadows and modelling. Instead of trying to give plastic depth, which damaged the flatness of his motif, the Art Nouveau designer used a *Wasserspiegel* device: a water-image that gives a double outline usually in simple black and white, repeating or emphasizing contours by a "streak-technique." The first rococo also rejected plasticity in favor of surface contours, and the rococo C-curve reappears in Art Nouveau along with open space like the airy background of the rococo neutral plane. Beardsley and other graphic artists often relied on the silhouette because they wanted to simplify their line and get rid of the exuberant historical details and realism.

In short, Art Nouveau is an atelier manner, depending openly on artifice. The heavy-handed, somewhat boisterous designs of William Morris and the arts-and-crafts mediaevalists were carefully chastened by the later pre-Raphaelites themselves; Burne-Jones reacts against Morris by his atelier manner and leads to Beardsley and Whistler, just as the Scottish designer Mackmurdo simplified the furnishings done by Morris and Company. Mackmurdo's use of the curve in tapestries and textiles shows how the linear patterns in Art Nouveau in some cases derive from the neo-mediaeval motifs not only of Morris but also of Viollet-le-Duc and others who imitated gothic floral decoration. The naturalism was rejected, leaving a waving gothic curve, especially in the ironwork of the 1870's, which evolves realistic metal flowers and stems into functional brackets, gratings, openwork capitals, bannisters, or plaques. Similarly the mediaeval naturalism of Rossetti's ballads is purified into an almost abstract design in his sonnets; for the sonnet, Rossetti says, must be carved in ivory or ebony, its flowering crest impearled and orient.

Rossetti's art has some of the evocative power of symbolism, and the fluid designs of Art Nouveau were occasionally a subjective deformation of nature. The exquisitely meandering Art Nouveau line sometimes could be mistaken for a phase of symbolist-synthetist art as well as for rococo. Toorop's fragile visionary designs are as musically cadenced as a symbolist poem; and Beardsley repeats many of the expressive flat patterns found in Gauguin—especially Gauguin's wood carving, which resembles the subjective art of Munch. Pottery designed by Gallé is a *décor symbolique,* the vases so subtly curved as to fix in crystal the diaphanous meanings of Baudelaire's poetry: "le fuyant, l'insaisissable, la vapeur des nuages . . . la langue des fleurs et des choses muettes" were what Gallé wished to suggest. He is an artist close to Maeterlinck, who has the same vaporous implications, and who designs his costumes for marionettes as if they were figures strayed from Art Nouveau into symbolist drama—"heavy mantles in red and yellow brocade, enormous fat jewels, chocolate or coffee-colored tights, giving the impression of unadorned dancing-jacks." Maeterlinck uses his highly stylized interludes in the theatre as an art that can open *le temple du Rêve.*

Gallé's vases have the flamelike movement of Beardsley's line, which is a sign of both neo-rococo and mannerism. Art Nouveau resembles rococo because the floral curve is worked up to ornamental clarity in a *field.* The fragile tendril and swirl are stated as significant motifs in an all-over pattern—a modern arabesque. Then too, rococo and Art Nouveau show a *loss of weight.*[16] Wrought iron made it possible for Art Nouveau to emancipate space from mass, as we see in the Galeries Lafayette in Paris. The great glass dome, bluish, rising over the three elaborate frail balconies with their fine wrought-iron balustrades and open stairways, gives a sense of space and freedom, a capricious play of light, that are typical of rococo. The Crystal Palace had used this same airy structure, without doubt a functional architecture. But the Galeries Lafayette also show the serpentine grace of renaissance mannerism, a tone of effeteness and unrest and over-refinement that is an aspect of the decadence of mannerist eras.

It is difficult to consider Art Nouveau apart from the decadent climate in which it was fostered. The mannerisms of Art Nouveau, for example, are apparent in the complicated, cloistral, and deliberate painting of Gustave Moreau, the painter most akin to Joris-Karl Huysmans and Walter Pater. When Pater described Leonardo's Mona Lisa with her sated placid beauty, he might have been speaking of almost any of the silvery canvases, often left unfinished, on which Moreau worked so secretively. Moreau's visions are vague sensual dreams of nudes studied again and again with his tortuous line in decorative settings that are like the *mise en scène* for some dim theatre. This seductive flesh is obviously begotten of Ingres and is mannered to a degree that recalls Luini or the unhealthy nudes of the School of Fontainebleau. Moreau is beguiled by jewelled, weightless, anemic figures crowded into fantastic palaces or temples or moving quietly through misty forests. *La Promenade des Muses* has the atmosphere of Rossetti's "deep dim wood where light falls in hardly at all," and *Les Rois Mages* has the pseudo-Arthurian gloom of Tennyson's *Idylls.* Sometimes Moreau's mediaevalism has the decorative design of "The Lady of Shalott" with intently inscribed graphic passages. He is given to mythical subjects and blurs them to indue them with a symbolic tone. *La Fleur Mystique* might be taken for some strange image dreamed by Redon, and *Les Licornes* appear on some alien melancholy shore where afternoon light falls wearily over damsels attended by horned beasts. Moreau was professor at the Beaux-Arts and teacher of Rouault; and the synthetic painting of the Nabis may owe a good deal to works like

La Mort de Promethée, so traditional in its references. There is something, also, of the cruel Art Nouveau line in Moreau's *Messaline,* and his attraction to the figures of Leda and Salome implies that behind the hieratic ornamentation there is a sensuality or sadism common to the decadents. One notes that in the seventies Moreau was working a short block from rue de la Tour des Dames, where George Moore was living in carefully devised sin with his friend Marshall. Moore says he had a pet python which he fed on live guinea pigs while Marshall (who did not like pets) sat at the organ in the hall playing Gregorian chants. The fantastic scene of Moreau's *Les Prétendants* with its blue baroque columns and regal furnishings may, after all, have inspired Moore and Marshall to adorn their drawing room with cardinal red hung from the middle of the ceiling to give the effect of a tent, and to make their rooms "unconventual" with terra-cotta fauns, Turkish couches, an altar, a bust of Shelley, censers, palms, and a gardenia tree in full bloom.

In spite of this abundance, the decadents had a flair for design that caused Gautier in 1852 to call his poems *Émaux et Camées,* and to explain that his title implied his aim to "treat little subjects within restricted limits of form as if they were a surface of gold or copper with the bright hues of enamel." Whatever it owes to the decadents, Art Nouveau cleansed itself of the excesses of Moreau, Tennyson, and Huysmans. Its line dominates color and mass, and its arabesques appear in "lunar clarity." The clumsy naturalism of the realists and the finicking anecdotal details of the pre-Raphaelites vanish along with the sensualism of the decadents. Art Nouveau succeeds in stripping even the arts-and-crafts movements of their archaeology, their museum vision, their concern for nature. William Morris had many functional notions of decoration, but he was always laboring under the burden of the antiquarian, half-picturesque, and pseudo-naturalistic methods; and he distrusted the machine. Consequently his designs were often quaint. Art Nouveau takes us from Morris' Red House in Kent with its quasi-gothic functionalism, to Horta's stripped façades, and from Morris' opulently flowered tapestry and woodcarving to the svelte ironwork of Guimard's Paris Metro stations.

If Morris and Viollet-le-Duc lead to Guimard, Tennyson's

Idylls and Rossetti's Dantesque sonnets lead inevitably to late-Victorian and Edwardian poetry, which has its own arabesque and neo-rococo quality; a verse on the verge of becoming functional, purifying its language and treating the poem as a series of stanzas carefully worked up into a decorative field. The motif in such poetry is carefully chosen and freed from the encumbrances of Tennyson's elegance—the impression is enough. And the impression presently leads to imagism, Hulme, and a new poetry in Pound and Eliot. Take Oscar Wilde's "Les Silhouettes" as an instance of artifice liberated as pure design—Japanese enough, no doubt, but also proto-imagist:

> The sea is flecked with bars of gray,
> The dull dead wind is out of tune,
> And like a withered leaf the moon
> Is blown across the stormy bay.
>
> Etched clear upon the pallid sand
> Lies the black boat . . .
>
> And overhead the curlews cry,
> Where through the dusky upland grass
> The young brown-throated reapers pass,
> Like silhouettes against the sky.

This is minor poetry in the sense that a great deal of rococo poetry is minor. The pattern dominates the details, however, as it did even in Browning's "Meeting at Night"—which is, in contour, Japanese and imagistic. Impressionistic, Japanese, symbolist, imagist, Art Nouveau—the characterization does not matter; the late nineteenth-century poetry was stylized for many reasons and in many ways. Even the nebulous verse of Swinburne accommodates these neat synthetic designs, in some instances resembling the Celtic contrivances in early Yeats:

> There were three men with her, each garmented
> With gold and shod with gold upon the feet;
> And with plucked ears of wheat
> The first man's hair was wound upon his head.
> His face was red, and his mouth curled and sad. . . .
>
> ("*Ballad of Life*," 1866)

In all this verse there is a kind of *cloisonnisme*—a sharp stanzaic outline superscribed on a few calligraphic details, often written with a Japanese stillness, with maximum visibility. Housman's *cloisonnisme* takes "classic" form, although it is related to the sophisticated motifs in *The Yellow Book* or to the severe restraint in Mackintosh furniture and walls [36]. Housman's verse has neatly beaten contours, a stripped and lapidary statement that seems to be functional. There is the economy of Art Nouveau design. His immaculate stoicism, which approaches the studied cynicism of characters in Oscar Wilde, has a late-century air, and is perilously close to artificiality and perilously close to the cliché.

> Loveliest of trees, the cherry now
> Is hung with bloom along the bough,
> And stands about the woodland ride
> Wearing white for Eastertide....
>
> And since to look at things in bloom
> Fifty springs are little room,
> About the woodlands I will go
> To see the cherry hung with snow.
> (1887)

Pope turned conventional themes to his own use in much the same way, and the exquisitely *repoussé* designs on brass plaques by Margaret and Francis Macdonald in the 1890's have the same decisive motifs, the same tact in statement.

Housman's poem is an artifice stated against the neutral field of a conventional notion. His celebrated irony is due to a tone that is negative and seemingly indifferent, an assumed impersonality that he shares with Hardy and the scientist of the day. The temper of his poetry is distinctly Art Nouveau because along with the cleansed statement there is a certain sterilization; behind the simplicities of Art Nouveau is a hardness or incapacity for feeling. Housman is forced to work with deficits—distrust, perhaps fears, so that his reduction of sensibility is more complete than in the first rococo. His disillusion and pathos are minus values; and he leaves them only implied since he is reacting against the exclamatory poetry of the romantics.

The foreground images take their meaning from what Housman does *not* say. Similarly the black-and-white Art Nouveau silhouette has an effective contour because the background is negative, a foil for the hyper-sophisticated décor with its artful naturalism. Housman's technique is neo-rococo because all parts of the decorative design are in sight, held in the same plane; his verses make their byzantine effect as mosaic does, by a decisive pattern on a vanished ground. In a figurative sense he flattens the surface, presenting his neat inscriptions on a theme that is almost a stereotype, like the theme of Gray's *Elegy,* although Gray's melancholy does not cause him to take the constant precautions to which Housman is driven. These precautions give Housman's verse its peculiar sterility, which is another aspect of its extreme artfulness, the aestheticism that explains the "loss of weight" in Art Nouveau. Housman's is not the crashing Byronic irony but a resignation in the face of odds bitterly accepted. The fragility of Art Nouveau design is sometimes an expression of a loss of confidence disguised as wit. The same loss of weight occurs in Wilde's facile *Picture of Dorian Gray,* with its cursory moral, and in Pater's *Marius the Epicurean,* with its carefully evasive spirituality.

The *japonaiserie* of Art Nouveau appears in Oscar Wilde, who doubtless had in mind Whistler's porcelain graces when Dorian Gray "devoted himself entirely to music, and in the long latticed room, with vermilion-and-gold ceiling and walls of olive-green lacquer, he used to give curious concerts." Pater's aesthetic hero Florian Deleal exists in this breathless synthetic atmosphere, seeking "single sharp impressions" that come floating to him in his "sealed place" through a window left ajar or between garden walls framing his vision to "comeliness":

> . . . and thus it happened that, as he walked one evening, a garden gate, usually closed, stood open; and lo! within, a great red hawthorn in full flower, embossing heavily the bleached and twisted trunk and branches, so aged that there were few green leaves thereon—a plumage of tender, crimson fire out of the heart of the dry wood. . . .
>
> (*Child in the House*)

36 MACKINTOSH (CHARLES RENNIE): *The Hall, Hill House, Helensburgh, 1902–3*

Pater has reduced Ruskin's purple prose, his dispersed light and color, to the graphic imagery of the Japanese print.

The carefully arranged asymmetries in Whistler's neo-rococo painting and his dreamlike quiet are everywhere in William Sharp's poems like "The White Peacock," which shows how symbolism adopted Art Nouveau motifs and gradually slipped over into an early imagism:

> Here where the heat lies
> Pale blue in the hollows,
> Where blue are the shadows
> On the fronds of the cactus,
> Where pale blue the gleaming
> Of fir and cypress,
> With the cones upon them
> Amber or glowing
> With virgin gold. . . .
> White as the snow-drift in mountain valleys
> When softly upon it the gold light lingers,
> White as the foam o' the sea that is driven
> O'er billows of azure agleam with sun-yellow,
> Cream-white and soft as the breasts of a girl,
> Moves the White Peacock, as though through the noontide
> A dream of the moonlight were real for a moment. . . .
>
> (1891)

In these passages of flimsy *vers libre* details from nature are isolated, sharply framed, and reduced to ornament; and Sharp's blue-china nocturnes are a transition from symbolism and Art Nouveau to imagism and Yeats's hushed twilight:

> In a hidden valley a pale blue flower grows,
> It is so pale that in the moonshine it is dimmer than dim gold,
> And in the starshine paler than the palest rose.
>
> (*"The Valley of Pale Blue Flowers,"* 1901)

The *fin de siècle* motif so carefully excerpted from nature brings Oscar Wilde into relation with the aesthetic of T. E. Hulme, whose *Speculations* in 1924 announced a return to poetry that would give you "the exact curve you want." Hulme is considered a herald of neo-traditionalism, neo-classicism, or imagism. Having rejected "romantic sentiment" in favor of verse controlled by "architect's curves—flat pieces of wood with all different kinds of curvature," Hulme seeks "accurate, precise, and definite description." Art Nouveau did not give this unsentimental image; but it did develop from "the exact curve" what Oscar Wilde called "those decorative conditions that each art requires for its perfection." Hulme's anxiety to get "the exact curve" arises from the same anti-romanticism that caused Wilde to say "the art that is frankly decorative is the art to live with"—"For the real artist is he who proceeds, not from feeling to form, but from form to thought and passion." Wilde, who serves as middleman for all sorts of aesthetic notions, is here bridging the ideas of Baudelaire and the ideas of Hulme. Wilde's sense of form is more abstract than Hulme's, for Hulme hoped to precipitate out of an impression a granular image that is a microcosm for the feelings clustered about it. Wilde, instead, means what Gauguin meant when he thought of artistic form as "outside things." Thus Wilde is close to symbolism when he states, "Mere colour, unspoiled by meaning, and unallied with definite form, can speak to the soul in a thousand different ways. The harmony that resides in the delicate proportions of lines and masses becomes mirrored in the mind. The repetitions of pattern give us rest. The marvels of design stir the imagination."

Wilde is close to Art Nouveau, however, when he says, "Form is absolutely essential to art," for he thinks of form as a surface design. The distinctively surface quality of Art Nouveau is illustrated by Austin Dobson, who almost parodies Wilde's notion that a poem must move from form to feeling, from a pattern in verse to any possible emotional effect. The result in Dobson's case is *vers de société,* a feat performed in a poetic vacuum:

> You bid me try, BLUE-EYES, to write
> A rondeau. What!—forthwith?—tonight?
> Reflect. Some skill I have, 'tis true;
> But thirteen lines!—and rimed on two!
> "Refrain" as well. Ah! Hapless plight!
>
> Still, there are five lines—ranged aright.
> These gallic bonds, I feared, would fright
> My easy Muse. They did, till you—
> *You* bid me try!
>
> That makes them eight. The port's in sight—
> 'Tis all because your eyes are bright!

> Now just a pair to end in "oo"—
> When maids command, what can we do?
> Behold!—the Rondeau, tasteful, light,
> You bid me try!
>
> (1876)

This has the accent of early eighteenth-century verse, the artfulness of Gay and Pope's conversation pieces; and it reminds us that Oscar Wilde's witticisms are also a neo-rococo verbal skill. The faculty for *touching* a subject is one evidence of rococo taste, a refusal to be pedantic or heavy-handed; and taste reappears in poetry and design with Art Nouveau. *The Yellow Book* is neo-rococo in its amateur note, making life an art by finesse. The romantics tried to translate life to art without play. Wilde revives the rococo tone of play in his high aesthetic line. He is able to exist in exquisite style on the glaciers of Beauty where Mallarmé lost his breath, and Pater faltered.

Walter Pater and Paul Valéry wrote essays on Leonardo da Vinci, both proposing that Leonardo's genius was his ability to transmute his impressions to abstract beauty. "This curious beauty," Pater thinks, "is seen above all in his drawings, and in these chiefly in the abstract grace of the bounding lines. . . . No one ever ruled over the mere *subject* in hand more entirely than Leonardo, or bent it more dexterously to purely artistic ends." It goes without saying that this is a somewhat byzantine impression of Leonardo. Valéry follows further the theme of Leonardo's "mysterious clarity" until he discovers that art is a form of consciousness almost like a mathematical concept, and that the contours of ornament become "the formations of thought." "The characteristic of man is consciousness," Valéry says in *Variété, I,* "and that of consciousness is a perpetual emptying, a process of detachment without cease." Valéry's emptied consciousness is a last phase of symbolism; but his notion of form is a phase of Art Nouveau, for, he says, "The conception of ornament bears the same relation to all the arts that mathematics bears to all the sciences." By means of the "architectural imagination"—rhythms felt in consciousness—ornament becomes an abstraction reconciling art and science. As late as 1938 Valéry was lecturing on "Poetry and Abstract Thought," asserting that verse is essentially a pure music liberating us from the world of objects. Poetry is like dance, a configuration of the spirit. If poetry is not identical with abstract ideas, the poet nevertheless "has his abstract thought" whenever he enters the realm of purified consciousness. Valéry's own *Cimetière Marin* arose, he states, as a rhythm in consciousness, a rhythm that finally found its images. The poem, along with architecture or music, exists "like a monument from another world."

In his dialogue on the architect, *Eupalinos,* Valéry says that poetry, music, and architecture all "invoke constructions of the mind," the intelligible forms which "borrow a minimum from natural objects" and "imitate them as little as possible." One wonders whether Valéry remembered what Delacroix, that passioniate romantic, wrote in his *Journal* in 1852 about architecture, an art that is "ideal": "Architecture, unlike sculpture and painting, takes nothing directly from nature, and here it resembles the art of music." One wonders whether Valéry knew the architecture designed by Mackintosh with its deletion of all naturalism and its use of the functional, mathematical plane as at Hill House (1902–3), a construction which might be taken for Bauhaus work. Valéry says that the poet "fabricates by abstraction," and, like the geometer, envisions a cleansed rigorous beauty, a "drama of consciousness" that Mallarmé and the symbolists tried to write. Valéry thinks of his consciousness as an invisible audience in a darkened theatre, never seeing itself but always watching the spectacle on the stage, a scene of intelligible and possible things. The mind of the poet intensifies life and art to a consciousness of forms; and in his "universe of words" he has "une conception si abstraite et si proche des spéculations les plus élevées de certains sciences." At his highest moments Valéry reports that "everything seems clear, fulfilled, and there are no problems." So nothing really attracts him, he says, "but clarity." Under the pressure of such conceptions Art Nouveau becomes a "crystalline system," an ultimate purification of decorative to abstract art.

The aestheticism of the nineteenth century took another crystalline form in James Joyce's epiphany. Like Valéry, Joyce finds that the decorative contours of Art Nouveau are capable of being facets of consciousness. To the young Stephen, Beauty reveals itself as an essence, a "luminous silent stasis," a recognition of Form that the artist must represent: an "arrest" when the image appears with its "wholeness, harmony, and radiance." Stephen Dedalus is an aesthetic immoralist who transvalues all his values to the artistic value of a Beauty which "is the first formal esthetic relation of part to part in any esthetic whole," the means of knowing the *quidditas* of things, an enchantment purifying life to an artistic image. "In the virgin womb of the imagination the *word* was made flesh" for Stephen, who turns from Dublin, from home and church and woman to become an artist by allowing "the rhythmic movement of a villanelle" to design itself within his consciousness:

> Are you not weary of ardent ways,
> Lure of the fallen seraphim?
> Tell no more of enchanted days.

Stephen "drew less pleasure from the reflection of the glowing sensible world through the prism of a language manycoloured and richly storied than from the contemplation of an inner world of individual emotions mirrored perfectly in a lucid supple periodic prose." He is lulled by a "soft liquid joy" when "long vowels hurtled noiselessly and fell away, lapping and flowing back and ever shaking the white bells of their waves in a mute chime and mute peal and soft low swooning cry." Joyce would agree with Proust that only by its language can we "judge the intellectual and moral level a work has reached." No writer was more directly affected by the stylization that came with Art Nouveau, which with its sophisticated rhythms cleansed the arts of bric-a-brac and defined the contours that gave Joyce's beauty its "wholeness, harmony, and radiance." Joyce believed that the town clock is capable of an epiphany, of becoming suddenly luminous and revealing itself as an aesthetic image.

Nevertheless Joyce's epiphany is probably not so influential in modern style as the technique Art Nouveau transmitted to the imagists—to Hulme, Pound, and Eliot. Imagism originates in the clean, sharp, isolated detail or passage seen as an "impression" in the carefully worked-up verses of minor writers like Arthur Symons, who had an eye for the emblematic feature, the significant motif or visual paradigm:

> Cool little quiet shadows wander out
> Across the fields, and dapple with dark trails
> The snake-gray road coiled stealthily about
> The green hill climbing from the vales.
> (*"Arques—Afternoon,"* 1896)

This is one of the impressions Art Nouveau borrowed from symbolist verse, a pan-impressionistic notation that is capable of being translated by Pound into an "ideogram," a modern "hieroglyph." Whistler was fond of these vignettes, and so were the minor impressionists and post-impressionists like Sisley and Utrillo. T. E. Hulme revolted against the moist and bleary outpourings of romantic art by seeking hard images of a finite classic precision. These pan-impressionist images were not often hard; however, they did offer a visual formula for misty feelings, and they often had an emphatic accent. "Images in verse are not mere decoration," says Hulme, who finds his new beauty in "small, dry things": "To take a concrete example," he adds—"if you are walking behind a woman in the street, you notice the curious way in which the skirt rebounds from her heels. If that peculiar kind of motion becomes of such interest to you that you will search about until you get the exact epithet which hits it off, there you have a properly aesthetic emotion." Hulme is not favoring a return to realism or even to nature but to the exactitude with which an image may be presented. He has accepted almost to a point of overstatement the very principle on which Art Nouveau is based: that the object must find its contour, its stylized *motif,* if it is to be a successful artistic design.

Hulme fixes the boundary where the vague impressionism and symbolism of the nineteenth century, having been clarified by Art Nouveau—with its penetration by *japonisme*—give rise to the new imagism of Pound and Eliot. The heavy emphasis on the image in modern verse—the evening spread out against the sky "like a patient etherized"—is caused by this fusion of symbolism and an imagism which translated itself into ideograms in Pound's cinematic *Cantos* and Eliot's *Waste Land.* Hulme's plea to "render particulars exactly," to concentrate, to get the clean rhythm of the Japanese *haiku,* marks imagism as deriving from the Art Nouveau that produced "impressions" like Sharp's "Valley of White Poppies":

> A white bird floats there like a drifting leaf;
> It feeds upon faint sweet hopes and perishing dreams
> And the still breath of unremembering grief.
>
> And as a silent leaf the white bird passes,
> Winnowing the dusk by dim forgetful streams.
> I am alone now among the silent grasses.
>
> (1901)

The fine details appeared long ago in Rossetti's poems; the tonality and design are Japanese; the emotional overtones are symbolist evocations; the isolated motif is a technique of Art Nouveau. There is a similarity to the "Blue Symphony" by John Gould Fletcher, one of the first imagists, who shows the "musical" color of the Nabis:

> Blue and cool:
> Blue, tremulously,
> Blow faint puffs of smoke
> Across somber pools.
> The damp green smell of rotted wood;
> And a heron that cries from out the water.
>
> (1913)

The imagist designs are sometimes scrupulously *japonais:*

> O golden-red and tall chrysanthemums,
> you are the graceful soul of the china vase
> wherein you stand
> amid your leaves.
>
> (F. S. Flint: *"Chrysanthemums"*)

Hulme's own poems—all five of them—have this Art Nouveau brand of imagism.

Pound claimed that imagism did not use images as ornaments. In a sense this is true; yet the imagists accepted the motif, on which they played less volubly than Pound does in the *Cantos*. Pound, in fact, complicated and toughened his imagism

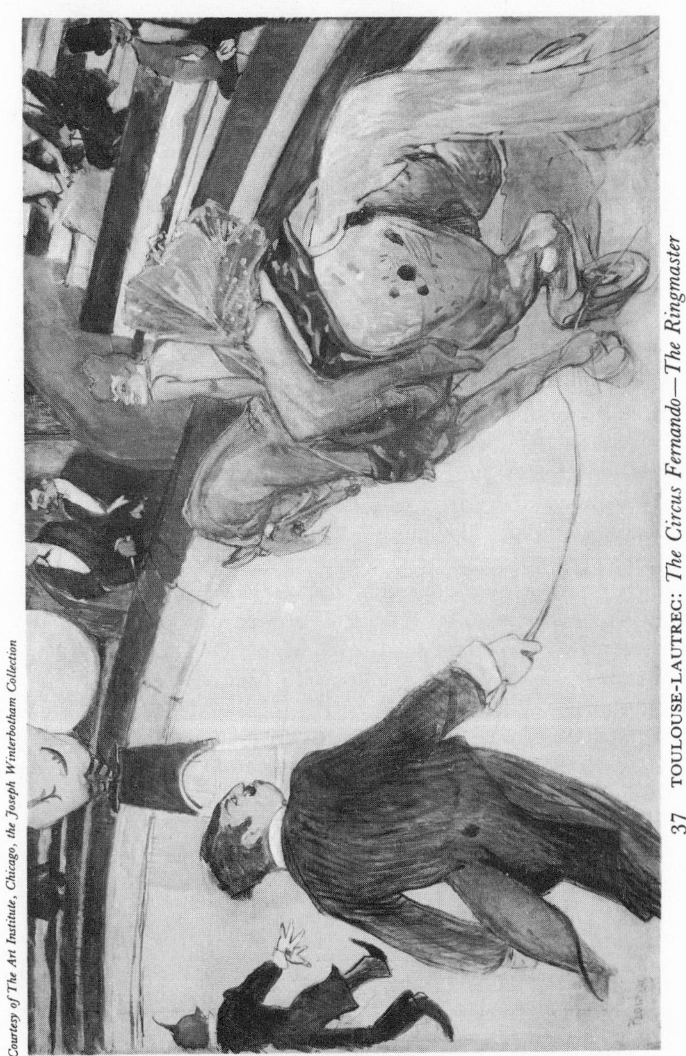

37 TOULOUSE-LAUTREC: *The Circus Fernando—The Ringmaster*

Courtesy of The Art Institute, Chicago, the Joseph Winterbotham Collection

by "superposition; that is to say it is one idea set on top of another." His ideogram is a means of abstracting the image to a higher, more cryptic level and giving it disruptive energy.

Pound has defined his ideogram as "an intellectual and emotional complex in an instant of time." It becomes cinematic by a kind of montage. Consequently Pound has endowed the early imagism deriving from Art Nouveau with a new concentration of meaning, new dimensions of reference, and turned imagist verse toward the expressionistic resources T. S. Eliot was able to exploit in *Prufrock,* where the yellow fog wraps itself about a window pane and falls asleep, malingeringly, in a London afternoon.

This expressionism traces back through another line of descent to Art Nouveau, too—the classic phase in Toulouse-Lautrec, whose poster art is a point of intersection for most of the stylizations reached by the nineteenth century [37]. Lautrec is indebted to the realists for his subjects and to the impressionists for his palette. He takes his angle from Degas, but his sense of design he shares with Gauguin, the *cloisonniste* painters, and Art Nouveau. He distorts space and abstracts forms, flattening his figures, abolishing shadows, making his line pictorial, simplifying his color to a decorative mosaic. His rhythm is borrowed from the Japanese print, but his drama is expressionistic. Lautrec is the most bizarre manifestation of Art Nouveau. If he looks backward to Manet, he looks forward to Matisse, another heir of Art Nouveau. Lautrec is a Nabi transfigured—and the earliest fauve. His documented scenes flicker before us with a cinematic mobility.

In Paris, at least, all the mannerisms of the century were drawing toward the art of a new era that was to find a major style—cubism, a painting that is more than a stylization because it was deeply rooted in a contemporary world-view and equipped to utilize the techniques refused by the nineteenth century until the last minute.

Part Four

THE CUBIST PERSPECTIVE

I

THE NEW WORLD OF RELATIONSHIPS: CAMERA AND CINEMA

"In the museum," Cézanne remarked, "the painter learns to think." By 1890, when he was painting *The Basket of Apples* [38], Cézanne was thinking hard, spilling these thoroughly realized apples across the top of a table that is speculatively broken upward on the right, tipping the surface until the fruit would, in nature, be rolling off, treating the napkin as a single white plane even if it droops over the edge of the table. The plate and other objects are warped into new gravitational fields of vision like those in Lautrec's scenes, where figures are buoyed up by steep graphic perspective.

This painting reminds us that a century earlier, at the close of the enlightenment, Immanuel Kant wrote that human experience is possible only when we have "a concept of an intelligible world." Dare to think, urged Kant: *sapere aude.* However faintly Pope thought, he had a concept of an intelligible world and could utilize the Newtonian world order in his verse. The nineteenth-century poet like Tennyson often dreaded to follow

Courtesy of The Art Institute, Chicago, the Helen Birch Bartlett Memorial Collection

38 CÉZANNE: *The Basket of Apples*

the scientist—perhaps because the scientists who most nearly affected men "as enjoying and suffering beings" were now biologists, not mathematicians. During the nineteenth century, art and science became alienated as they had not been alienated in the enlightenment; thus the intellectual roots of art were cut. Experiments such as impressionism and the naturalistic novel adapted certain methods from science; yet on the whole art and science seemed to be two incompatible kinds of experience or knowledge, and scientific theory and aesthetic theory seemed contrary. Matthew Arnold despairingly asked in his essay on "Literature and Science" how poetry can "exercise the power of relating the modern results of natural science to man's instinct for conduct, his instinct for beauty?" He was forced to admit, "I do not know how." He was in any case sure that science without poetry did not suffice. On an earlier page we have noted the effects of this alienation on poetry, for in his essay written in 1926 I. A. Richards asked whether the modern poet can be expected to deal with a God who is subject to a theory of relativity. Significantly enough, T. S. Eliot, whom Richards takes as an example of the plight of the modern poet, helpless before the science that has destroyed his beliefs, makes his maturest poetic statements by writing verse that is an "act of the mind" as well as a confession of faith:

> Time present and time past
> Are both perhaps present in time future,
> And time future contained in time past. . . .
> What might have been is an abstraction
> Remaining a perpetual possibility
> Only in a world of speculation.
> What might have been and what has been
> Point to one end, which is always present.
> (*"Burnt Norton"*)

Eliot is more intelligent than Pope, and has, perhaps unconsciously, made our most conceptual scientific theory—a theory of relativity—apposite to poetry now that this theory is "manifestly and palpably material to us as enjoying and suffering beings."

Wallace Stevens is another who insisted that the great feat of poetic imagination "lies in abstraction. The achievement of the romantic, on the contrary, lies in minor wish-fulfillment, and it is incapable of abstraction." Stevens does not of course mean rationalism; nevertheless he proposes that "we live in the mind." We have just noticed also how Paul Valéry argues that "the clear distinct operations of the mind" are not opposed to poetry; rather, poetry requires "our will to intelligence, and exercising to the full our powers of understanding." Valéry's hero is M. Teste, who holds, like Stevens, that "it is by a sort of abstraction that the work of art is constructed." The poem as a work of abstract thought demands what Stevens calls "liberty of the mind." Stevens goes on: "The truth seems to be that we live in the concepts of the imagination before the reason has established them." Immanuel Kant would have understood this statement. For Kant, at the height of the enlightenment, would have assumed that imaginative activity sometimes coincides with conceptual activity. Have we not been misled by the nineteenth-century romantic belief that the imagination means either emotional power or the concrete image, the metaphor alone. We have not supposed there is a poetry of ideas.

Cubism is above all an "art of conception," and it was born of thinking done by Cézanne and by Nabis like Sérusier, who said, "A painter must be intelligent." Gleizes and Metzinger repeat: "Without denying either sensation or emotion, the cubist has raised painting to the level of the mind"—*La peinture exigeait donc les connaissances solides.* This solves Baudelaire's problem of transposing *volupté* to *connaissance.* T. S. Eliot, speaking for the moderns, has said, "The only method is to be very intelligent."[1] We know what Eliot owes to the symbolists and the artists of the late nineteenth century who freed the motif from the anecdote, the illustrative, the weight of the object in its ordinary guise. Gleizes and Metzinger underscore the importance of this heritage of abstraction, to which Gauguin and the Nabis contributed so much, when they remark that "the visible world does not become the real world except by the operation of thought." They add: "It is not enough for a painter to see a thing; he must *think* it."

The fauvist painters, too, were able to abstract both line and color, and it is hard to say whether Picasso's *Demoiselles d'Avignon* (1907) is fauvist or cubist; yet it remains true that the cubists did what the fauves did not: they developed a theory—a theory that has the closest agreement with the theories of our science. Fauvism and cubism are alike quests for style, but the analysis of the world was pressed further in cubism, which undertook to represent the object in its "total existence."[2] In his *Theory of Figure Painting* André Lhote stresses what demands cubist art made on the mind: "The more the intelligence enters into the creation of a work of art, the more the painting can be said to have a maximum of existence." I. Rice Pereira, one of the neo-plastic painters, has said, "Every space has its own geometric structure and dimensions and belongs to different levels of experience." This sounds like a sentence from Alberti or another renaissance theorist; for in the renaissance, science was an aspect of art, and the painter, like the cubist or post-cubist, was aware of the mathematic of his day. The renaissance was creative partly because, like the enlightenment, it was eager to assimilate science to art.

Among the blockages in nineteenth-century art was the inability, or unwillingness, of the artist to utilize science intelligently, to make art genuinely contemporary. Or, worse, the science that most readily aroused a response was Darwinian biology, which seemed to sanction strong impulse and romantic feeling rather than intelligence.

Rodin's failures as an artist are informative. Temperamentally he was kin to Delacroix, and had a Wagnerian need to express energy, the nineteenth-century dynamism that disturbed Henry Adams and sent him, for refuge, to Chartres. To find an idiom for the titanic, Rodin experimented with wave-motions in his sculpture—the romantic motion that drove the great breaking billow in Géricault's *Raft of the Medusa*. Rodin's groups of figures curve inward, then are thrust horizontally outward in a surge leaping out of the block, like the head of *La Tempête* crying out in direct emotive attack. Rodin also specialized in the anatomical fragment—the hand, the head, the muscular body emerging from the unfinished marble. This is a brand of symbolism, for only a few details are stated. *The Last Vision* derives from Michelangelo's unfinished giants as well as from the techniques of symbolism—only a head, a suggestion of crossed hands, a translation of sculptural volumes into dim pictorial terms. It is significant that the Rodin Museum is hung with Carrière's gray misty paintings, for Carrière blurs everything he touches. Rodin substitutes vagueness for sculptural realization except in a few items like *La Femme Accroupie,* a massive simplification almost Egyptian. This evasive poetic technique is in sharp contrast to the sculptural value of Cézanne's proto-cubist planes. Rodin, in fact, never found his style, and there is an abiding conflict between his cloudy implications and his inherent fleshliness, a conflict from which Wagner also suffered. The vagueness reminds us of Maeterlinck; the mass reminds us of Michelangelo and the baroque. Rodin never reached any such conciliation as Renoir's sculptural abundance; and at moments he becomes a kind of John Singer Sargent in stone. Some of the Wagnerism is due to Rodin's quest for myth, leading him to subjects like *Eve, Orpheus, The Metamorphoses of Ovid,* the archetypal huge *Man Walking,* and the pompous cliché of *The Thinker*. Much of this titanism is merely emotional luxury, like *The Gates of Hell.* Some, like *The Kiss,* is simply vulgar.

Rodin's technical device is the intertwining of his figures, a tactic that gives the stone mobility and opens his volumes into a sculptural space later explored by Henry Moore. But Rodin never discovered the simultaneous space of an authentic modern like Cézanne or Calder, who uses the mobile as a solution to the problem of activity in sculpture. Instead, Rodin only complicates the old three-dimensional scenographic space: we must pass *around* his figures in spite of their intertwining and wave-motions; we do not see them in the cinematic perspective of cubist painting or abstract sculpture, a poly-dimensional space where time is "flattened" as it is in the montage-vision of Boccioni's *Bottle Developing in Space,* or Archipenko's openwork figures. Since Rodin's episodes develop in a Euclidean space-time system, the romantic forms of *Chute d'un Ange, Oceanides,* or *Fugit Amor* move within a space that is volumetric but not simultaneous. Rodin can render one profile at a given instant, episodically, and his surfaces appear, burst, and change within a succession of instants no matter how they intertwine. His work is endowed with the nineteenth-century sense of force; there is something Bernini-like in the explosion of his masses. But he lacks the architectural context of baroque sculpture, and his figures exist in a formless romantic infinity, not the framework of the baroque theatre. *The Gates of Hell* violates the architectural notion of a portal: their extreme mobility should have been expressed by a *revolving* door, and they are not baroque but picturesque. Rodin rebelled against the confines of Euclidean space without conceiving any other structure. He needed a relativity theory to make time another dimension of space, treated simultaneously as a field in which sculpture moves. He needed not the mythical poetry of the romantics and Wagner but the geometric constructions of Antoine Pevsner or Naum Gabo, who take motion in space as an aspect of contour in time.

With cubism these blockages disappear. They disappear in Cézanne, who was intelligent as Rodin was not. It is not desirable to depend heavily on Cézanne's often-quoted statement,

"Represent nature by means of the cylinder, the sphere, the cone. . . ." There are few cylinders, spheres, or cones in his painting. But there is a new occupation of space, for Cézanne was instinctively contemporary and somehow able to cope with the deeper problems behind the brushwork of Courbet and the early tachism of the impressionists, who broke up time by light, and space by their modular constructions. So in Cézanne the problem of sensation yielded to the problem of representation, which is the problem of Cézanne's conception of the world. It is a problem he attacks directly, without evasions. He did not read science or philosophy; like many great painters he seems to have been almost illiterate—certainly inarticulate. Nevertheless he was, in Gertrude Stein's sense of the word, contemporary because he felt strongly the new world of relationships in space being discovered in the philosophy of F. H. Bradley and the predecessors of Einstein—Riemann, Clifford, and Gauss.

In 1875 Clifford was writing that our ordinary laws of geometry do not apply to small portions of space, that these portions are comparable to little hills on the surface of a plane, and that distortion passes like waves from one portion of space to another. Van Gogh must have *felt* this motion when he painted the enormously powerful curved local spaces in ravines and water; much as Cézanne *felt* the dislocations of space in representing the masses of Montagne Sainte-Victoire [39], which appear to model the dimensions around them. In his landscapes Van Gogh forces the synthetist designs invented by Gauguin to bulge into the contours of a new topography that is nearly magnetic in direction.

In retrospect we can see the full significance of the cubist movement that made art contemporary and found a style. Cubism is a fruition of modern thought; for it was based, as Francastel states, on new conditions of life, on new formal techniques, and indirectly on a whole fund of scientific and philosophical speculation. I. Rice Pereira has said that modern painting is an image of our cognition, and that space is a symbolic extension of man's being. So it is with the cubists and their followers, since cubism is an art that expresses the condition of

39 CÉZANNE: *La Montagne Sainte-Victoire*

modern man, who has been forced to live in a world where there are, as Whitehead put it, no longer any simple locations, where all relations are plural.

Technically cubism is a breakdown of three-dimensional space constructed from a fixed point of view: things exist in multiple relations to each other and change their appearance according to the point of view from which we see them—and we now realize that we can see them from innumerable points of view, which are also complicated by time and light, influencing all spatial systems. Cubism is an attempt to *conceive* the world in new ways, just as renaissance art was an attempt to conceive the world in new ways. Thus the modes of abstraction that have grown from cubism have involved the intelligence. In a passage on "Art and Science" Naum Gabo indicates how these two are now interdependent:

> Whatever exists in nature, exists in us in the form of our awareness of its existence. All creative activities of Mankind consist in the search for an expression of that awareness. . . . The artist of today cannot possibly escape the impact science is making on the whole mentality of the human race. . . . The artist's task is not so pragmatic and straightforward as the scientist's; nevertheless, both the artist and the scientist are prompted by the same creative urge to find a perceptible image of the hidden forces in nature of which they are both aware. . . . I do not know of any idea in the history of man's culture that developed in a separate and independent compartment of the human mind. . . . To my mind it is a fallacy to assume that the aspects of life and nature which contemporary science is unfolding are only communicable through science itself. . . .[3]

Cubism may go beyond the modernity of science, for as Braque saw, "Art disturbs; science reassures." The truly contemporary artist is always slightly in advance of science for he is conscious of the atmosphere about him in a way the scientist or critic is not. Picasso painted *Guernica* long before Hiroshima was annihilated. Dostoevsky plumbed the unconscious before Freud. Braque and the early cubists eagerly accepted the challenge to deal with the object in all its new ambiguities: to disturb our vision of things, because as Braque remarks, "It is always desirable to have two notions—one to demolish the other."

The ideas behind cubist painting are reflected in all the modern arts. In writing on the music of poetry Eliot has seen that verse can suggest new "correspondences" in an age of relativity: "The music of a word is, so to speak, at a point of intersection: it arises from its relation first to the words immediately preceding and following it, and indefinitely to the rest of its context; and from another relation, that of its immediate meaning in that context to all the other meanings which it has had in other contexts, to its greater or less wealth of association."

Hence, also, the art of Joyce in *Finnegans Wake,* where each portmanteau phrase is an intersection in multidimensional meaning. Adrian Leverkuehn, the Faustian hero of Thomas Mann's novel, experiments with modulations between distant keys, "using the so-called relation of the third, the Neapolitan sixth," finding that "relationship is everything. And if you want to give it a more precise name, it is ambiguity."

Cubism exploited the rich ambiguity of the modern object exactly while science and the cinema were also discovering ambiguities in the modern view of things. The theory of relativity that evolves through F. H. Bradley, Whitehead, Einstein, and modern mathematics is only the scientific expression of "the new landscape" of the twentieth century, a landscape revealed for the first time in cubist painting and the cinema. Describing this landscape, Charles Morris has written: "Contemporary man must be able to move among and between diverse perspectives, cultural perspectives on the earth, spatial and temporal perspectives in the cosmos." Ortega y Gasset has furnished us with a philosophy of "perspectivism," which represents the complexity and ambiguity of our existence.

The changing perspectives on which we build our existence appear in the cinema, a modern form of illusion that relates motion, time, and space in a new kind of composition. It may well be that according to the law of technical primacy—the theory that in each era all the arts fall under the influence of one of the arts—the cinema has technical primacy during the years between the rise of cubism and the present. By the cinema one naturally means not Hollywood, which ordinarily uses the camera merely to record a nineteenth-century plot, but an artistic technique of presenting things as they exist in time by means of a composite perspective. The daguerreotype arrested things in space and time and used the old renaissance perspective, the closed scene, with posed figures, seen from a fixed angle. This rather documentary technique had its influence on the realistic novel, *trompe l'oeil,* and Degas' angle of vision. But the technique of the camera never produced a style until photography broke away from the old renaissance laws of composition and dealt with the problems of changing appearances in time and space. Then the camera, used with artistic consciousness, became the cinema and revised the stylizations of the daguerreotype into the multidimensional art that is deeply congenial to cubist painting. Whenever a technique produces a theory—that is, when a technique like photography becomes conscious—the groundwork for a style is laid. By 1912 Delaunay seems to have been conscious of a basically cinematic technique when he studied the *rythme tourbillant* of his colored disks. Gertrude Stein, with her sense that art must "live in the actual present," described all the modern arts as cinematic, although she doubted she had "ever seen a cinema" when she wrote *The Making of Americans* and claimed that "this our period was undoubtedly the period of the cinema and series production." "I was doing," she says, "what the cinema was doing, I was making a continuous succession of the statement of what that person was until I had not many things but one thing." Her early stories were "made up of succession and each moment having its own emphasis that is its own difference and so there was the moving and the existence. . . ."

By its revolution in thought and method of representing the world cubism created a cinematic style. The cubists began by rejecting the renaissance illusions of three-dimensional space and a closed orthogonal perspective. They renounced the figment of chiaroscuro along with the subterfuge of arranging solid volumes in a false distance. André Lhote boldly said he rejected "all the precautions which Old Masters took to cover up the arbitrariness of their chosen methods." So too, Ortega asked whether anything could be more artificial than Euclidean geometry—on which painting had been based. The cubists created a new flat perspective; they broke open the volumes of things by spreading objects upon shifting interrelated planes that did not violate the surface of the canvas, the space at the disposal of the painter as painter. This flat perspective meant also that painting could reintegrate itself with the wall, which could be treated like a cinematic screen. By representing the several faces of things simultaneously, the cubist dealt with the old problem of time and motion in new ways; objects "moved," but they were also immobilized in a complex design, offered to us in their calm being, their plural aspects conceived together. If the cubists "assassinated" objects, "so much the worse for objects"—as Picasso said to Zervos. This destruction was actually the reorganizing of the world by the mind. When Gleizes and Metzinger claim that the visible world becomes real only by the agency of thought, they are merely following Gauguin's principle that "art is an abstraction drawn from nature."[4] The cubist object no longer has a single or simple identity.

Yet this assassination of the object was not like the symbolist-expressionist distortion of things, for the cubists were nearly scientific in their destructions, loving the object and seeking to study it in its silent, dynamic power. In his talks with Zervos, Picasso said, "There isn't any such thing as abstract art. You must always start with something. Afterward you can remove all traces of actuality. There's no danger then anyway, because the idea of the object will have left its indelible mark." The cubist object remains even after it "is no longer discernible." The cubist found his reality among the shifting appearances of things. Gleizes and Metzinger saw in an object a multiple reality that can be defined only by multiple images: "An object hasn't any absolute form. It has many: as many as there are planes in the domain of meaning . . . Autant d'yeux à contempler un objet, autant d'images essentielles." In the same way Picasso took the painter's task as recording *une impression multidimensionelle*. Daniel-Henry Kahnweiler says that the main interest of cubists was to state in two dimensions what seems to have three—a form of polyphonic vision counterpointing the many facets of objects into a whole. Therefore, Kahnweiler insists, cubist painting is close to the new music of Satie and Schoenberg, which is horizontal in melody and vertical in harmony.

Cubist painting resolves the old conflict, disturbing to Descartes and John Locke and the academicians, between the "primary" qualities of an object (those features known to abstract thought—its mathematical properties) and its "secondary" qualities (those felt by the senses—its material properties). For the cubist both are aspects of the object, and neither is the ground of its reality. The cubist object is a point at which thought about the object (our conception of it) penetrates and reorders sense impressions and feelings. In its purity cubist painting refuses to attract us by appealing strongly to the eye or the emotions. It uses low hues and restrained lines; it breaks up the potent rhythm of the romantic line and confines itself to neutral greys, greens, tans, blues, black, and white. The cubist painter does not make a violent attack upon the object or upon us; he reduces the glaring fauvist color and surging line to an idiom of transparencies and a pictorial, instead of a spatial or emotive, depth. It is noted that the influence of Cézanne eventually killed fauvism.

At its extreme purity—in Braque's painting—cubism is a study of the very techniques of representation—painting about the methods of painting, a report on the reality of art. With Braque's intelligent and lyrical vision cubism devoted itself to what the French call the *tableau-tableau*—the painter's painting—which investigates both the object and the means of painting this object. As a *tableau-tableau* cubism reaches its most refined introspections, its most acute self-consciousness. Yet cubism was not at first doctrinaire; its relation to the world was too genuine. Braque's painting is a formal but not, however, an abstract world, since he never loses contact with the texture of objects he studies and destroys, the bottles, violins, fruits, and musical scores he fixes in the "luminous silent stasis" which James Joyce believed is the artistic triumph. Braque has a deep, long attachment to the still life [40], but the still life becomes for him a "poetic creation": "The painter," he explains, "doesn't try to reconstruct an anecdote but to establish a pictorial fact."[5] The *fait pictural*—the tableau-object—has complex and ambiguous modes of existence, belonging to different orders of reality, different levels of being, between the worlds of art and life. Sometimes to show how his painting adjusts to any level of reality the cubist assimilated into his pictorial world the very elements of actuality alien to painting—fragments of cord, cloth, newsprint, wood. Indeed, to show the equivocal relationships into which his work could enter—and also to affirm the existence of a world of art—the cubist needed collage, the texture of objects themselves, to underscore the points of intersection. The device of collage is one of the guarantees of the integrity of cubist art, its refusal to accept subterfuge, its denial of the single identity of things.

To prove that art and life intersect, that thought enters things, that appearance and reality collide, or coincide, at the points we call objects, the cubist relied on certain technical devices: a breaking of contours, the *passage,* so that a form merges with the space about it or with other forms; planes or tones that bleed into other planes and tones; outlines that coincide with other outlines, then suddenly reappear in new relations; surfaces that simultaneously recede and advance in relation to other surfaces; parts of objects shifted away, displaced, or changed in tone until forms disappear behind themselves.[6] This deliberate "oscillation of appearances" gives cubist art its high "iridescence." However we describe it, cubist painting is a research into the emergent nature of reality, which is constantly transforming itself into multiple appearances, at once fact and fiction. Cubism is a moment of crisis in the arts when "description and structure conflict" in a world of plural vision and classic form. Above all cubism refused any melodramatic stress, the literary subject, the "big" anecdote; it was not interested in the isolated episode, or the climax. Instead cubism was an ingenious examination of reality in its many contingencies, an experimental painting with the hardihood of modern science and thought.

Thus cubists gradually disengaged the object from three-dimensional space, from a limited, fixed point of view, and "dismantled" it into planes which give an illusion of closure and depth but which are always moving and readjusting themselves to one another. The cubist world knows both change and permanence; it is a region of process, arrest, transition, where things emerge into recognition, then revise their features; an Uncertainty Principle operates here as it does in the new science.

While the cubists were living in the Bateau Lavoir on the Montmartre slope their friend Princet, an amateur mathematician, used to talk with some of them about the science that has conceived our world as a structure of emergent relationships determined by one's point of view. The cubist world is the world of a new physics, of F. H. Bradley, who in 1893 in *Appearance and Reality* stated that reality can have no absolute contours but varies with the angle from which one sees it: "We

Courtesy of the Louse and Walter Arensberg Collection, Philadelphia Museum of Art

40 BRAQUE: *Still Life (c. 1917–18)*

have to take reality as many, and to take it as one, and to avoid contradiction." Anticipating Whitehead's theory of the essential relevance of every object to all other objects in the universe, Bradley defined the identity of a thing as the *view* we take of it—what Whitehead later called our prehension of it. Appearances belong to reality, and reality is intrinsic in varying appearances. Space is for Bradley only "a relation between terms which can never be found." Like Whitehead and the relativists, Bradley accepts the "irreducible plurality of the world" and affirms that "plurality and relatedness are but features and aspects of a unity." The absolute manifests itself in change, and changes reveal the nature of reality: "appearance without reality would be impossible, and reality without appearance would be nothing." Bradley's ingenious diagram makes this notion clearer than Whitehead ever did: many relations are possible within reality, which allows us to construct appearances from many points of view—

A B C D
B A D C
C D A B
D C B A

If these terms are given, we may read them in many directions and make contrary senses. The appearance of any item like A makes a design, though this design has no independent existence apart from the whole situation in which it appears. If we see only diagonals, then our reality will be limited to a pattern of A and D. But the configuration of the A items as a diagonal takes meaning only in relation to the other items B, C, D, which are relevant to any patterns we are able to select. In fact, any shifting of B, C, or D at once alters the appearance of A. Bradley lays the foundation for an existentialist approach, since each of the features of a situation is engaged in a total complex.

Whitehead expanded this theme of the essential relevance of all aspects of reality to reality itself: "all entities or factors in the universe are essentially relevant to each other's existence" since "every entity involves an infinite array of perspectives." In theory there is no such thing any longer as "simple location" in a universe where nothing can be located without involving everything else. By the same token there is no such thing in theory as an isolated instant in time, which becomes a function of motion: things cannot be placed by simple here and now when all speeds seem to be the same in relation to the speed of light. Thus

> The misconception which has haunted philosophic literature throughout the centuries is the notion of "independent existence." There is no such mode of existence; every entity is only to be understood in terms of the way in which it is interwoven with the rest of the Universe.
>
> (*Essays in Science and Philosophy*)

The world is a structure of variable relationships and multiple appearances.

To see why perspectives in cubist painting were "inquisitorial" and why the cubist world was a complex of shifting planes, we need to consider what Whitehead means by an event, which is the ultimate concrete entity in reality. A thing is an event which focusses out of process a certain complex of relations from a certain point of view; but every event or thing involves the rest of the universe—all other events and all other points of view. "An event," Whitehead remarks, "has to do with all that there is." It seems to be independent, but it is not; its independence is seen only by cutting away its relations to everything else and regarding it in isolation—that is, taking a very limited view of its actuality:

> The event is what it is, by reason of the unification in itself of a multiplicity of relationships. The general scheme of these mutual relationships is an abstraction which presupposes each event as an independent entity, which it is not, and asks what remnant of these formative relationships is then left in the guise of external relationships. The scheme of relationships as thus impartially expressed becomes the scheme of a complex of events variously related as wholes to parts and as joint parts within some one whole . . . the part evidently is constitutive of the whole. Also an isolated event which has lost its status in any complex of events is equally excluded by the very nature of an event. So the whole is evidently constitutive of the part.
>
> (*Science and the Modern World*)

Nature is therefore a structure of "emergent relationships"—emerging, according to our point of view, from the substrate neutral activity which must be called process because it has no features of itself and is like a fog out of which appear the various objects taking form for us depending on our prehension. Forms will differ as our prehensions change. And our prehensions change according to our situation in time and space. Things are merely an area of tension in constantly emerging conditions. An object or a fact is only a residue from the process continually under way in our universe.

In such a universe where things have no simple locations the old Newtonian values of absolute space and absolute time have gone. The only constant left is the speed of light, which is so nearly instantaneous that all spaces, times, and motions seem levelled when measured against it. The speed of light consumes differences in space and time until each location seems to be only an illusion depending on a local point of view. Suppose, for example, the eye could move with the speed of light and see, instantaneously, all the separate still shots along the outspread reel of a movie: these separate still shots, which appear extended in time and space when they are projected on a screen, would appear together, simultaneously, in a configuration that is static—as if the reel were run off instantaneously. Then we should be able to take in the total course of events at a glance; the sequence of episodes on the film would not be a plot unfolding in time or even by cause-and-effect, but a certain pattern of relationships that was there all the while, as a "given" in the first place. But for any eye unable to take in the total situation with the speed of light, the various events will emerge in time and space and motion according to the speed with which the still shots are projected. At either end of the scale of motion, there is no motion—and the time of the unfolding of these events is an illusion created by the rate at which the reel is run off.

Furthermore, the total configuration would have no meaning apart from the individual shots, each of which is an event in which all the other events are involved. The concrete event—the individual shot—is one aspect of a total configuration, which becomes only an abstraction without the individual shots or events of which it is composed. The film has no meaning apart from its separate shots; yet the meaning of the separate shots derives from their situation within the abstraction of the total film. Permanence has no meaning apart from change; the abstract and the concrete are two facets of a total structure. In Bradley's phrase, we must take this reality as many and as one, and avoid contradiction. But as Whitehead also says, "the very character of what is real is the transition of things, the *passage* one to another." Our world is a manifold of changing relationships which expresses itself as a "community of occasions" where every concrete actuality takes its place as an "irreducible stubborn fact" in an emergent total design.

If we assume, therefore, that abstract ideas are the basis of reality, we "misplace our concreteness" because all values are rooted in "matter-of-fact events" which are real enough but do not exist independently of other events. "The actuality is the value." Once again Whitehead foreshadows the existentialism of Sartre or Camus, who believe that individual man's existence is the ultimate reality of human experience, and that each man is inalienably free to act; yet in acting he involves himself in an engagement or commitment with all the Others. Whenever I choose, as I must, I choose for *you* also. Sartre says that "the destiny of man is placed within himself" since each must choose for himself and the value of one's life is generated by these choices. In this sense existence precedes essence. Yet by a contradiction inherent in reality when a man acts he commits himself to all other men, "deciding for the whole of mankind" and taking on "complete and profound responsibility." As with Whitehead, the concrete and the abstract are only two aspects of the same situation. The reality of human experience is always singular; but in choosing for myself I make history by choosing for others who impinge upon me. The existentialist says: I define myself by my relations with others who are *not* me; the Other is not the Self, but the Self needs the Other to realize the identity of the Self. Existentialism, then, is a philosophic extension of Whitehead's notion that the salvation of reality is the concreteness of the actual event, which loses meaning, however, apart from all events that have ever been or will ever be. The sum of Whitehead's relativity and our existentialism is that there is no simple location or independent existence in the sense of isolated existence. The essence of reality is in the relations entered into by each concrete event, each thing and person.

In all these ways cubism was modern since it was an analysis of the multiple identity of objects, their emergent relationships and engagement with other objects and events. Theo van Doesburg wrote: "A style comes into being when, after achieving a collective consciousness of life, we are able to set up a harmonious relationship between the inner character and the outward appearance of life."[7] Or as Gertrude Stein put it, "the composition in which we live makes the art which we see and hear." The cubist was not only contemporary; he was prophetic. The techniques of passage, transition, and transformation within and about the object expressed the collective consciousness of modern experience as nineteenth-century art did not. In Delaunay's *Tour Eiffel* (1910) the oscillations of the modern movement, the flickering consciousness of the new century with its cinematic eye and its laminated space were apparent. The atmospheric continuum of the impressionists was broken up into a dynamic collision of shots taken from different angles.

Delaunay uses the simultaneous perspective which finds its technique in the cinema and is common to all the modern arts, being adapted after cubism to the methods of abstract and nonobjective painting and sculpture and reappearing as tachism. Eisenstein notes that while cubism was flourishing in France, montage was thought to be "everything" in the cinema. In his words, montage is "a complex composed of film strips containing photographic images" so arranged that two or more shots are seen together, or nearly together, in a compound image. Thus "the polyphonic structure achieves its total effect through the composite sensation of all the pieces as a whole." Based not on sequence but counterpoint, montage compels us to see things in multiple perspective, telescoping time and fixing representation in a spliced image like the flattened cubist perspective.

Eisenstein explains the montage principle by quoting from René Guilleré's article on the jazz age, which equates the cinematic technique with syncopation:

> In both art and literature creation proceeds through several perspectives, simultaneously employed. The order of the day is intricate synthesis—bringing together viewpoints of an object from below and viewpoints from above.
>
> Antique perspective presented us with geometrical concepts of objects—as they could be seen only by an ideal eye. Our perspective shows us objects as we see them with both eyes—gropingly. We no longer construct the visual world with an acute angle, converging on the horizon. We open up this angle, pulling the representation against us, upon us, toward us. . . . That is why we are not afraid to use close-ups in films: to portray man as he sometimes seems to us, out of natural proportions. . . .
>
> In other words, in our new perspective—there is no perspective.
>
> (Quoted in *Film Sense*)

Guilleré means there is no one perspective, but synchronization or jazz syncopation with rhythms stated in sharp profiles brought up into the foreground.

Cézanne's still lifes had already synchronized perspectives in this way, tipping surfaces and breaking the horizon, bending the edges of plates and deforming curves into flat patterns. The deformation takes on a cinematic motion in Picasso's *Demoiselles d'Avignon* (1907), showing how the expressionistic distortions invented by Gauguin, Lautrec, and Art Nouveau were adapted to the cubist analysis of space. Whether or not under the influence of African sculpture, the *Demoiselles* proves that expressionism was influenced by the analysis of perspective in early cubism; and this analysis led to the filmlike montage passages at the right of Picasso's painting. The fragmented bodies of the *Demoiselles* flicker into multiple vision, the sliding planes of Braque's chessboards and tables. Cubism absorbed much of the disturbance in fauvist painting and theorized it into a style, a representation of modern time and space which could be treated only by means of the compound image with its simultaneous changing relationships. If Art Nouveau led toward fauvism and abstract art, cubism after the *Demoiselles* transcribed both Art Nouveau and fauvism into contemporary cinematic statement.

The intricate synthesis of the cinema was used with great

virtuosity in Picasso's *Atelier de la Modiste* [41] in 1926, a painting that seems to be projected on a screen in black and white in mobile complications adapting the double outline (*Wasserspiegel*) technique of Art Nouveau to a jazz syncopation. The painting is nearly a full illustration of the cinematic perspective defined by Eisenstein: there is even the effect of the close-up, the representation being pulled upon us, with flattening and distortion of outlines. These involved and shifting silhouettes give a new dimension to the graphic art of Beardsley, and they have the expressive foreshortening of Matisse's fauvist space. They are also closely related to the biomorphic forms of Joan Miró. The three figures and their reflected images, the mirror (or the doorway), the table, the chair are seen "with both eyes" in several perspectives—a montage study of activity held "close to the wall." As in a movie, the third dimension is reduced to an optical illusion, and space becomes an ideogram, losing its realistic value to enter a pictorial composition. There *is,* of course, an ingenious triptych-like basic organization, although the extraordinary passage of the images over the entire surface is another result of impressionist experiments with the fleeting appearances of things. All these cinematic

Musée d'Art Moderne, Paris, Archives Photographiques

41 PICASSO: *Atelier de la Modiste*

Gift of Mrs. Simon Guggenheim, Collection, The Museum of Modern Art, New York

42 PICASSO: *Girl Before a Mirror*

techniques are carried over into *Guernica* (1937), which adds to the montage of the *Atelier* the implication of being a cartoon, thus bringing a note of contemporary journalism. Again Picasso works in black and white, perhaps suspecting that the cartoon-strip in the press is like the movie. The syncopation is much more frantic in *Guernica,* convulsing and compounding the jazz of the *Atelier* to a progressive phase.

Picasso's use of montage is increasingly learned, as it is in James Joyce. He extracts, for example, a mythical dimension from his montage in *Girl Before a Mirror* (1932) [42]. Resorting to the archetypal theme of Vanity—the mediaeval motif of Beauty regarding her own image—he treats his Girl in a stained-glass technique, adapting to boudoir uses a *Belle Verrière* diapered background as basic geometry along with the leaded mediaeval medallion. Who is this Girl? If we "read" the two parts of the painting—the Girl and her Image—we discover that she is a contemporary Mary who is also Isis, Aphrodite, the Adolescent before her Mirror. There is also a Freudian image of the self, the daylight or conscious self at the left echoed in the Id-image on the right, the dark self. So the Virgin or Vanity or Venus here presents herself under two more guises: Diana and Hecate, the light and dark phases of the moon-goddess; or, perhaps, Persephone, the goddess who leads a double existence during the fertility-cycle. The dark self also suggests the savagery of the maenad; or the figures on a totem pole; or the shrouded body, the mummy, about to be laid in the grave; or the Fayum portraits on Coptic sarcophagi. The shrouded figure, in turn, suggests the veiled image of the nun who has died to the world, to vanity. And the breasts are not only breasts but apples; so here is a modern Eve, her womb seen in two different perspectives. Anticipating the X-ray technique of Tchelitchew, Picasso has analyzed the organs of the two images by a roentgen-view; there is an X-ray of the skeleton, the ribs, in the darker image; then the ribs become a quite different motif in the Girl herself, who seems to be wearing a striped bathing suit and thus becomes a bathing-beauty—again the modern Venus. The multiple images of the full and crescent moon, the full and profile body and face, the skeletal and fleshly features create a montage that has psychological, religious, and legendary meaning as well as abstract design in line and color. The fauvist distortions have been intellectualized into a cinematic style that synchronizes.

The principle of synchronization has been the basis of even the mechanical devices of the new century—the synchromesh gear is a means by which varying speeds and parts are brought into adjustment. Gertrude Stein suspected that the cinema is the primary art of the twentieth century because it synchronizes. If, she says, the artist is to be contemporary he must have the "time-sense" of his day; and the time-sense of this century is symbolized in the American assembly-line method of production; the automobile is conceived as a whole and assembled from its parts by a process of prefabrication. In the nineteenth century, with its historical and evolutionary time-sense, its plotted novels with their cause-and-effect sequence of events, their climactic scenes, their logical denouements, there was "the feeling of beginning at one end and ending at another." Now there is a "conception of the whole," the synchronization corresponding to cinematic montage or juxtaposition of elements. The twentieth-century mobile design synchronizes changing forms into patterns where time is a function of space; not only in Calder's mobiles, but as early as 1912, when Boccioni's sculpture *Bottle Developing In Space* opened up composite views of the solid object by means of syncopation, which is jazz movement and the inherent tempo of the early twentieth century.

Gertrude Stein remarks that melodramatic events have lost their meaning for us; there are no longer "decisive" battles but, instead, total wars during which the irreducible concrete fact is the G.I. standing on a street corner waiting for something to happen. Our perspective has been flattened even historically. "And so what I am trying to make you understand," Gertrude Stein wrote, "is that every contemporary writer has to find out what is the inner time-sense of his contemporariness." Our time-sense is cinematic because, as she says, "In a cinema picture no two pictures are exactly alike each one is just that much different from the one before." There is a writer's "building up" of an image from recurrent statements each a little different from the one before and after.

Whitehead has pointed out that what looks like permanence is actually only recurrence. Therefore from our sense of movement emerges a total pattern, the montage that brings Representation A into counterpoint with Representation B in a design that is at once mobile and static. Gertrude Stein remarks, "The better the play the more static." This strange opinion is due to her contemporary sense of a total configuration—a modern law of fatality that has some resemblance to a Greek sense of fatality in a drama where man suddenly finds himself in a certain *situation*. The cubist-cinematic time-sense is classic in this way, for all classic art has a certain stillness that is a synoptic view of action.

In some of her short stories Gertrude Stein attempted to catch the time-sense of the cinema to illustrate the notion that there is no such thing as repetition and that recurrence is the genuine modern movement, the recurrence of separate "shots" in the film—images differing from each other only minutely but giving a sense of existence in time and space. Nothing happens in these stories, which are static and must be read as if they presented in "flattened" form a situation to be taken only in its total configuration. "Miss Furr and Miss Skeene" (1922) is this sort of experiment in a cinematic mode:

> Helen Furr had quite a pleasant home. Mrs. Furr was quite a pleasant woman. Mr. Furr was quite a pleasant man. Helen Furr had quite a pleasant voice a voice quite worth cultivating. She did not mind working. She worked to cultivate her voice. She did not find it gay living in the same place where she had always been living. She went to a place where some were cultivating something, voices and other things needing cultivating. She met Georgine Skeene there who was cultivating her voice which some thought was quite a pleasant one. Helen Furr and Georgine Skeene lived together then. . . .
>
> They stayed there and were gay there, not very gay there, just gay there. They were both gay there, they were regularly working there both of them cultivating their voices there, they were both gay there. Georgine Skeene was gay there and she was regular, regular in being gay, regular in not being gay, regular in being a gay one who was not being gay longer than was needed to be one being quite a gay one. They were both gay then there and both working there then.

The last paragraph suggests Whitehead's idea that events are a form of recurrence taking place in process. Indeed this prose gets as close as it can to the process from which events emerge.

Eisenstein intends, like Gertrude Stein, to do away with theatre, the nineteenth-century story. Instead, he bases his cinematographic technique on the Japanese ideogram, which he sees as a form of montage. Once again, then, we come to

Pound's use of the ideogram for "superposition"—"that is to say it is one idea set on top of another." If Eisenstein seems to have taken some of his notions about montage from the Japanese *kabuki,* a stylized dramatic form, Pound, we know, took his "superpository images" from Fenollosa's studies of the ideogram. Apollinaire developed his "calligrams" almost at the same hour while Pound, Eisenstein, and the cubists were using the same perspective. The short poem known as the *haiku* also led imagist verse toward a cinematic technique, which appears in the synchronization and syncopation of Eliot's *Waste Land,* in turn indebted to Pound's ideogrammatic methods. In effect both Pound and Eliot began writing as imagist poets who developed a technique much like Eisenstein's in the film; for Eisenstein says he wanted to "dismember" events into a montage of various shots, and "by combining these monstrous incongruities, we newly collect the disintegrated event into one whole." He uses an "optical counterpoint" like the counterpoint in the traditionalist verse of Eliot, who closes *The Waste Land* with a syncopated passage resembling the syntax of the film—a "graphic conflict"—or the collisions in Japanese theatre, where two features or sides of an actor are sharply posed:

> London Bridge is falling down falling down falling down
> *Poi s'ascose nel foco che gli affina*
> *Quando fiam uti chelidon*—O swallow swallow
> *Le Prince d'Aquitaine à la tour abolie*
> These fragments I have shored against my ruins
> Why then Ile fit you. Hieronymo's mad againe.
> Datta. Dayadhvam. Damyata.
> Shantih shantih shantih

In his essay on the cinema Malraux says that the nineteenth century had a fanatic need of the Object in painting which went along with the plotted narrative in literature. The new method is, instead, *découpage,* truncating the object and making a symbol of it in cinema and literature. The *découpage* in Eliot's passage is really the method in Pound's *Cantos,* which are built about certain motifs treated by superposition of images excerpted from Eastern and Western history and literature. These superpositions—an extremely complex montage—are striking in Pound's use of Chinese history in Cantos LII–LXI, and in the Chinese ideograms embedded throughout the later stretches of his ambitious work with its flattened and timeless perspective or syncopation. In Canto LXXV the mention of Buxtehude and the "Stammbuch of Sachs in yr/luggage" is followed by a musical score, serving for the rest of the Canto. Thus Pound and Eliot create a multidimensional vision, and even their irony is due to a montage-principle of placing together statements having an entirely different poetic tone, as when Eliot opens the third section of *The Waste Land* by complicated and most divergent references and images, causing incongruities that are like the intentional discords in our music or painting.

> The river's tent is broken: the last fingers of leaf
> Clutch and sink into the wet bank. The wind
> Crosses the brown land, unheard. The nymphs are departed.
> Sweet Thames, run softly, till I end my song.
> The river bears no empty bottles, sandwich papers,
> Silk handkerchiefs, cardboard boxes, cigarette ends
> Or other testimony of summer nights. . . .

The lines show that Eliot's impersonal theory of poetry is also a form of montage, for, as he says, the contemporary poet works with the poetry of the past, employing it in new relations for new effects. He exploits traditional motifs, as Picasso did in *Girl Before a Mirror;* he has only a medium to use, not a personality—and in this he parts from the symbolists, and the fauves. So Eliot uses Marvell's lines

> But at my back I always hear
> Time's winged chariot hurrying near

in wholly unexpected relations:

> But at my back in a cold blast I hear
> The rattle of the bones, and chuckle spread from ear to ear.

This is what Eliot calls, in his essay on Joyce, the "mythical" method of the novel: "manipulating a continuous parallel between contemporaneity and antiquity." It is Eliot's own means of "making the modern world possible for art."

Joyce's *Ulysses* illustrates the montage principle in its widest application. Leopold Bloom is a modern Ulysses who during his day in Dublin re-creates in "mythical" episodes the events of the *Odyssey,* meeting his Telemachus in the young Stephen, confronting the Sirens and Circe, descending to the underworld when Paddy Dignam is buried, returning to that unfaithful Penelope in the person of Molly Bloom, who, like Picasso's Girl, is an archetypal image of the great goddess debased by Joyce's composite vision. The portmanteau language here and in *Finnegans Wake* gives instantaneous cross references between myth, philology, psychology, and music; and it adapts itself to stream-of-consciousness, which is likewise montage. As Leopold Bloom walks through the cemetery after Paddy's funeral he invents a new "eulogy in a country churchyard":

> Besides how could you remember everybody? Eyes, walk, voice. Well, the voice, yes: gramophone. Have a gramophone in every grave or keep it in the house. After dinner on a Sunday. Put on poor old greatgrandfather Kraahraark! Hellohellohello amawfullyglad kraark awfullygladaseeragain hellohello amarawf kopthsth. Remind you of the voice like the photograph reminds you of the face. Otherwise you couldn't remember the face after fifteen years, say. For instance who? For instance some fellow that died when I was in Wisdom Hely's.

The montage at Paddy's grave is more simultaneous, since Leopold is aware, instantaneously, of the need to take off his hat, the sickening plunge of the coffin, the chap in the mackintosh he doesn't know, Ned Lambert's nice soft tweed, his own dressy suits when he lived in Lombard Street, the spatter of rain. The portmanteau texture is most complex in *Finnegans'* multiple layers of language, an X-ray technique applied to syntax as well as consciousness.

As early as *Portrait of the Artist* Joyce was doing away with conventional perspective, opening up the narrative in Eisenstein's sense, pulling it against us in a new immediacy like a film close-up, shifting its language from prose to poetry and giving an impression of the various facets of consciousness, changing from the texture of the diary to the sermon to dialog to meditation—devices already exploited in that freakish eighteenth-century novel *Tristram Shandy,* one of the first experiments in montage, dislocations in time, double exposures of sensibility.

Even the "metaphysical complexities" admired by the New Critics are cinematic, for "ambiguity" and "irony" are said to bring together conflicting moods, and do not arise from *alternations* of mood, as in comic relief, but from juxtaposition. We now see that Shakespeare had his own montage; he did not alternate comic and tragic (as the nineteenth-century critics used to explain) but fused his comic and tragic meanings in a truly modern way in his intenser plays like *Hamlet,* where the Prince's antic disposition makes his jesting with Ophelia and Polonius a sign of disgust nearly unbearable, as it is in the graveyard when he asks Horatio, "Why may not imagination trace the noble dust of Alexander till 'a find it stopping a bunghole?" Similarly Eliot's Prufrock by a wrenching irony says he should have been a pair of claws scuttling across the floor of silent seas.

Montage effects are deep in the absurdist themes of our existential thought. Man's existence as we now see it is a conflict or collision of opposites. These contradictions in present experience are not reconcilable by logic; yet they are, as Kierkegaard said, reconciled in *me.* Man is free only when he is engaged; he is heroic but comic; he must act rationally without having any rational premises to stand on; he finds his self only in the face of "the others"; his being is grounded in nothingness; his very consciousness is a form of *dédoublement,* a splitting open of experience by an awareness that he is aware, a dissociation of the self watching the self. One's personality dissolves into changing profiles, which must be seen together. Existentialism is an "ethic of ambiguity."

Ortega y Gasset, like the cubists, supposes that the structure of reality depends on the view we take of it: there are as many views as there are modes of consciousness. His philosophy of perspectivism is an attempt of the contemporary mind to cope with contradictions between doubt and belief, between the mind and reality outside the mind: "Perspective is the order and form that reality takes for him who contemplates it," Ortega writes. The grave philosophic error is to suppose there is an absolute perspective. That is to do in philosophy what renaissance perspective did in space—to presume there is only one system. There is no absolute space because there is no absolute perspective. To be absolute, space would cease being real and become only an abstraction; and thus Ortega accepts the premises from which Bradley and Whitehead began, namely, that many differing perspectives co-exist in reality:

> Perspective is one of the component parts of reality. Far from being a disturbance of its fabric, it is its organizing element. A reality which remained the same from whatever point of view it was observed would be a ridiculous conception. . . .
>
> Every life is a point of view directed upon the universe. Strictly speaking, what one life sees, no other can. . . . The persistent error . . . is the supposition that reality possesses in itself, independently of the point of view from which it is observed, a physiognomy of its own. . . . But reality happens to be, like a landscape, possessed of an infinite number of perspectives, all equally veracious and authentic. The sole false perspective is that which claims to be the only one there is.
>
> *(The Modern Theme)*

To confine a view of reality to a single or orthodox conception is to empty it of meanings. To suppress the individual is to amputate the content of reality and impoverish it for all of us. That is why Ortega defines liberalism as the supremely civilized virtue, the capacity to live with the enemy. Once Ortega remarked that no two cameras can take the same photograph of a scene. As man changes his point of view, reality changes its nature for him. In a world of private and changing perspectives "the reality of the object increases as its relationships increase."[8] The meanings of reality emerge within reality itself. Or, as Ozenfant put it, "Cubism is painting conceived as related forms which are not determined by any reality external to those related forms." Ortega and the cubists yield us a fuller vision of reality than was possible in any art based on a single angle. If one of the properties of reality is to reorganize itself from different points of view, then the cubist dismantling of the object is one of the amplest readings of reality in Western art.

The cubist painter never deceived himself that his images represented the world as it "is," or that his imitation was issued on any gold standard of reality. For the cubist, reality is at once actual *and* fictitious, depending on our approach to it and our situation within it. During his cubist phase Picasso said, "From the point of view of art there are no concrete or abstract forms, but only forms which are more or less convincing lies." Our illusion conditions the nature of reality, and reality produces our illusions. As Bradley once remarked, without reality there is nothing to "appear" although these "appearances" are not reality. Thus cubists accepted the object; for them the world exists as it did not for their forebears the symbolists. Cubist painting is a scene of conciliation between the naïve opposites of nineteenth-century art—realism and symbolism. The cubist destroyed the solid factual world of photography, penetrating this world by thought, making it real, as Gleizes and Metzinger said, by the impact of the mind upon it, by studying its relation to consciousness. He achieved what Cézanne hoped to achieve, something solid *and* artificial. Kahnweiler said that the cubist object appears "simultaneously," its multidimensional existence signified by intersections of planes on the surface of the canvas. The cubist painted object is reconstructed into another order of being, removed from the injuries of time and space, for depth is no longer equated, as it was in renaissance vision, with the time it takes to enter that depth. Yet the cubist does not deny the value of time, for it is time that causes changing appearances. The time in which cubist objects exist is a new co-ordination—inherent in space. The cubist object has an ambiguous contemporary mode of being, a plural identity apparent only as a passage between thing and idea, fact and fiction. Cubism is a structure emerging from process. It has literary as well as painted and sculptured forms.

II

CUBIST DRAMA

When Luigi Pirandello wrote *Six Characters in Search of an Author* in 1921, he called it a "comedy in the making." It is a very highbrow study of oscillation of appearances in the theatre. Just as the cubist broke up the object into various planes, or as photomontage gave its own sort of polyphonic vision by means of combined shots, so Pirandello offers a compound image in drama. He surrenders the literary subject while the cubist is surrendering the anecdote, and treats his theatre as a plane intersecting art and life, explaining in his prefatory note that "the whole complex of theatrical elements, characters and actors, author and actor-manager or director, dramatic critics and spectators (external or involved) present every possible conflict." He is concerned with the collision between art and actuality, the theatrical crisis where the imitation of life and life itself appear as a passage between events on the stage and events in our existence. His play is a research into the plural aspects of identity, and he concludes that there are many possible levels of reality at which things can happen. He has penetrated the old theatrical plot by thought, much as the cubist penetrated objects, and having conceived his problem as an encounter of art with life, he has discovered a "way to resolve it by means of a new perspective"—a perspective like a flat-pattern cubist illusion.

In *Six Characters* the action (which is not a "play" at all) improvises upon certain dramatic situations as being reality and upon certain events in life as being art. While a company of actors is rehearsing a play—by Pirandello himself, for the planes of reality begin to shift at once—six members of a family (father, mother, legitimate *and* illegitimate children) enter the bare stage and ask to be allowed to act out (or "realize") the drama of their lives; for an author has conceived them but not written them into any script. Theirs is a history of a broken home caused by the mother's infidelity. Against the manager's inclination, against the inclination of the actors, the six characters try to represent their sad lives in acted form, which at once brings the difficulty that they cannot interpret for the professionals the meaning of the plot they have lived and are attempting to realize. "The drama," explains the Father, "is in us, and we are the drama." In other words, theatre breaks down. The effort of the characters to represent themselves on the stage is finally blocked when one of the six, the unhappy Boy, in a fit of despair, shoots himself. Some of the professional actors take this to be an artistic climax; but it is a genuine suicide. The Father shouts "Pretence? Reality, sir, reality!" By this time the director does not care: "Pretence? Reality? To hell with it all. . . . I've lost a whole day over these people, a whole day!" The ambiguity of the illusion is emphasized when at the close of the second "act" a stage hand drops the curtain by mistake, leaving the Father and the director in front of it, before the footlights, isolated from both audience and the "characters" and other actors. The end of the first act comes when the director, to gather his wits, calls off rehearsal—which is not rehearsal at all, but an equivocal passage from life that is being translated into art by characters who wish to express their life in dramatic form.

By refusing the momentum of plot Pirandello is left with the formal art-problem of writing a drama about the writing of a drama, a final purification of the nineteenth-century problem of treating life as art, or taking the art-view of life. Like the cubist painting about the painting of a painting, Pirandello's play is a sort of *tableau-tableau* showing the relation between actuality and its representation. The cubists used the textures of actuality in the form of collage to bring their art-structure into proper focus; and they used it impromptu. Sometimes they quoted a few legible details of objects in a frankly photographic way so that the clichés of painting could be better contrasted with the fictions of flat-pattern perspective. In thus avoiding the tyranny of the literary subject they discovered what Piet Mondrian a little later emphasized, that "the expression of reality cannot be the same as reality." Into his formal study of the writing of a drama Pirandello has deliberately inserted a good many theatrical clichés as a sort of collage: the professional actors, whose vocation is like that of the traditional model or lay figure used by painters, rely on all the customary mechanisms of the stage; and the director takes the attitude of the commercial theatre toward doing a play. He fails entirely to mediate between the professional troupe who are rehearsing a Pirandello script and the six displaced characters who have blundered into the commercial theatre from reality.

These six belong to life yet at the same time they do not belong to it; they are like the things Picasso "assassinated" in the interest of total representation. Their impromptu appearance on the "legitimate" stage is a double exposure of reality and illusion. There is also the bona-fide audience (which may or may not represent actual life). All these levels of representation are held together in a simultaneous perspective of transparent dramatic planes to be read in many directions at the same time. The final test, of course, is whether the events of life are susceptible of being interpreted by drama anyhow, or whether the experience of the six characters can be realized until they appear in some artistic composition. The Boy's suicide is a shocking collage. We cannot say that these persons exist off the stage; and we cannot say they live on the stage. Above all, what is the stage? Hamlet had already raised Pirandello's questions about drama's being a mere dream of passion. The six characters, the director, the actors rehearsing Pirandello come into every sort of encounter. If the six exist at all, they do so in some state of emergence. When they enter, "a tenuous light surrounds them, almost as if irradiated by them—the faint breath of their fantastic reality." This is their cubist iridescence of form.

The instant the six appear, the planes of representation are displaced. The Father tries to state their situation: "The drama consists finally in this: when that mother re-enters my house, her family born outside of it, and shall we say *superimposed* on the original, ends with the death of the little girl, the tragedy of the boy, and the flight of the elder daughter. It cannot go on, because it is foreign to its surroundings. So after much torment, we three remain: I, the mother, that son." But the Son stands in the background refusing to be identified with the rest of the six, commenting upon the whole enterprise as being merely "Literature." In vain the Father protests, "Literature indeed! This is life, this is passion." Yet the Son will not take his part in any theatrical representation; nor does he belong to life either. "Mr. Manager," he insists, "I am an 'unrealized' character, dramatically speaking; and I find myself not at all at ease in their company. Leave me out of it, I beg you." There he is, a figure to be fitted into the composition against his will, adding a further difficult dimension as if he had broken loose from the terms of the problem as Pirandello posed it. We cannot even place him as collage.

For the Father the drama lies in taking a point of view on events—a prehension, Whitehead would call it. He argues, "For the drama lies all in this—in the conscience that I have, that each one of us has. We believe this conscience to be a single thing, but it is many-sided. There is one for this person, and another for that. Diverse consciences. So we have this illusion of being one person for all, of having a personality that is unique in all our acts. But it isn't true. We see this when, tragically perhaps, in something we do we are, as it were, suspended, caught up in the air on a kind of hook." This is the cubist suspension of the object. When the Father sees the professional actors trying to play his "role," speaking his "part" in the clichés of their art, he exclaims, getting more and more confused, "I don't know what to say to you. Already I begin to hear my own words ring false, as if they had another sound."

Pirandello invites us to examine the texture of his drama exactly as the cubist invites us to examine the contrasting textures in his painting, the very invitation raising doubt about holding the mirror up to nature. The most "natural" scene in the rehearsal comes when two of the characters, Madam Pace and the Step-Daughter, begin to speak so quietly and casually that the actors—who are trying to learn the "parts"—object it's impossible to play the scene that way. The director agrees: "Acting is our business here. Truth up to a certain point, but no farther." Pirandello thus parodies Cézanne's approach to art: "I have not tried to reproduce nature," Cézanne said: "I have represented it." The manager wishes a single, simple illusion of reality. The Father points out that any such illusion makes drama only "a kind of game." Naturally the actors think it no game: "We are serious actors," they protest; they are artists. In desperation the Father then asks, "I should like to request you to abandon this game of art which you are accustomed to play here with your actors, and to ask you seriously once again: who are you?" The director, badly upset by this remark, resents having his identity questioned by a mere dramatic character: "A man who calls himself a character comes and asks me who I am." By the Father's reply, Pirandello hints that represented forms may be more real than actualities: "A character, sir, may always ask a man who he is. Because a character has really a life of his own. . . ." The reality may be an appearance; as the Father says, "You must not count overmuch on your reality as you feel it today, since, like that of yesterday, it may prove an illusion for you tomorrow." Gide would agree, and T. S. Eliot, who writes

> You are not the same people who left that station
> Or who will arrive at any terminus. . . .
>
> (*"Dry Salvages"*)

Pirandello is only characteristic of the many others in modern theatre who have tried to break through the boundaries between the stage and life; and besides, the problem became a traditional one anyhow after Hamlet's advice to the players. This does not, however, make it less contemporary.[9]

With Pirandello it was almost obsessive, and coincided with the cubist analysis of illusion and reality. *Each In His Own Way*

(1923) returns to the dramatic illusion "based upon an episode in real life." In this play the audience takes part, for among them are "real" persons whose lives have been dramatized in the "play" going on behind the footlights. These persons, objecting that "the author has taken it from real life," gather in the "lobby" after the first act to attack Pirandello and to break up the performance on the stage, which deals with a love affair between "a certain Moreno Woman" and "Baron Nuti," whose names have been in the newspapers. The directions Pirandello wrote for this interlude show how he was experimenting with multidimensional theatre:

> This scene in the lobby—Spectators coming out of a theatre—will show what was first presented on the stage as life itself to be a fiction of art; and the substance of the comedy will accordingly be pushed back, as it were, into a secondary plane of actuality or reality. . . . The Moreno Woman and Baron Nuti are present in the theatre among the spectators. Their appearance, therefore, suddenly and violently establishes a plane of reality still closer to real life, leaving the spectators who are discussing the fictitious reality of the staged play on a plane midway between. In the interlude at the end of the second act these three planes of reality will come into conflict with one another, as the participants in the drama of real life attack the participants in the comedy, the Spectators, meantime, trying to interfere.

Pirandello "destroys" drama much as the cubists destroyed conventional things. He will not accept as authentic "real" people or the cliché of the theatre any more than the cubist accepts as authentic the "real" object, the cliché of deep perspective, the contour of volumes seen in the light of the studio—or under sunlight either. The object, say Gleizes and Metzinger, has no absolute form; it is only a passage in possible relationships, with many relevances that are never fixed. Except by a blunder we cannot drop the curtain on Pirandello's drama because there is no clear boundary between life and art. Nor can the cubist painter isolate or define his object. He can, however, represent its emergence into reality.

III

THE CUBIST NOVEL

Pirandello's "desperate theatricality" was not a laboratory fully equipped for research into the new perspectives in reality; and his plays seem to be artful rather than art, perhaps resembling some of the experiments Picasso should have performed in his studio, not in public. Yet Pirandello, like Picasso, was seeking a "way beyond art" and, like the scientists, accepted reality as a continual transformation where fiction impinges on fact, where art intersects life. In writing of Picasso, Gertrude Stein explains that "because the way of living had changed the composition of living had extended and each thing was as important as any other thing . . . the framing of life, the need that a picture exist in its frame, remain in its frame was over. A picture remaining in its frame was a thing that had existed always and now pictures commenced to want to leave their frames and this also created the necessity for cubism." The cubists changed the status of the easel picture and deliberately, as modern artists, broke open the boundaries between their composition and the process going on outside the frame; the easel painting was no longer a work of art isolated from the world about it. To emphasize the relevance of their interlocking planes to the situation outside, they "bled" their composition, or sometimes arbitrarily cut off their constructions without completing the motif or extending it to the edge of the canvas. Thus they affirmed Whitehead's principle that there is no isolated or independent existence, that the whole is constitutive of each part and each part constitutive of the whole. Art is no longer a window into another world but an aspect of reality, a mode of transformation, another angle on process. The obliteration of punctuation in Apollinaire's "calligrams" is the same sort of elision between images that occur simultaneously, like the montage of rhythms in Delaunay's whirling colored disks.[10]

Cubist paintings had the enormous advantage, which nineteenth-century illustrative or symbolist painting did not have, of *approaching* reality without attempting either to identify art with things or to alienate art from things. This is the difference between the cubist *découpage* and *découpage* in Degas, who relied on the camera-shot, the excerpt from life, for unexpected quotation. The cubist quoted otherwise, by collage or the inserted clichés of the studio. Thus the cubist separation of painting from actuality, when it occurs, is shown to be arbitrary, not deceptive; the limits of cubist representation are not set by the limits of the canvas, for by implication cubist painting belongs to the world outside. The canvas is no longer "other." Neither the romantics nor the realists were able to make this adjustment of art to life. Apollinaire was exact in saying that cubist structures are endowed with the fulness of reality; they gave up the nineteenth-century "game of art" to pass "beyond painting." The cubists were able to *situate* the art-object more satisfactorily, more intelligently, more provocatively than at any time since the renaissance—when painters also tried to bring the art-object into adjustment with real space by means of deep perspective.

Many novelists like Aldous Huxley and Philip Toynbee have used the cubist simultaneous perspective, but no modern writer has been more concerned with situating his narrative than André Gide, who has been called cubist, but only in the trivial sense that he liberated the novel from conventionalities. This is the Gide who surprises us as Picasso has often sought to surprise; but, as Ozenfant remarked, surprise works only once. There is more in Gide than surprise, for his novels are not mere revolt but experiments with new means of representing reality. Gide constantly examined the transformations of fact to fiction and the effects of the Discontinuity or Uncertainty Principle: there he followed current scientific theory even more successfully than Valéry, who doubtless knew science far better.

Much of Gide's "fiction" is a factual record seen from a certain angle and thus transformed. As he suggested in *Les Caves du Vatican* (1914) "fiction is history that *might* have taken place, and history is fiction that *has* taken place." *Les Cahiers d'André Walter* (1891) was his early attempt to give a fictional dimension to autobiography, and four years later in *Paludes* he explained, "I arrange facts in such a way as to make them conform to truth more closely than they do in real life." The ground of Gide's fiction was usually his *Journals,* equivocal testaments produced somewhere between Gide's life and Gide's art in a domain where cubist sculptors created what has been called "The Object Purified" or "The Object Dissected." Are we, for example, to think that the episode in *La Porte Étroite* (1909) when Jérome finds Alissa weeping because of her mother's adultery is fact or fiction? We know that here, as in *L'Immoraliste* (1902), Gide was consciously treating in some duplex way the events he mentions not only in his *Journals* but also in that more tantalizing "record" *Et Nunc Manet In Te.* Gide's ingenious transformations of actuality to fiction culminated in *Les Faux-Monnayeurs* (1919–1926); and at once he complicated these transformations by printing *Le Journal des Faux-Monnayeurs,* which is for the most part Gide's own journal documenting the writing of the novel. Deliberately Gide turned his back on the modern quest for myth in literature and devoted himself, instead, to the cubist problem of the distance of art from actuality. "What will attract me to a new book," he says in the *Journal des Faux-Monnayeurs,* "is not so much new characters as a new way of presenting them. This novel must end sharply, not through exhaustion of the subject, but on the contrary through its expansion and by a sort of blurring of its outline."

The blurring occurs precisely along the margin between art and life. As he said in his tenth Imaginary Interview, the novelist can dispose of his materials as he sees fit, but his materials are actualities—"You cannot do without them."

Beginning, like a cubist painter, with actualities, Gide then affirmed the difference between actuality and the representation of actuality. When Gide was very young, another writer asked him, "If you had to sum up your future work in a sentence, in a word—what would that word be?" Gide replied, "We must all represent." From the first he saw that representation is a challenge to actuality. Any representation is a counterfeit that daringly invites us to detect what is fraudulent in resemblance. It is an act of defiance in which the artist stakes his skill in rendering a notion of reality. The counterfeiting becomes a creative act. Gide based *Les Faux-Monnayeurs* on Oscar Wilde's paradox that nature imitates art: "The artist's rule should be never to restrict himself to what nature proposes, but to propose nothing to nature but what nature can and should shortly imitate." So Gide accepts the significant motif from the decadents and symbolists and yet amends art-for-art into the more penetrating inquiry of the relation between art and life.

What Gide finds is that life is not art, that art is not life, that art cannot occur without life, but that life may be less significant than art: life and art are two aspects of consciousness, perhaps. The cubists were working in the same direction, for as Juan Gris told Kahnweiler: "My aim is to create new objects which cannot be compared with any object in actuality. . . . My *Violin,* being a creation, need fear no competition." Here was the trouble with the novel, Gide thought—it had always been clinched to actualities (*cramponné à la réalité*). Defoe and Stendhal had written "pure" novels by a kind of counterfeiting that interested Gide, who says in *Journal des Faux-Monnayeurs:* "On the one hand, the event, the fact, what is given from without; on the other hand, the special effort of the novelist to write his book with these. And *there* is the real subject, the new axis that unbalances the narrative and projects it toward the imaginative. In brief, I see this notebook where I record the composing of the novel, turned entire into the novel itself, forming the main interest, for the greater irritation of the reader." This is a novel centering in a novelist (in some respects Gide himself?) who is writing a fiction about the very events in which he himself, as novelist, is involved. All relations in Edouard's novel are reflexive and at the same time open to actuality, uncertain, shifting.

It has been said that the great cubist achievement was *camouflage.* In cubist painting and Gide's stories the relations between the painted object and the object, between plot and autobiography, are unresolved and reciprocating. Similarly in the film which "broke with the theatre," Eisenstein presented a "graphic conflict" by montage: "Headlights on speeding cars, highlights on receding rails, shimmering reflections on the wet pavements—all mirrored in puddles that destroy our sense of direction (which is top? which is bottom?)."

Edouard says he sets himself before reality like a painter. Later Strouvilhou asks why modern painting has gone so far ahead of literature by daring to discard the fine subject. Curiously, Strouvilhou is wrong. Painting did not outdistance *Les Faux-Monnayeurs,* which, like Pirandello's comedy-in-the-making, surrenders the fine subject and dismantles plot with its cause-and-effect certainties while the cubists were setting about their diffractions of reality. *Les Faux-Monnayeurs* is an inquiry, like Picasso's *Arlésienne,* into the innumerable transitions between the object and the conception of the object. Gide personally seems not to have seen the resemblance, being insensitive to contemporary painting. One of his friends was surprised that he admired Chardin. "It was natural," Gide remarks, "that but little gifted to like painting instinctively, I should attach myself particularly to a painter whom I could like only quite specifically for the qualities of which I had been most particularly deprived. . . . There are few painters who more authentically taught me to enjoy painting." Evidently Gide liked Chardin for the same reason he liked Defoe: they both confidently offer the actualities Gide did not permit himself. In *Les Faux-Monnayeurs* Edouard does not set himself in front of actuality like Chardin and Defoe but, instead, like Braque, La Fresnaye, and early cubists who destroyed things, then formally rebuilt them to compete with the actuality they had demolished. Gide notes that his novel "must not be neatly rounded off, but rather disperse, disintegrate."

In 1937 Gide wrote "Some Reflections on the Relinquishing of Subject in Plastic Arts," in which he says he was never tempted to take still lifes by Chardin or Cézanne for "actual objects." Gide knew that the cubists were eager to explore the contradiction between the object and their representation of the object. Cézanne wanted his paintings to be solid *and* artificial "like paintings in museums." Braque used to take his paintings out into the fields "to have them meet things," to see whether his representation could hold its own against the natural world from which he had excluded it. Picasso also exchanged actuality for representation, stating in his painting what the world is *not.* At the outer margin of cubist purity Mondrian protests that "art has been liberated from everything that prevents it from being truly plastic"—a last corollary to the significant motifs of Art Nouveau. For all these painters art is an equivalent. More consciously than any other novelist Gide practiced an art of counterfeit, which is a camouflage of the "document" (the journal) and a representation of the document at some uncertain level of fiction. As Edouard explains about the false ten-franc piece, "It will be worth ten francs so long as no one recognizes it to be false." Gide asks whether we recognize it. First Edouard writes in his journal that he has never been able to invent anything; then he corrects himself: "Only this remains—that reality interests me inasmuch as it is plastic, and that I care more—infinitely more—for what may be than for what has been." The textures of actuality over against the textures of fiction—that is the problem in Gide's research, which repeats in the novel the cubist analysis in the *tableau-tableau,* the art-form in the making.

Picasso has asked whether anybody ever saw a "natural" work of art. His own paintings, he claims, are a course of destructions: "I do a picture—then I destroy it. . . . In each destroying of a beautiful discovery, the artist does not really suppress it, but rather transforms it . . . makes it more substantial." The novel Edouard intends to write will be a sum of destructions, or a "rivalry between the real world and the representation of it which we make to ourselves. The manner in which the world of appearances imposes itself upon us, and the manner in which we try to impose on the outside world our own interpretation—this is the drama of our lives." It is a drama nineteenth-century art, with its anxiety about nature, never wrote; the nineteenth century either tried to find the drama in nature or else, with the symbolists, refused nature, but did not welcome the rivalry of the mind with what nature offers. This rivalry produces a style—which is more than a technique: it is an assertion that man takes a *view* of nature. Trying to justify his method, Edouard says he would like his book to be as close to *and as far from* actuality—as human and fictitious—as Racine's *Athalie.* Edouard allows himself no finer subject than Strouvilhou's painter; everything will go into his novel, yet the result will not be reportage. There will be no suppressions, but only a translation of events into fiction: "What I want is to represent reality on the one hand, and on the other that effort to stylize it into art." The artist's struggle, which causes style, is "between what actuality offers him and what he himself desires to make of it." During his cubist phase Picasso studies how the features of *Man with Violin* transform themselves into his conception. The painter or novelist becomes "a spectator at the birth of his work."[11] Here is another facet of the double-consciousness of modern man, the *dédoublement* of existential experience.

Bernard objects about Edouard's novel: "A good novel gets itself written more naïvely than that." Bernard misses the point —this is not the nineteenth-century "good novel," for the modern artist is aware of actuality in a new way. In fact Edouard says actuality "puts him out." He must, like Braque, compete with it. Edouard is trying to liberate his narrative from easy identifications. His journal (which is, in part, Gide's novel) uses a tactic of collage by imposing excerpts from life (documents!) upon a fictional texture for the sake of affirming the competition between fiction and history. Apollinaire calls this tactic the cubist "enumeration of elements," of which actuality is merely one. Edouard says his novel will be a "formidable erosion of contours." The erosion had begun in the cubist destruction of objects; for, as Picasso said, if they are damaged by representation, "so much the worse for objects." Edouard transvalues the document as the cubists transvalued ordinary things like bottles, tables, newspapers. For the cubist, objects are residual; they are borrowed into another order of reality.

The cubists gave counterfeit a prestige, recovering the formalities of artistic vision by passing objects through a repertory of planes, not by reportage. The skill of the counterfeiter exerts itself against great pressures from the world outside. His resistance to this world is the warrant of his art, since actuality must be used only as collage—a fragment that guards the integrity of representation. Cubist painting is an impartial examination of textures, a résumé of the various levels of identity at which things appear. Apollinaire said that the great revolution in art Picasso achieved almost unaided "was to make the world his representation of it." Cézanne's proto-cubism was solid geometry, entirely untheoretical, a realization of the strength of the world, the thick contours of houses and dovecotes and hills, the mass of trees, roads, sea, rocks, and headlands. Of its own weight, almost, this world fell open into shifting planes that dazzle in Braque, Gris, and Picasso, who make many hypothetical adjustments by a cinematic vision through which things flicker, come and go, recede and approach, yet are held in formal composition. As the artist penetrated nature by his thought, cubism turned conceptual in its approaches and structures. Cézanne's volumes were leveled to planes until the object, at first dismantled, was reconstructed on the surface of the canvas within two dimensions, an entirely pictorial displacement with *ruptures subites des plans géométrisés*. The erosion of contours was complete, and cubism, disciplined by the mind, went from its massive to its transparent, synthetic, cinematic phase.

This is how Gide erodes his events and characters. Edouard complains that the novel, too long hindered by fidelity to facts, must be stripped of its encumbrances—its "literature." Now that photography, he argues, has "freed painting from its concern for a certain sort of accuracy," the phonograph should rid the novel of nineteenth-century dialog. He does not describe his characters; he is concerned only with the "formal adjustments" in his fiction. The cubist world and the world of *Les Faux-Monnayeurs* are not the world we ordinarily know. Just when we are about to feel Braque's things, reassuringly, "there," they disappear in a complex of planes, lines, colors, with interpolations of wood, paper, cloth, which are—and are not—within the composition, and are only one more insolent value in reality. Gide's fiction uses all the simulated and literal textures of cubism. Is Edouard's notebook a fiction? If so, then what is the status of Gide's own journal, transcribed into the formalities of Edouard's novel-in-the-making? More annoying, what is the status of Alfred Jarry, that legendary *fauve* let loose in person, pistol and all? This *trompe l'oeil* is a sardonic version of the outworn actualities of the novel. What of the coiners themselves, whom Gide "borrowed" from stories in the daily press? And what of Edouard's scandalous closing remarks about Boris: Edouard will not use Boris' suicide in *his* novel—"I have too much difficulty in understanding it. And then I dislike police court items. There is something peremptory, irrefutable, brutal, outrageously real about them." Wherever these facts are most obviously used as facts they appear fictional. In contrast to the collage-figure of Jarry, the figure of Lady Griffith is deliberately set "outside the action," like the Son in Pirandello's play. What are the relations between Gide's journals, the intermediate *Journal des Faux-Monnayeurs,* the journals displaced into Edouard's notebooks, and Gide's encompassing fiction—if it be fiction? In his notes Gide said he wanted this book to be "a crossroad—a meeting of problems."

Apollinaire said that the cubist analysis of the object is "so complete and so decisive of the various elements which make up the object that these do not take the shape of the object." Gide disliked the naïve logic of the older novel and admired Defoe's ability to gain a fictional perspective on literal facts. However useful, Defoe's experiment with actuality was limited. Gide experiments with other dimensions, from the internal dimension of Edouard's journal to the wholly unexpected Thackeray-like intrusion when he remarks to us by shocking direct address, "I am afraid that Edouard, in confiding little Boris to Azais' care, is committing an imprudence." To vex us again Gide opens another fictional dimension when Edouard records in his notes for his novel-in-the-making (which is, reflexively, these notes themselves) how he submitted these notes to

Georges for scrutiny ("I wanted to know what Georges' reaction might be; . . . it might instruct me"). These mirror-inversions are so complicated that reality becomes only a theoretical perspective upon reality.

Gide treats the events in *Les Faux-Monnayeurs* at a distance that gives him *access* to actuality without any naturalistic false resemblances and encumbrances. Edouard complains that previous novels have been like pools in public gardens: "their contours are defined—perfect, perhaps, but the water they contain is captive and lifeless. I wish it now to run freely. . . . I choose not to foresee its windings. . . . I consider that life never presents us with anything which may not be looked upon as a fresh starting point, no less than as a termination." He wants his novel to end with the phrase "might be continued." Comparably, Gertrude Stein left unfinished her *Making of Americans* when she was convinced that her cinematic fragments had caught the rhythms of reality. *Les Faux-Monnayeurs* closes with Edouard's wish to know Caloub, the boy who was only casually mentioned at the start of the book. Caloub's unfinished profile carries the fiction "outside."

Edouard says that for him "Everything hangs together and I always feel such a subtle interdependence between all the facts life offers me, that it seems to me impossible to change a single one without modifying the whole." This means there can be no isolated stress on "big" events, no major crisis, no emotive fragments, no melodramatic passages; the perspectives are too complex to allow this heavily personal accent. Neither Gide nor the cubist painter needs the climax. That would be romantic. The cubist view of the world is an unexcited sense of possible meanings and contours. This undisturbed perception is the privilege of classic art, which makes its formal arrangements without being victimized by its emotional momentum. The cubist novel, the cubist painting displace and adjust their figures arbitrarily with, perhaps, the control of Racine's drama, or with any of the classic disciplines that destroy, then reconstruct, the world.

The cubist imagination, or Racine's, brings the world clearly and firmly into focus between our sensations and our ideas. Gide's experiment was to find out precisely where he must set the plane of his fiction, which must purify facts by ideas of these facts. This is what the nineteenth-century realists never determined, for they accepted Courbet's belief that "the art of painting should consist solely of the representation of objects visible and tangible to the artist." Gide began by distancing autobiography, like Picasso insisting there are no concrete or abstract forms in art but only more or less successful lies which occur when actualities are transposed to representation. Picasso's art, or Gide's, is a counterfeit erected arbitrarily between the physical world and the formations of thought. This it shares with "pure" science. For the modern painter, novelist, and scientist the world exists to be violated by the mind, which excerpts from it what it needs. The cubist counterfeit does not refuse the splendor of things and events. But it can also approach the condition of music. Edouard says, "I can't see why what was possible in music should be impossible in literature." It is possible, as Gide must have known when he hoped his novel would be like a fugue. The cubist, subduing the world by the activity of his mind, achieves fugue-like variations upon the themes reality affords.

To have art approach music was the aim of the symbolists. But the symbolist distance from actuality is not the cubist distance. The symbolist imagination—a belated romanticism—demolished the world by feeling, emotively possessing objects as hieroglyphs for a state of soul. The symbolist imagination suffers among its own ruined images of things. The cubists revered the world as the symbolists and fauves did not—for the fauves were often inheritors of the symbolist emotional distortion. The violence of the cubist imagination is intellectual; objects are destroyed at an impersonal distance, as if by theorem. Cubist refractions of objects are "disinterested." The cubist painting or novel is not the art of fugue in the nineteenth-century sense that art is music; for then music meant emotional suggestion. Poe and Baudelaire wrote musical compositions, but did not purify their music of their emotional involvements. It was left for the cubists to detach themselves from their moods, to speculate dispassionately about objects, to gain nuances by thought and vision rather than by feeling. Braque said, "I love the rule that controls emotion." Cubist color, like cubist line, has architectural, not emotive, value. Some have complained that cubism dehumanizes art; Ortega y Gasset feared it did.

The cubists were not really *fauves* in spite of their close kinship; for the fauvists were descendants of the first romantics, and fauvism approached a style only when it was decorative, or when it used rhythm and color architecturally and mastered its urgent vision as Van Gogh did under the still glare of a southern sun. Then the ornamental motifs of the Nabis and Art Nouveau were endowed with monumental presence. Matisse, the greatest fauve, inscribed romantic feeling in joyous liberated flat patterns; composition, he said, is reducing violent movement to decoration. The cubists passed from plane to plane without romantic impetus. Their fugal compositions are neutral in tone—intelligent variations upon a few themes worked out in series: figures with guitar, harlequins, tables, carafes, fruits, and the furnishings of urban life. The cubist investigated the uses of actuality by diffractions and discontinuities, a structure of contrasting textures adjusted within monochromatic transparencies and reflections as if within receding mirrors. With cubist asceticism Gide reduced mannerisms of style until his surface is "pure," for, as he decided, in this novel "everything must be said in the most neutral way" (*la manière la plus plate*). His statement is as disinterested as a Braque *nature morte*. His narrative refuses sensuous color, purple passages, romantic inflections. It has the lucid quality of Braque's manipulation, the facile touch of a gallic hand.

He will improvise, improvise upon an ordinary motif until he has examined its possibilities. Like the cubist, Gide is impartial. What he called his irresolution, an incapacity or unwillingness to endorse any one perspective, was typical of the cubist temperament, the indecision of the early twentieth-century intellectual who, having accepted the notion of relativism, was aware of all the attitudes that could be held, but perhaps not acted upon: neutrality in art and life, and a clever investigation of alternative angles on every problem. In 1932 Gide wrote, "Each of my books up to now has been the exploitation of an uncertainty." Gide discovered, along with the cubists, the artistic value of impromptu. He notes again: "Everything in me calls out to be revised, amended, re-educated." Picasso has a cubist temperament—mercurial in his experiments, his diversities, his departures, and his returns. Another cubist, André Lhote, once said, "Each aspect of an object demands a new perspective, a new space to create."

Under such scrutiny the cubist object gradually tended to disappear [43]. Once the figure broke up into planes, these planes broke up, and there was no way to halt the destruction short of reabsorbing these smaller and smaller facets into the neutral continuum of process, which is featureless. We see the fragmentation beginning rather savagely in Picasso's *Demoiselles d'Avignon* (1907) and ending in the depersonalized, minutely fractured passages of *Man with Violin* (1911) [44]. After the first bold—nearly fauvist—regard of the object, cubism diffused its momentums, accepting what Whitehead calls the "startling discontinuity of spatial existence," which also appeared in the quantum theory and cinematic *découpage,* syncopation, and the "collision of independent shots." Gide intended the action in *Les Faux-Monnayeurs* to be a continual discontinuity: "every new chapter should pose new problems, serve as a new beginning, a new impulse, a plunge ahead." His law of composition was, "Never keep on—Ne jamais profiter de l'élan acquis." Begin again. Check the velocity. Break the rhythm. Try another profile. His novel is a form of "creative incoherence." From *André Walter* on Gide gave himself and his characters to the ethical impromptu, *la vie spontanée.* "Inconsistency. Characters in a novel or play who act all the way through exactly as one expects them to . . . This consistency of theirs, which is held up to our admiration, is on the contrary the very thing which makes us recognize that they are artificially composed." Thus Edouard explains his psychology. Or again, Protos in *Caves du Vatican:* "Do you know what is needful to turn an honest man into a rogue? A change of scene—a moment's forgetfulness suffice . . . a cessation of continuity—a simple interruption of the current." The *acte gratuit* is a psychological mechanism congenial to the cubist artist, who in his readiness to shift perspectives takes the impromptu approach. At the close of the nineteenth century Pater had urged the artist to be inquisitive: "What we have to do is to be for ever curiously testing new opinions and courting new impressions." The cubist turned

Courtesy of the Louise and Walter Arensberg Collection, Philadelphia Museum of Art

43 PICASSO: *Nude Female, 1910–11*

this *fin de siècle* aesthetic receptivity into a principle of style.

Gide's art has the excitement of interruption, of fracture. His fiction is a daring intellectualism that constantly re-organizes appearances into adjustments that look very strange, if not inexplicable, to the older logic of continuity. As Gris said, "Cubism is a state of mind." As Braque said, "Art is made to disturb." Gide repeats: "My role is to disconcert."

Gide's detachment is not hostile or in any way emotional, but cubist. His distance from the events he presents is not determined by intensity of feeling; he does not betray disillusion; he is not surprised; he does not exclaim. Instead, his tone is exploratory, uncommitted. The very question of "sincerity" vexes him: "I am never anything but what I think myself—and this varies so incessantly that often, if I were not there to

Courtesy of the Louise and Walter Arensberg Collection, Philadelphia Museum of Art

44 PICASSO: *Man with Violin, 1911*

make them acquainted, my morning's self would not recognize my evening's. Nothing could be more different from me than myself." So remarks Edouard, underscoring what Gide says in his journals. This "dissociation of sensibility" in Gide is not tormented (that would be romantic) because he recruits, indifferently, from all ranges of possible experience without predisposition. His protestant scepticism and scruple are a disguise for a discontinuity of temperament and inconsistent motives—his outlook is a "flat" perspective that is not cynical but open to alternative angles. Gide is capable of sympathy, of crime, of faith, of blasphemy, but never of unintelligence. The cubist invents with disconcerting curiosity, by severe and ingenious experiment.

Before the cubists investigated the world we did not know what an object is *capable of.* Chardin must have surmised; but he was not venturous enough. Defoe must have guessed; but his research was local. Gide systematically investigates his moralists and immoralists, subjecting them to irresistible strains suddenly and cleverly applied. Man in the cubist novel, like the object in cubist painting, is capable of all features, and at the same instant. Yet Gide's curiosity is not the bohemian curiosity of Baudelaire and Rimbaud, which was essentially a means of escaping from the world, or rejecting it. Gide says, instead, "I love life, but I have lost confidence in it."

Cubism was a sign of destruction as well as creation. Both cubist and fauvist destructions of the world suggest possibilities of splendor and disaster the nineteenth century could hardly have imagined—even after the flaming devastations of Turner's painting. When Gertrude Stein first flew over the American landscape in 1934–35 she understood what art means for our century, for the air-vision gave her a new and terrifying perspective:

> . . . when I looked at the earth I saw all the lines of cubism made at a time when not any painter had ever gone up in an airplane. I saw there on the earth the mingling lines of Picasso, coming and going, developing and destroying themselves, I saw the simple solutions of Braque, I saw the wandering lines of Masson, yes I saw and once more I knew that a creator is contemporary, he understands what is contemporary when the

> contemporaries do not yet know it, but he is contemporary and as the twentieth century is a century which sees the earth as no one has ever seen it, the earth has a splendor that it never has had, and as everything destroys itself in the twentieth century and nothing continues, so then the twentieth century has a splendor which is its own and Picasso is of this century, he has that strange quality of an earth that one has never seen and of things destroyed as they have never been destroyed.
>
> *(Picasso)*

First the artist's destruction of the world, the painted object, the prose fiction. Then the larger and more public destructions, *Guernica* and Hiroshima. Cubism was an art of frightening conceptions.

IV

WORLD WITHOUT OBJECTS: NEO-PLASTICISM AND POETRY

September, 1939, changed everything, and may conveniently be taken as a boundary beyond which ideas of destruction became military instead of artistic. The armies put an end to cubism, which had done all its important researches anyhow and had already mutated into neo-plasticism—the logical outgrowth of the cubist attempt to purify the world of painting into a statement of relationships within objects, between objects, beyond objects. It was not, perhaps, until the 1940's, when Mondrian was living in New York and a new generation of painters was changing abstract expressionism to tachism, that the trend became official. As early as 1913 Malevich by his "suprematism" hoped to "deliver art from the dead weight of the object." The new "retreat from likeness" also appeared early in Kandinsky, Delaunay, Severini, and Marcel Duchamp, whose versions of *Nude Descending a Staircase* pointed toward the future. By 1912 Frank Kupka had reached very high levels of abstraction in work like *Ordonnance Sur Verticales*

Jaunes. The Second World War simply emphasized the break with the classic methods of cubist art and brought a new wave of iconoclasm with "disappearance of subject in painting."

The need for abstract idiom when the armies plunged into total war might have been predicted by anyone familiar with Wilhelm Worringer's theory that in periods when man is at home in his world naturalistic art flourishes, and that in periods when man is alarmed by his world non-figurative art appears. The Gauleiters meant, among other things, that cubists would be followed by painters who more completely obliterated the object. Once again Mondrian proves how the artist often serves as a sensorium of society when at least as early as 1920 he confessed, "Gradually I became aware that Cubism did not accept the logical consequences of its own discoveries; it was not developing abstraction toward its ultimate goal, the expression of pure reality. I felt that this reality can only be established through *pure plastics*." Pure plastics: the recoil from things toward a non-figurative geography was inherent in the cubist experiments, which had to end in something like field equations.

In 1933, four years before Gide wrote his note on "The Relinquishing of Subject in Plastic Arts," T. S. Eliot was evidently entertaining very kindred notions in a lecture he gave upon the possibility of writing "poetry which should be essentially poetry, with nothing poetic about it, poetry standing naked in its bare bones, or poetry so transparent that we should not see the poetry." He did not write much poetry of this kind until the years between 1936 and 1942, when *Four Quartets* appeared with their thoughtful language—a language permeated by oriental contemplation and in many ways resembling Dante's speculative tongue in the *Paradiso* and other places where he versifies Aquinas:

> The detail of the pattern is movement,
> As in the figure of the ten stairs.
> Desire itself is movement
> Not in itself desirable;
> Love is itself unmoving,
> Only the cause and end of movement,
> Timeless, and undesiring

Except in the aspect of time
Caught in the form of limitation
Between un-being and being.

This transparent tough verse, clear as a dogmatic concept, is doubtless in Eliot's case a result of formal religious beliefs. It is no less intelligent for that reason, and it marks a phase in Eliot's course from his early symbolist-metaphysical poetry to a more genuinely contemporary idiom he was using in the theological passages of *The Hollow Men* and *Ash Wednesday*. We must recall that Eliot's poetic career has consistently led him away from Laforgue toward Dante and the orient. This progress suggests that while the New Critics and many of Eliot's followers have been occupied with so-called "metaphysical" complexity, metaphor, and irony, Eliot himself has moved beyond these problems toward the neo-abstract poetry of the *Quartet*

To be conscious is not to be in time.

To recapitulate: In 1917 Eliot, a beneficiary of symbolism, began by writing a kind of imagist poetry. In this vein he recorded his impressions of the Waste Land in hard, dry, and very ironic language:

The winter evening settles down
With smell of steaks in passageways.
Six o'clock.
The burnt-out ends of smoky days.

In *Prufrock* and other poems of this time he was obviously dependent on the "ironic inheritance" from French verse, using metaphors like the yellow fog licking its tongue into the corners of the evening, an image vividly drawn from the world of objects. He was hardly less dependent on the concrete images of Donne and the "metaphysicals":

Webster was much possessed by death
And saw the skull beneath the skin;
And breastless creatures under ground
Leaned backward with a lipless grin.

These extremely material images highly charged with expressionist (almost fauvist) feeling were "objective correlatives" capable of evoking what Eliot then wished to stimulate, a sense of the disorientation of the jazz age. Then came the cinematic montages of *The Waste Land,* a series of "shots" excerpted in the manner of Pound's *Cantos* from all periods of Western history, legend, and poetry, with composite images of great power and suggestiveness: Madam Sosostris with her bad cold and wicked pack of cards, bats with baby faces in violet light, typists seduced by young men carbuncular and putting records on a gramophone with automatic hand, and the slain god suffering his hour of trial in red stony places where he is betrayed. This poetry had a Donne-like crystallization of image arranged in counterpoint, motif answering motif in certain movements, the theme of sterility and sexual frustration being carried through glimpses of Marie, the hyacinth girl, Elizabeth and Leicester, Philomela, shopgirls violated in rented canoes, and Lil's abortion. Toward the end of the poem the language becomes different when the cinematic sliding statements overlap from line to line in a technique that is not really enjambment but a released double-syntax resembling the free functionalism in Le Corbusier's architecture; the language is "modular"—

If there were water we should stop and drink
Amongst the rock one cannot stop or think.

In *The Hollow Men* (1925) the language surrenders more of the metaphysical concreteness and takes on the conceptual phrasing of theology:

Between the conception
And the creation
Between the emotion
And the response
Falls the Shadow. . . .

By *Ash Wednesday* (1930) this intellectual language is in many passages stripped to the statement of the *Quartets,* a new mode of abstract poetry, a Dantesque scholastic discourse. Eliot turns from "the infirm glory of the positive hour"—

> Because I know that time is always time
> And place is always and only place
> And what is actual is actual only for one time
> And only for one place. . . .

Along with this non-figurative discourse comes, we may guess, Eliot's sense that the concrete image no longer suffices because

> . . . Words strain,
> Crack and sometimes break, under the burden,
> Under the tension, slip, slide, perish,
> Decay with imprecision, will not stay in place,
> Will not stay still.

When one finds that words cannot present an "objective correlative," then, presumably, one lets them "slip" into a poetry so transparent it dismisses the concrete image as far as it is possible for poetry to do so. So Eliot's verse now works like a Calder mobile, accepting a new sort of movement where the contours are like a wave-effect. The poem has a new illusion, a new complexity, more transparent than the tortuous metaphysical involutions.

In some such way Eliot comes to the discourse of the great opening passage of the *Quartets,* which abandons the object and has a purer figuration, grave, bare, controlled, abstract:

> Words move, music moves
> Only in time; but that which is only living
> Can only die. Words, after speech, reach
> Into the silence. Only by the form, the pattern,
> Can words or music reach

> The stillness, as a Chinese jar still
> Moves perpetually in its stillness. . . .
> Or say that the end precedes the beginning,
> And the end and the beginning were always there
> Before the beginning and after the end.
> And all is always now.

This passage approaches the purity in Mondrian, who believed that the simple relations stated in his geometric forms unburdened painting "from the tragic content of material and individual things; thus it becomes the purest expression of the universal." It is a poetry of thought, and shows, perhaps, that Will Grohmann was right in saying that conception is not only the cause but the result of painting.[12] This would be true of music, an essentially non-figurative art. It is a change in style, taking poetry out of the metaphysical tradition, bringing it into line with abstract painting, which also rises in the mind and speaks to the mind without much reference to the concrete image. Eliot has said, in effect, that the older mode of poetry was not adequate:

> That was a way of putting it—not very satisfactory:
> A periphrastic study in a worn-out poetical fashion,
> Leaving one still with the intolerable wrestle
> With words and meanings. The poetry does not matter.
> It was not (to start again) what one had expected.

There he was "between two wars" feeling he had wasted twenty years trying to learn how to use words, then finding that after one learns, one is not disposed to say the same thing.

This résumé of Eliot's course will indicate that the experiments in drama and novel have been no more contemporary than what happened in poetry. We say that it is a bad age for poets; and it is. But it may be that Eliot was more responsive than Pirandello or Gide and that the poet's sensitivity to what is contemporary sends him to the farthest outposts of the *avant-garde*.

Eliot seems constantly to have been more aware of his position than Wallace Stevens, who in certain ways is a better illustration of the trend toward abstraction, since he approaches an art that is almost decorative. Though Stevens' explanations of his own work were so veiled as to seem almost coy, it is clear from his poems that he spent his career exploring the relation between the mind and the world, trying to find how far poems can be purified by Ideas of an Order. Whether or not he was influenced by Valéry, Stevens proposes that the poet's imagination must somehow create a "non-geography" in the mind, for the imagination must be "a violence from within that protects us from a violence without. It is the imagination pressing back against the pressure of reality." The poetic mind must invent its world: "the inconceivable idea of the sun." This is the almost platonic imaginative abstraction which, unexpectedly, has a close rapport with post-cubist art and recent scientific thought. In his lectures at Princeton, Stevens said the poet must be measured "by his power to abstract himself, and to withdraw with him, into his abstraction, the reality on which the lovers of truth insist. He must be able . . . to abstract reality, which he does by placing it in his imagination." This sounds like Socrates' praise in the *Philebus* of arts that have a vision of pure forms. It also sounds like a rephrasing of Baudelaire's notion that poetry resembles mathematics and music. Stevens spoke of "the acute intelligence of the imagination," enabling us to create the "unreal" out of what is "real," endowing objects with "light" and comprehending "the opposite of chaos in chaos." Or again, "To regard the imagination as metaphysics is to think of it as part of life, and to think of it as part of life is to realize the extent of artifice."

Stevens' imagination is not a rational activity but, rather, takes its dominance in musical form. Indeed his play with words is often a figure in pure sound; and he develops many poems upon abstract motifs of color: the *blue* guitar theme, which modernizes the designs of Art Nouveau. He is heavily indebted to painting, as well as to music, for other motifs like Hartford in a purple light. By imagination we must, Stevens says, make a "Supreme Fiction" that must be "abstract," must "change," must "give pleasure." By feats of vision we ranscend the object and realize, like Shakespeare's Theseus, hat in this kind the best are but shadows, and the worst no worse if imagination amend them. Imagination is the satisfaction of the mind:

> The central poem is the poem of the whole,
> The poem of the composition of the whole,
> The composition of blue sea and of green,
> Of blue light and of green, as lesser poems,
> And the miraculous multiplex of lesser poems,
> Not merely into a whole, but a poem of
> The whole, the essential compact of the parts,
> The roundness that pulls tight the fatal ring.
>
> (*"A Primitive like an Orb"*)

The imagination is an organ by which we achieve those supreme fictions necessary to "cleanse" romantic desires—for Stevens repudiates the romanticism in symbolist art, although he, too, wishes to triumph over mere objects:

> We feel, without being particularly intelligent about it, that the imagination as metaphysics will survive logical positivism unscathed. At the same time, we feel, and with the sharpest possible intelligence, that it is not worthy to survive if it is to be identified with the romantic. The imagination is one of the great human powers. The romantic belittles it. The imagination is the liberty of the mind. The romantic is a failure to make use of that liberty. It is to the imagination what sentimentality is to feeling. It is a failure of the imagination precisely as sentimentality is a failure of feeling. The imagination is the only genius. It is intrepid and eager and the extreme of its achievement lies in abstraction.
>
> (*Imagination as Value*)

The great problem with Stevens, as with Kandinsky, was to know with what to replace the mere object; and he found that the imagination must prey upon objects but finally release itself from them into pure fictions, the figurations of the mind:

The prologues are over. It is a question, now,
Of final belief. So, say that final belief
Must be in a fiction. It is time to choose.
(*"Asides on the Oboe"*)

Stevens speaks for the modern mind. A fiction: not a myth, for myth is romantic and anthropomorphic, projecting, like a daydream, the human drama into the universe. The fiction is impersonal, getting at reality without romantic "gestures" as Stevens apparently explains in "So-and-So Reclining on Her Couch":

. . . To get at the thing
Without gestures is to get at it as
Idea.

To get at the thing as idea is what Stevens calls "Projection C," the trajectory of the mind toward reality. The fiction is intellectual without being logical. It is a "poem of the mind," imposing its order, its design, on the world of things—colored things, which also have their own textures and satisfactions. Following the tradition of Valéry, Stevens writes:

The poem of the mind in the act of finding
What will suffice. It has not always had
To find: the scene was set; it repeated what
Was in the script.
Then the theatre was changed
To something else. Its past was a souvenir.
It has to be living, to learn the speech of the place.
It has to face the men of the time and to meet
The women of the time. It has to think about war
And it has to find what will suffice. It has
To construct a new stage. It has to be on that stage
And, like an insatiable actor, slowly and
With meditation, speak words that in the ear,
In the delicatest ear of the mind, repeat,
Exactly, that which it wants to hear. . . .
. . . The poem of the act of the mind.
(*"Of Modern Poetry"*)

We float "in the contention, the flux / Between the thing as idea and / The idea as thing." The mind in the act of finding itself in a world of things—this is Stevens' theme; it is the theme of Naum Gabo, who says, "Whatever exists in nature, exists in us in the form of our awareness of its existence." Yet Stevens also believes it is the greatest poverty not to live in a physical world: "the plastic parts of poems / Crash in the mind." The mind must find itself amid things. We must create our fictions, find the motifs of imagination, while the world is crashing plastically. Then we can write a "Description Without Place"—

> It is possible that to seem—it is to be,
> As the sun is something seeming and it is.

Description without place is, for Stevens, a "spirit's universe," indifferent to the eye, like the future, which is also "description without place." Almost like Andrew Marvell, Stevens is able to annihilate the world to a green thought: "Her green mind made the world about her green." The mind makes the music of the world; like the jar that is set on a hill in Tennessee it rises up to "take dominion everywhere."

It is not, however, among the poets but among the painters that the object tends completely to "disappear from sight," as it eventually does in Mondrian, theorist of the neo-plastic. His rigorous intellectual composition is a statement of relationships purged of all reference to the world outside, attaining by geometric imagination "what is absolute in the relativity of time and space." (One thinks of Eliot's "What is actual is actual only for one time / And only for one place.") Mondrian wants his painting "to be able to express these relationships" by a "new vision" that eradicates the old romantic personality. (One thinks, again, of Eliot's notion that the poet must escape from the burden of personality by means of his medium, which is all he has to employ.) For Mondrian sees that modern man lives impersonally in a cosmology where his perspectives are defined by scientific concepts. "The life of a cultivated man in our time," Mondrian wrote in 1917, "is gradually being divorced from natural objects and is becoming more and more an abstract existence." This marks a final emancipation from the object as an isolated fragment of reality, and from all forms of realism that were merely an "accumulation of objects."

Cubism began the cancellation of the object, a trend that has continued through increasingly severe deletions in neo-plastic and non-objective painting, which has produced the "anti-object," just as the novelist has produced the "anti-hero." Now the scientist has detected "anti-matter," so-called "strange particles" causing trajectories which, when photographed, might be taken for a painting by Pillet. The object has been lost in an activity the scientist calls a field. "The particular in art will disappear," according to Mondrian, who describes not only what has happened in his own simplified patterns but also in the recent development known as tachism, which absorbs and annihilates all figuration into a seemingly random texture dribbled over the surface of the canvas. Mondrian and the tachists reach a last phase of futurist painting, which attempted to prove that a pattern in time is only a pattern in space, and vice-versa. The futurist Severini wanted painting to express a "plastic dynamism, the absolute vitality of matter." Boccioni, another futurist, said, "We must open up the figure or shape and fill it full of the environment in which it has its being." Bazaine tells us that a tree, a face, a landscape is only a network of directions or lines of force: "The more we get inside the object, the less it closes in on itself; it opens on the whole universe." Matta has remarked, *à propos* of his painting in the UNESCO building in Paris, that "the image of man is no longer anthropomorphic but a complex of forces"—the principle of the anti-hero in painting. The crisis in the easel picture brought on by cubists who wanted painting to leave its frame has resulted in the annihilation of objects in neo-plasticism, which treats time as a field of space.

The withdrawal of the object into complex fields of time and space is illustrated by one of Singier's abstract paintings with the significant title *Le Quatuor;* for Singier is deliberately invoking the temporal art of music. In *Le Quatuor* space opens into musical time, as it does in the mobile, in a pictorial field that is a variant on the quartet, showing lines that extend or expand through transparent green planes, with four major nodes or curves intersecting in a classic symphonic movement. The intersecting planes and lines are notations for the violin, the cello, the score, signature, bars, crescendo and diminuendo, repeats, and rests; and the composition is made architectural by transposing four musical movements in time into simultaneous, cinematographic space with its complex of rectangles forming a flat design.

Singier's composition demonstrates the inexhaustible fertility of cubist techniques as a means of representing the gradual withdrawal of the object or the cancellation of the outside world progressively taking place in neo-plastic painting. As in the first cubism, Singier's references still hover between the object and the constructs of the mind. The older generation of cubists limited the area over which the object might hover by a rather ascetic geometry and color; the neo-abstract painters dare to remove the object further before reconstructing it. Singier's recrystallizations are somewhat more private than those in classic cubism, without, however, submerging the object wholly in the self or in the neutral field of forces outside. This level of submergence gives Singier's painting a new transparency, such as we also see in Lapoujade's lyric and highly mobile *Adolescent,* a whitish evaporation of early futurist studies in motion, like Duchamp's *Nude Descending a Staircase,* into an opalescent perspective that is rococo and very feminine. The movement in Lapoujade's figure is still cinematic, as it is in Singier's study.

The object hovers somewhat differently in an abstraction like Busse's *La Carrière: La Cathédrale,* a post-cubist cinematic development of a double motif in gray, black, and white, ambiguously a treatment of cathedral, quarry, and flat pattern. Here the film-movement takes on deep architectural space, for beyond the cinematic flicker of the rectangles the third dimension reappears in almost coulisse form in a composition that restricts its color more severely than original cubism. This work by Busse shows how abstract painters generally have returned to cubist problems with a tradition behind them, and have used Cézanne, Braque, and Picasso much as Poussin used Raphael. In Busse, who thinks out his work strongly, the flat-pattern cinematic motion adds a plastic implication without sacrificing the surface. This intelligent reconstruction has the firmly built surfaces of paintings by De Staël, whose dense areas of pigment mount the old cubist planes in a texture resembling inlay. De Staël's *Roofs of Paris,* a capacious mosaic, hovers more remotely than Braque's pitchers and chessboards. Busse revises not only cubism but impressionism in his *Rayon de Lumière,* a flat pattern of bright blue and green chips across which fall two gay yellow diagonals in a forest-perspective harking back to divisionist methods in Seurat, or, further, to Renoir's archaic *Moulin de la Galette* or even Courbet's woodland glades. Now the present generation of Spanish painters has discovered still other ingenious ways to hover between the world and the autonomous abstraction.

As the object withdraws, there is a cancellation of color too. Picasso often worked in black, white, and gray, as did the movie before technicolor; one of the cubist discoveries was that black heightens the value of colors. The abstract painting deriving from cubism has continued to use black as a means of reducing the problem of painting to a mode of absence. The cubists presented their objects in neutral terms; the neo-plastic painters have moved farther along the scale toward the negative. Hartung has found a wild black *écriture;* Soulages uses black in plastic strips; Busse works out his depths against black verticals.

Along with this negation of color there has come another sort of response to the modern situation—an internal fluorescence in the work of Soulages, Pillet, Lancelot-Ney, and others. This deep radiation is unlike the calm and faceted light of cubist painting, the prismatic beams of Feininger, the X-ray penetration of Tchelitchew, the gay thin brilliance of Dufy, or the joyous blare of Matisse. It appears within a grid of surface geometry and has little to do with color, since any hue can be excited to activity in abstract painting. It modernizes Claude's diffused sunshine, Fragonard's somnolent noonday, and Turner's burning romantic color. It arises like an aurora from the neon-lighted city, glowing within modular structures. It is different from the daylight spectrum of impressionism and even from the strained white gas flare in which Degas caught his dancers—for Degas, like every painter, was sensitized to the light of his day. This recent fluorescence seems to signify the existence of the object, like an atomic manifestation, even after the object itself has disappeared.

In short, painting since cubism has been a new iconoclasm,

a further repudiation of a too-solid world that had existed since the renaissance. Bazaine claims that "the object has to disappear as object in order to justify itself as form." Instead of objects there are only notations of relationships and of textures that occur in process.

What determines relation and texture in "the new world of space," as Le Corbusier calls it? To answer this question we must turn to some notions in post-Einsteinian science, which apparently has replaced early twentieth-century concepts of space and energy by a theory that both space and energy are aspects of field-behavior.[13] Einstein treated space as a function of mass-energy distribution in accordance with field equations, and it is on this basis that gravitation is now generally taken to be a certain kind of behavior of time-space structures in fields of force. Space is interpreted to be no absolute system in the nature of things but only a function of our own conceptual scheme: it is a mode of perceiving objects, not characteristic of things in themselves. Thus any geometry we use seems to be a matter of convenience, and since we cannot get outside the system we use, we select a system that allows us to deal best with the aspects of nature we are trying to observe. From another point of view the structure of space is only a function of the distribution of matter and energy. Indeed, energy or force may itself prove to be only one more fiction like space. The idea of force, essential to Keplerian physics, was accepted in nineteenth-century mechanics as a value in itself; furthermore the notion of force was endowed with psychological meanings when Schopenhauer, Nietzsche, and the romantics transferred this value from physics into ethics under the semblance of the will.

Relativity and field theories have dispensed with the notion of force except as a formula to indicate the appearance of objects together in a field. Aside from this technical meaning, the idea of force becomes as empty a concept as the old notions of ether or the absolute space and time of a Newtonian world-system. Force now seems like the middle term of a syllogism, a means of getting from premise to conclusion, dropping away after it has served its methodological purpose. Contemporary science suggests that force is only a certain relation between objects in a field. Object A moves in a certain path when it is surrounded by objects B and C. The only way we can explain the behavior of A under these conditions is by a notion of force, which then vanishes when we understand the whole configuration, the appearance and interaction of objects together. Thus the idea of force has been displaced by an idea of the functional dependence of objects, and the nineteenth-century "energy" becomes merely the description of a field. Force, in sum, seems to be only a name for the conditions under which things exist together. Gravitation is not a "force" but a property of a given space-time system. And space is a function of the distribution of matter, or its behavior, in a field. Nothing could more effectively dismiss the romantic belief in freedom, individualism, and the importance of the decisive act—the heroism of Ahab and creatures whose destiny seemed in their own power.

Matta is one of the painters who has interpreted these field-effects, especially in his later work, when he seems to have turned from abstract surrealism toward compositions whose very titles intimate his sense of post-Einsteinian space. *The Turning of the Earth* (1955), for example, employs planes and orbits in relations so intricate that the space of the composition is not homogeneous; each passage appears to be a special complication with its own contours, and the galaxies of "things" expand almost explosively in a strange universe that is at once finite and infinitely extensible. The relations of planes to clusters of granular objects are restated more troublingly in *The Unthinkable* (1957), where trajectories intersect or surround two-dimensional surfaces that dissolve into atmospheric light. Even the earlier works like *Vertigo of Eros* can be read as a series of deviations in space-time occurring in an incoherent field that requires alternative mathematical equations to deal with it intelligibly. Matta's space is organic and inorganic at the same time, but certainly not anthropomorphic in the sense that the space of any preceding painting has been anthropomorphic. It is space that cannot be conceived, or even seen, without invoking some unfamiliar mathematic to deal with its discontinuities. At least no uniform structure can be given it by the unaided eye.

To repeat what Mondrian said: the neo-plastic painter tries to think of his composition as "an abstract expression of relations." Whether it is called neo-plasticism or tachism, recent painting appears to be a variety of field equation, a symbol of the way in which space and energy are conceived as *situations*. This art may indeed be iconoclastic; but it expresses a world-view where the object disappears into patterns of behavior, an abstract orchestration of relational functions. Neo-plastic painting, at least in its tachist mode, is a depiction of the distribution of matter and energy without any absolute reference-system. The interlaced dribbles of pigment in Mathieu's huge *Les Capétiens Partout* develop from seemingly random splashes or doodles an emergent movement that is a sort of magnetic flow of brushwork. The horizontals and verticals in red, black, and yellow pigment, wavering, thickening, vanishing, reappearing as if by chance, exist together as a field equation bracketed by wild meteor-like splatters of white paint in orbital motions disintegrating as they sweep away from the galaxy that threw them off. It is, as written, an equation for the release of great energy under conditions of extreme instability—an *écriture* that seems also to be a form of play. The "distribution" that emerges is something like a complex statistical pattern or rhythm. The great brown canvas reaches its graphlike design only by a kind of hazard, representing what apparently happens in the atom or in the self. The heightened sensitivity of the most recent painting to the negative is probably part of this aspect of hazard in a field. The black holes punched in the canvas of Lucio Fontana's *Concetto Spaziale* are a significant intrusion of the negative into the composition; for these holes are an ultimate version of collage, and scattered in a seemingly random distribution or, at best, a direction, appear against thin, wavering rectangular "background" outlines in black. In sculpture Henry Moore has for a long time been interpolating the value of negative space—the holes in the material that create form from what is *not* there.

Jackson Pollock's tachism shows that distribution in a field may be almost random; here the effect is very similar to a Brownian movement of particles in solution. Actually, however, the random movement in pigment creates a texture. The difference between texture and pattern is that texture resembles molecular activity, suggesting uniformity, whereas a pattern formulates the relations between independent parts and a constant design. The tachist method of spurting or drooling pigment on the surface to be covered gives only a very low level of structure, at times approaching uniformity. But a texture results. Although this painting has been called "standardized chaos," it takes on meaning in an age when force has become a fiction, when matter is an aspect of the behavior of forces in a field, when a surrender of the romantic will and individuality seems necessary. The field has become more important than objects in the field: objects detach themselves from a field only when we give them a higher level of structure to disengage them from their background.

The notion of "togetherness" has cosmic import. Tachism seems to reflect in painting the situation in which we think of ourselves as now existing; for as Francastel says, any system of space is only an expression of the world in a certain epoch. If so, then tachism is a sign of a new law of necessity (*ananke*) that is thoroughly anti-romantic, assigning to fatality a very negative meaning in a totalitarian world. With its aspect of neutrality, its tactic of subtraction, its resignation of what is individual or even personal, tachism may be read as a recent form of despair—at least of compliance—or of a loss of a sense of freedom. A disturbing indifference is inherent in tachist painting, which employs the streak, the blot, the little touch or standardized unit from which the whole composition is made. This modular principle was implicit in impressionist painting, notably in Monet, whose last compositions obliterate the object, absorbing it into an atmosphere that is a field-effect, and also an abstraction. A modular technique underlies our age of mass observation and human engineering in which the self is treated only by statistical laws like particles in Brownian movements.

Does Meursault, at the close of Camus' *Stranger,* feel the operation of some such law of neutrality, and yield to it as a result of an insight into a universe he sees in its overwhelming indifference just before he dies? His extreme subtractions—the meaninglessness of the behavior of things, the irrelevance of purpose, will, or even desire that cause him to react toward the pole of anti-romanticism—would represent the mood in which some tachist painting is done. Meursault accepts the random. His existence is emptied of figuration until it is almost an abstraction. Levelling to the random seems complete in Beckett's plays and novels.

The random texture reappears in a trend that seems contrary to abstract art—what in France is called "aliterature" among those like Alain Robbe-Grillet who have turned back to "the surface of things," avoiding point of view by a new reportage, placing the personality on the same neutral level with the scene to which it belongs. Robbe-Grillet does not disengage character from background; there is a low level of structure in his seemingly indiscriminate account that merges psychology with an unceasing description of things. The "figure" is reabsorbed into the "ground." These writers say, like Gautier, that the world "quite simply *is*" and must be taken on its own obvious evidence, at first glance. Their attempt to avoid the old "depth" of a personal view has led "aliterary" writers to record, in a kind of *neue Sachlichkeit,* not the "essence" of experience but only the superficial appearances, which *are* reality. The tachist method in aliterature is illustrated by the episode in *The Voyeur* when Mathias sees—and slowly recognizes what it is—a poster announcing a movie: it is not stream-of-consciousness in the older sense of the term because it entirely represses awareness to the plane of perception:

> The new advertisement represented a landscape.
>
> At least Mathias thought he could make out a moor dotted with clumps of bushes in its interlacing lines, but something else must have been superimposed: here and there certain outlines or patches of color appeared which did not seem to be part of the original design. . . .
>
> On the upper section appeared the names of the leading actors. . . .

And so on. If tachism in painting had already appeared in the later Monet, one wonders whether aliterature had not already appeared in Arnold Bennett's novels with their heavy accumulations of things. Except that Bennett's indiscriminate realism did not level people and things as Robbe-Grillet does in his attempt to decerebrate his fiction. His experiment is cinematic since it is based upon film-shots to "draw us out of our interior comfort toward this proffered world" and give us the sense of the "presence" of things. The complete submergence of the person in the milieu is managed by a technique that seems to be the most random form of the random: "The coffee pot is on the table. It is a round table with four legs, covered with an oil-cloth checkered red and gray. . . ."

Tachist painters have eliminated the object without even asking with what the object is to be replaced; but the replacements have nevertheless been made, and sometimes seem more valuable than the objects. Hartung, for instance, has resorted to an automatism of the brush that conveys the extreme neurosis of the modern self as well as the explosive behavior of things in the contemporary field. The world-without-object—the world as a statement of pure relations—is thematically presented in the openwork sculpture of Antoine Pevsner, Richard Lippold, Ibram Lassaw, or Naum Gabo, purifying the cinematic methods of cubist art into a spatio-temporal disembodied montage, to be thought rather than seen. This form of neo-plasticism gives us only the paradigms of process, not objects.

At one of the recent symposiums on non-figurative art Berto Lardera summarized the meaning of this revision of cubism into the iconoclastic art of Mathieu or De Staël: "The problem of space is really the problem of man's situation in his world. Actually the analysis of space, its problems, is merely the analysis of all man's problems in today's world." So, says Lardera, we must find new laws of gravity for sculpture—which Calder seems to have done. The modern artist can believe only in a reality having an infinity of profiles: profiles that appear only by accident and are constantly mobile. And, in Lardera's words, it may be that all these profiles will be "devoured in space by light"—the light, perhaps, of twentieth-century destructions which are brighter than the sun?

Notes

I ROCOCO: THE IDEA OF AN ORDER

1 Maynard Mack: Introduction to Pope's *Essay on Man,* Twickenham ed., 1950. This aspect of Pope is also treated in chapter vii of Reuben A. Brower's *Alexander Pope,* 1959, which appeared after this book was in press.

2 Chapters iii and iv, *Science and the Modern World,* 1925.

3 Arthur O. Lovejoy, "The Parallel of Deism and Classicism," *Modern Philology,* XXIX, 1932, 281–299.

4 Jeremy Bentham, *Works,* Edinburgh, 1843, chiefly Vol. VIII and the "Fragment on Ontology." See also *Bentham's Theory of Fictions,* ed. C. K. Ogden, 1932.

5 In *The Philosophy of "As If,"* London, 1924.

6 Obviously my whole discussion of rococo style is based upon this book by Fiske Kimball, whose opinions and phrasings I have adopted.

7 See Louis Gillet, *La Peinture de Poussin à David,* 1935, 124.

8 Mack, Introduction to *Essay on Man,* Twickenham ed., lxiii.

9 Mack, lxxv.
10 Geoffrey Tillotson, *On the Poetry of Pope,* 1938, 138.
11 Tillotson, 49.
12 My account of *genre pittoresque* is drawn from Kimball, *Creation of the Rococo* and from W. G. Constable's unpublished lectures on *vedute* painters.
13 By Yvor Winters in *Primitivism and Decadence*, 1937, 1947.

II PICTURESQUE, ROMANTICISM, SYMBOLISM

1 Robert Langbaum in *The Poetry of Experience,* 1957, stresses the point.
2 Jean Prévost in *Baudelaire,* 1953, studies "Les Rythmes" in Baudelaire to prove that the poet transcended his feelings as the romantics did not.
3 Kenneth Clark, *Landscape Into Art,* Penguin ed., 96.
4 Bernard Weinberg, *French Realism: The Critical Reaction,* 1937, reviews the many interpretations of realism during the century.
5 This passage (from Odilon Redon's *À Soi-Même*) is discussed in Roseline Bacou's *Odilon Redon,* Geneva, 1956, a commentary I have used.
6 The best study of this change in the romantic imagination is probably M. H. Abrams' *The Mirror and the Lamp,* 1953, 1958.
7 This passage is quoted in Guy Michaud's *Message Poétique du Symbolisme,* 1947, which with its supplemental *Documents* has been a source invaluable to the present chapter. See *Documents,* 85.
8 Georges Poulet followed his *Études Sur le Temps Humain,* 1949, by an essay on "Timelessness and Romanticism," *Journal of the History of Ideas,* XV, 1954, 3–22.
9 Nikolaus Pevsner, *An Outline of European Architecture,* 1951, 246.
10 The tournament is described in John Steegman, *Consort of Taste,* 1950, 93–99.
11 "The Existence of Symbolism," *Kenyon Review,* Summer, 1957.
12 On this whole relation see Guy Michaud, *Mallarmé,* Paris, 1953.

13 Langbaum, *The Poetry of Experience,* especially the Introduction.

14 Throughout this chapter I have often cited passages from Bradford Cook's edition of *Selected Prose Poems, Essays, and Letters of Mallarmé,* 1956.

15 My interpretation of Baudelaire rests upon Margaret Gilman's two books, *Baudelaire as Critic,* 1943, and *The Idea of Poetry in France,* 1958, and on Joseph Chiari, *Symbolism from Poe to Mallarmé,* 1956.

16 My passages on Mallarmé follow, in general, Jacques Gengoux, *Le Symbolisme de Mallarmé,* Paris, 1950, and Guy Michaud, *Mallarmé,* Paris, 1953. The essay on Mallarmé in Georges Poulet's *Interior Distance,* 1952, 1959, explains how this poet creates his dream even more daringly than Shelley through an act of annihilation—by withdrawing existence from what exists.

III NEO-MANNERISM

1 Pierre Francastel, *Art et Technique aux XIXe et XXe Siècles,* Paris, 1956, 184. This book, along with Francastel's other work like *Nouveau Dessein, Nouvelle Peinture,* Paris, 1946, and *L'Impressionisme,* 1937, is the basis for a great deal of the present chapter: his interpretations of blockage, the technical revolution, the conflict of sensation and representation, the significance of the tachist method, the disharmony between style and perception in the nineteenth century, and the impressionist revolution and contribution all appear in my own discussion. The "cultural patchwork" of nineteenth-century architecture is treated in detail in Henry-Russell Hitchcock's *Architecture: 19th and 20th Centuries,* 1958, on which I have depended in this chapter as well as in the two adjoining chapters. The influence of techniques on art is treated in Francis D. Klingender's *Art and the Industrial Revolution,* 1947, which has also proved valuable.

2 Henri Focillon, *La Peinture aux XIXe et XXe Siècles,* Paris, 1928, 113–114.

3 This is held by Ernst Curtius, *European Literature and the Latin Middle Ages,* chap. xv.

4 Rudolf Wittkower, "Principles of Palladio's Architecture," *Journal of the Warburg and Courtauld Institutes,* VIII, 1945, 68–106.

5 Notably, Karl Scheffler, *Verwandlungen des Barocks,* Vienna-Zuerich, 1947, and *Das Phaenomen der Kunst,* Munich, 1952; also Gustav René Hocke, "Manier und Manie in der Europaeischen Kunst," *Merkur,* June, 1956, and Walter Friedlaender, *David to Delacroix,* 1952.

6 Throughout my treatment of impressionism I have drawn upon not only the works by Francastel mentioned in preceding notes, but also on his article "Destruction d'un Espace Plastique," in *Formes de l'Art, Formes de l'Esprit,* Paris, 1951; and, in addition, I am much indebted to Ruth Moser, *L'Impressionisme Français,* Geneva-Lille, 1952; Lincoln F. Johnson, Jr., *Toulouse-Lautrec, the Symbolists, and Symbolism* (Harvard thesis), 1956; and François Daulte, *Frédéric Bazille et Son Temps,* Geneva, 1952. Besides, one is always using John Rewald's *History of Impressionism,* 1946. The quotations from critics of impressionism like Albert Aurier are to be found in Jacques Lethève's irreplaceable source book on contemporaneous matters, *Impressionistes et Symbolistes Devant la Presse,* Paris, 1959.

7 Francastel's analysis of impressionist innovations in "Destruction d'un Espace Plastique," in *Formes de l'Art, Formes de l'Esprit,* is here indispensable.

8 Quoted in John Rewald, *Post-Impressionism,* n.d., 244.

9 Roger Fry, *Characteristics of French Art,* 1932, 128. Lincoln F. Johnson, Jr., in *Toulouse-Lautrec* discusses the "atmospheric continuum" in impressionism.

10 My sketch of the Lyonnais derives chiefly from Agnès Humbert, *Les Nabis et Leur Époque,* Geneva, 1954, and Henri Focillon, *La Peinture au XIXe Siècle,* Paris, 1927. See also Friedlaender, *David to Delacroix,* chap. ii.

11 The following account of the Nabis is a composite of information in Charles Chassé, *Le Mouvement Symboliste,* Paris, 1947; Anne Armstrong Wallis, "Symbolist Painters of 1890," *Marsyas,* 1941, 117–152; Agnès Humbert's *Les Nabis et Leur Époque;* and Bernard Dorival, *Les Peintres du XXe Siècle,* Paris, 1957, I, and his *Les Étapes de la Peinture Française Contemporaine,* Paris, 1943–46. For material on Gauguin especially I have drawn on John Rewald's *Post-Impressionism,* though this book is also relevant to Art Nouveau.

12 So the Nabis are classified by Dorival in *Les Peintres du XXe Siècle,* I, 17–23.

13 My treatment of Art Nouveau and its characteristics is grounded primarily in Stephan Tschudi Madsen, *Sources of Art Nouveau,* 1955; but I have also often drawn on Alf Bøe, *From Gothic Revival to Functional Form,* Oslo, 1957; Henry F. Lenning, *The Art Nouveau,* 1951; Henry R. Hope, *Sources of Art Nouveau,* an unpublished Harvard thesis, 1943; Fritz Schmalenbach, *Jugendstil,* Wuertzburg, 1934; Friedrich Ahlers-Hestermann, *Stilwende: Aufbruch der Jugend,* Berlin, 1956; and the classic sketch in *Pioneers of the Modern Movement,* 1936, by Nikolaus Pevsner, who stresses the "long, sensitive curve" behind Art Nouveau.

14 The next paragraphs on the primary role of architecture and the importance of *métier* are indebted to Henri Van Lier, *Les Arts de l'Espace,* Tournai, 1959, and to Jean Cassou, "La Nostalgie du Métier," in *Formes de l'Art, Formes de l'Esprit,* Paris, 1951.

15 On the whole matter of Japanese influence in literature and decadence, see Earl Miner, *The Japanese Tradition in British and American Literature,* 1958. I have adopted Miner's useful term "pan-impressionism."

16 This aspect of Art Nouveau is treated in Lincoln F. Johnson, Jr., *Toulouse-Lautrec.*

IV THE CUBIST PERSPECTIVE

1 Alfred Alvarez, *The Shaping Spirit,* 1958, 21.

2 André Salmon, *La Jeune Peinture Française,* Paris, 1912, 50.

3 Quoted in Gyorgy Kepes, *The New Landscape,* 1956, a book that has proved valuable throughout the entire chapter, especially his study of "laminated" space.

4 André Lhote, *La Peinture Liberée,* Paris, 1956

5 "Pensées sur l'Art," *Confluences,* Mai, 1945.

6 My résumé of cubist techniques is drawn from Winthrop Judkins' article, "Toward a Reinterpretation of Cubism," *Art Bulletin,* XXX, December, 1948, 270–278, and from Daniel-Henry Kahnweiler, *The Rise of Cubism,* 1949. See also John Golding, *Cubism,* 1959, which appeared while this book was in press.

7 Quoted in *Dictionary of Abstract Painting,* ed. Michel Seuphor, 1957, 43.

8 On Ortega's perspectivism I am generally indebted to Leon Livingstone's article "Ortega y Gasset's Philosophy of Art," *PMLA,* LXVII, 1952, 609–655.

9 Perhaps the most notable recent attempt to break the barriers between theatre and life is the "epic" theatre of Bertolt Brecht, a discussion of which might obscure (or at least greatly retard) matters here because of Brecht's involvements with Marxist ideology. However, Brecht's epic theatre is technically an extension of the cubist methods in Pirandello, as the excellent account in John Willett's *Theatre of Bertolt Brecht,* London, 1959, explains. Willett describes how Brecht uses montage, and fractures the continuity of his drama by counterpointing effects, deliberately interrupting the action by songs and using the film for background and subtitles. Brecht subjects his audience to a sort of shock treatment by his so-called *Verfremdungseffekt* ("V-effect")—"jerking" the actor out of relationship, breaking the illusion of the conventional theatre, making the spectators continually reorient themselves by unfamiliar changing angles. Above all Brecht is analytical, and has said of his plays, "The process of showing must itself be shown." He writes a "non-Aristotelian" drama and has said of his presentations, "I am the Einstein of the new stage form." Willett has treated all these questions in relation to Brecht's social realism and his use of the new music of Kurt Weill, Milhaud, and others. Eisenstein has had his influence on Brecht, also, as well as the Japanese *Nō* play. But it is difficult to talk of Brecht's theatre apart from his social point of view.

10 In *The Banquet Years,* 1958, Roger Shattuck explains the relevance of Apollinaire's calligrams to the art of juxtaposition.

11 Max Ernst, *Beyond Painting,* 1948, 20–21.

12 Will Grohmann as quoted in Marcel Brion, *L'Art Abstrait,* 1956, 241.

13 The next paragraphs dealing with field-behavior and modern theories of force, together with the random texture of tachist painting, rephrase explanations in Max Jammer's two books *Concepts of Space,* 1954, and *Concepts of Force,* 1957, and in a very suggestive article by Rudolf Arnheim, "Accident and Necessity in Art," *Journal of Aesthetics and Art Criticism,* XVI, 1957, 18–32.

Bibliographical Note

The following lists indicate the chief secondary material on which I have drawn or from which I have quoted in the preceding chapters.

ROCOCO

AINSWORTH, EDWARD GAY: Poor Collins, 1937
CASSIRER, ERNST: The Philosophy of the Enlightenment, 1951
EVANS, JOAN: Pattern, 1931
FLORISOONE, MICHEL: Le Dix-Huitième Siècle, 1948
GILLET, LOUIS: La Peinture de Poussin à David, 1935
HAZARD, PAUL: La Crise de la Conscience Européene, 1935
HAZARD, PAUL: La Pensée Européene au XVIIIème Siècle, 1946
KAUFMANN, EMIL: Architecture in the Age of Reason, 1955
KIMBALL, FISKE: The Creation of the Rococo, 1943
LOVEJOY, ARTHUR O.: "The Parallel of Deism and Classicism," *Modern Philology,* XXIX, 1932, 281–299
MACK, MAYNARD: "Introduction" to Pope's Essay on Man (Twickenham ed.) 1950
OGDEN, C. K.: Bentham's Theory of Fictions, 1932

TILLOTSON, GEOFFREY: On the Poetry of Pope, 1938
VAIHINGER, HANS: The Philosophy of "As If," 1924

PICTURESQUE, ROMANTICISM, SYMBOLISM

ABRAMS, M. H.: The Mirror and the Lamp, 1953, 1958
BACOU, ROSELINE: Odilon Redon, 1956
BAKER, JAMES VOLANT: The Sacred River, 1957
BEGUIN, ALBERT: L'Âme Romantique et le Rêve, 1946
CAZAMIAN, LOUIS: Symbolisme et Poésie, 1947
CHARLTON, D. G.: Positivist Thought in France, 1959
CHIARI, JOSEPH: Symbolism from Poe to Mallarmé, 1956
CLARK, H. F.: "Eighteenth Century Elysiums," *Journal of the Warburg and Courtauld Institutes,* VI, 1943, 165–189
COOK, BRADFORD, ED.: Selected Prose Poems, Essays, and Letters of Mallarmé, 1956
FREY, JOHN ANDREW: Motif Symbolism in the Disciples of Mallarmé, 1957
FRIEDLAENDER, WALTER: David to Delacroix, 1952
GENGOUX, JACQUES: Le Symbolisme de Mallarmé, 1950
GILMAN, MARGARET: Baudelaire as Critic, 1943
GILMAN, MARGARET: The Idea of Poetry in France, 1958
HAUTECOUER, LOUIS: Littérature et Peinture en France, 1942
HIPPLE, WALTER JOHN, JR.: The Beautiful, the Sublime, and the Picturesque, 1957
HITCHCOCK, HENRY-RUSSELL: Architecture: 19th and 20th Centuries, 1958
HUSSEY, CHRISTOPHER: The Picturesque, 1927
JOHANSEN, SVEND: Le Symbolisme, 1945
JONES, P. MANSELL: The Background of Modern French Poetry, 1951
JONES, P. MANSELL: Verhaeren, 1957
KLINGENDER, FRANCIS D.: Art and the Industrial Revolution, 1947
KNIGHT, EVERETT: Literature Considered as Philosophy, 1957
LANGBAUM, ROBERT: The Poetry of Experience, 1957
LEHMANN, A. G.: The Symbolist Aesthetic in France, 1950
MICHAUD, GUY: Mallarmé, 1953
MICHAUD, GUY: Message Poétique du Symbolisme (and Documents), 1947
MONK, SAMUEL H.: The Sublime, 1935

PEVSNER, NIKOLAUS: "Genesis of the Picturesque," *Architectural Review,* XCVI, 1944, 139–146
PEVSNER, NIKOLAUS: An Outline of European Architecture, 1951
PEVSNER, NIKOLAUS: "Richard Payne Knight," *Art Bulletin,* XXXI, 1949, 293–320
PEYRE, HENRI: Shelley et la France, 1935
POULET, GEORGES: Études sur le Temps Humain, 1949
POULET, GEORGES: "Timelessness and Romanticism," *Journal of the History of Ideas,* XV, 1954, 3–22
PRÉVOST, JEAN: Baudelaire, 1953
RAYMOND, MARCEL: From Baudelaire to Surrealism, 1933, 1950
SANDSTRÖM, SVEN: Le Monde Imaginaire d'Odilon Redon, 1955
SCARFE, FRANCIS: The Art of Paul Valéry, 1954
STEEGMAN, JOHN: Consort of Taste, 1950
TEMPLEMAN, WILLIAM D.: Life and Work of William Gilpin, 1939
TURNELL, MARTIN: Baudelaire, 1953
TODD, RUTHVEN: Tracks in the Snow, 1947
WEINBERG, BERNARD: French Realism: The Critical Reaction, 1937
WITTKOWER, RUDOLF: "Principles of Palladio's Architecture," *Journal of the Warburg and Courtauld Institutes,* VIII, 1945, 68–106

NEO-MANNERISM

AHLERS-HESTERMANN, FRIEDRICH: Stilwende: Aufbruch der Jugend, 1956
ANTAL, FREDERICK: Fuseli Studies, 1956
BALSTON, THOMAS: John Martin, 1947
BAZIN, GERMAIN: French Impressionists in the Louvre, 1958
BØE, ALF: From Gothic Revival to Functional Form, 1957
CABANNE, PIERRE: Edgar Degas, 1958
CHASSÉ, CHARLES: Le Mouvement Symboliste, 1947
CLARK, KENNETH: Landscape into Art, 1949, 1956
CURTIUS, ERNST ROBERT: European Literature and the Latin Middle Ages, 1948, 1953
DAULTE, FRANÇOIS: Frédéric Bazille et Son Temps, 1952
DORIVAL, BERNARD: Les Étapes de la Peinture Française Contemporaine, 1943–46
DORIVAL, BERNARD: Les Peintres du XXe Siècle, 1957
DURET, THÉODORE: Manet and the French Impressionists, 1910
FOCILLON, HENRI: La Peinture au XIXe Siècle, 1927

FOCILLON, HENRI: La Peinture aux XIXe et XXe Siècles, 1928
Formes de l'Art, Formes de l'Ésprit, 1951
FRANCASTEL, PIERRE: Art et Technique aux XIXe et XXe Siècles, 1956
FRANCASTEL, PIERRE: L'Impressionisme, 1937
FRANCASTEL, PIERRE: Nouveau Dessein, Nouvelle Peinture, 1946
FRIEDLAENDER, WALTER: David to Delacroix, 1952
FRY, ROGER: Characteristics of French Art, 1932
GAUNT, WILLIAM: The Aesthetic Adventure, 1945, 1957
GAUSS, CHARLES EDWARD: Aesthetic Theories of French Artists, 1949
GOLDWATER, ROBERT: Gauguin, 1957
HITCHCOCK, HENRY-RUSSELL: Architecture: 19th and 20th Centuries, 1958
HITCHCOCK, HENRY-RUSSELL: Early Victorian Architecture in Britain, 1954
HOCKE, GUSTAV RENÉ: "Manier und Manie in der Europaeischen Kunst," *Merkur,* June, 1956
HOCKE, GUSTAV RENÉ: "Ueber Manierismus in Tradition und Moderne," *Merkur,* April, 1956
HOPE, HENRY R.: Sources of Art Nouveau (Thesis, Harvard University), 1943
HUMBERT, AGNÈS: Les Nabis et Leur Époque, 1954
HUNTER, SAM: Modern French Painting, 1956
IRONSIDE, ROBIN: Pre-Raphaelite Painters, 1948
JOHNSON, LINCOLN F., JR.: Toulouse-Lautrec, the Symbolists, and Symbolism (Thesis, Harvard University), 1956
JONES, HOWARD MUMFORD: "The Pre-Raphaelites," *The Victorian Poets,* 1956
KERMODE, FRANK: The Romantic Image, 1957
LENNING, HENRY F.: The Art Nouveau, 1951
LETHÈVE, JACQUES: Impressionistes et Symbolistes Devant la Presse, 1959
MADSEN, STEPHAN TSCHUDI: Sources of Art Nouveau, 1955
MARTINO, PIERRE: Parnasse et Symbolisme, 1954
MINER, EARL: The Japanese Tradition in British and American Literature, 1958
MOSER, RUTH: L'Impressionisme Français, 1952
PEVSNER, NIKOLAUS: Academies of Art, 1940

PEVSNER, NIKOLAUS: Pioneers of the Modern Movement, 1936
RAMSAY, WARREN: Jules Laforgue and the Ironic Inheritance, 1953
REWALD, JOHN: History of Impressionism, 1946
REWALD, JOHN: Post-Impressionism, n.d.
SCHEFFLER, KARL: Das Phaenomen der Kunst, 1952
SCHEFFLER, KARL: Verwandlungen des Barocks, 1947
SCHMALENBACH, FRITZ: Jugendstil, 1934
SCHMUTZLER, ROBERT: "The English Origins of Art Nouveau," *Architectural Review,* CXVII, 1955, 108–116
SHIRLEY, ANDREW: John Constable, 1944
VAN LIER, HENRI: Les Arts de l'Espace, 1959
VENTURI, LIONELLO: Impressionists and Symbolists, 1950
VENTURI, LIONELLO: Modern Painters, 1947
WALLIS, ANNE ARMSTRONG: "Symbolist Painters of 1890," *Marsyas,* 1941, 117–152

CUBISM

ALVAREZ, ALFRED: The Shaping Spirit, 1958
APOLLINAIRE, GUILLAUME: The Cubist Painters, 1913, 1944
ARNHEIM, RUDOLF: "Accident and Necessity in Art," *Journal of Aesthetics and Art Criticism,* XVI, 1957, 18–32
Arte Figurativa e Arte Astratta, 1955
BARR, ALFRED, JR.: Picasso: Fifty Years of His Art, 1946
BRADLEY, F. H.: Appearance and Reality, 1893, 1902
BRAQUE, GEORGES: "Pensées sur l'Art," *Confluences,* Mai, 1945, 339–342
BRION, MARCEL: L'Art Abstrait, 1956
BRU, CHARLES-PIERRE: Esthétique de l'Abstraction, 1955
DORIVAL, BERNARD: Les Étapes de la Peinture Française Contemporaine, 1943–46
DORIVAL, BERNARD: Les Peintres du XXe Siècle, 1957
DORNER, ALEXANDER: The Way Beyond "Art," 1947
EISENSTEIN, SERGEI: Film Form, 1949
EISENSTEIN, SERGEI: Film Sense, 1942
ERNST, MAX: Beyond Painting, 1948
ESCHOLIER, RAYMOND: La Peinture Française: XXe Siècle, 1937
GIEURE, MAURICE: G. Braque, 1956
GIEURE, MAURICE: Initiation à l'Oeuvre de Picasso, 1951

GLEIZES, A. AND METZINGER, J.: Du Cubisme, 1912, 1947
GRAY, CHRISTOPHER: Cubist Aesthetic Theories, 1953
JAMMER, MAX: Concepts of Force, 1957
JAMMER, MAX: Concepts of Space, 1954
JUDKINS, WINTHROP: "Toward a Reinterpretation of Cubism," *Art Bulletin,* XXX, December, 1948, 270–278
KAHNWEILER, DANIEL-HENRY: Juan Gris, 1947, 1948
KAHNWEILER, DANIEL-HENRY: The Rise of Cubism, 1949
KEPES, GYORGY: The New Landscape, 1956
LE CORBUSIER (CHARLES-ÉDOUARD JEANNERET-GRIS): The New World of Space, 1948
LHOTE, ANDRÉ: La Peinture Liberée, 1956
LHOTE, ANDRÉ: Theory of Figure Painting, 1954
LIVINGSTONE, LEON: "Ortega y Gasset's Philosophy of Art," *PMLA,* LXVII, 1952, 609–655
MALRAUX, ANDRÉ: Esquisse d'une Psychologie du Cinema, 1946
MARCH, HAROLD: Gide and the Hound of Heaven, 1952
MATTHIESSEN, F. O.: The Achievement of T. S. Eliot, 1958
MOHOLY-NAGY, LASZLO: Vision in Motion, 1947
MONDRIAN, PIET: "Natural Reality and Abstract Reality," in *Piet Mondrian,* ed. Michel Seuphor, 1957
MONDRIAN, PIET: Plastic Art and Pure Plastic Art, 1945
OZENFANT, AMADÉE: Foundations of Modern Art, 1931, 1952
PAULHAN, JEAN: "Braque, le Patron," *Horizon,* XI, May, 1945, 329–339
PEREIRA, I. RICE: The Nature of Space, 1956
SALMON, ANDRÉ: La Jeune Peinture Française, 1912
SEUPHOR, MICHEL: Dictionary of Abstract Painting, 1957
SHATTUCK, ROGER: The Banquet Years, 1958
STEIN, GERTRUDE: Lectures in America, 1935, 1957
STEIN, GERTRUDE: Picasso, 1938, 1939
Témoignages Pour l'Art Abstrait, 1952
VENTURI, LIONELLO: Four Steps Toward Modern Art, 1956
WHITEHEAD, ALFRED NORTH: Essays in Science and Philosophy, 1947
WHITEHEAD, ALFRED NORTH: Science and the Modern World, 1925

Index

Wylie Sypher is professor of English, dean of the graduate division and chairman of the department of language, literature and arts at Simmons College in Boston. Born in Mount Kisco, New York, Mr. Sypher was graduated from Amherst College, received master's degrees from Tufts College and from Harvard, and a Ph.D. from Harvard. He has taught summers at the University of Wisconsin, the University of Minnesota, and at the Bread Loaf School of English, and twice has been awarded a Guggenheim fellowship for research in the theory of fine arts and literature. His book, *Four Stages of Renaissance Style,* published in 1955, has become an influential work on its subject. His other books include *Enlightened England* and *Guinea's Captive Kings.*

V-212	Rossiter, Clinton	CONSERVATISM IN AMERICA
V-220	Shonfield, Andrew	THE ATTACK ON WORLD POVERTY
V-179	Stebbins, Richard P.	U. S. IN WORLD AFFAIRS, 1959
V-204	Stebbins, Richard P.	U. S. IN WORLD AFFAIRS, 1960
V-222	Stebbins, Richard P.	U. S. IN WORLD AFFAIRS, 1961
V-53	Synge, J. M.	THE ARAN ISLANDS, *etc.*
V-231	Tannenbaum, Frank	SLAVE & CITIZEN: *The Negro in the Americas*
V-206	Wallerstein, Immanuel	AFRICA: THE POLITICS OF INDEPENDENCE
V-145	Warren, Robert Penn	SEGREGATION
V-729	Weidlé, W.	RUSSIA: ABSENT & PRESENT
V-208	Woodward, C. Vann	BURDEN OF SOUTHERN HISTORY

VINTAGE HISTORY AND CRITICISM OF LITERATURE, MUSIC, AND ART

V-22	Barzun, Jacques	THE ENERGIES OF ART
V-93	Bennett, Joan	FOUR METAPHYSICAL POETS
V-57	Bodkin, Maud	ARCHETYPAL PATTERNS IN POETRY
V-51	Burke, Kenneth	THE PHILOSOPHY OF LITERARY FORM
V-75	Camus, Albert	THE MYTH OF SISYPHUS *and Other Essays*
V-171	Cruttwell, Patrick	THE SHAKESPEAREAN MOMENT
V-4	Einstein, Alfred	A SHORT HISTORY OF MUSIC
V-177	Fuller, Edmund	MAN IN MODERN FICTION
V-13	Gilbert, Stuart	JAMES JOYCE'S "ULYSSES"
V-56	Graves, Robert	THE WHITE GODDESS
V-175	Haggin, Bernard	MUSIC FOR THE MAN WHO ENJOYS "HAMLET"
V-114	Hauser, Arnold	THE SOCIAL HISTORY OF ART, Volume I
V-115	Hauser, Arnold	THE SOCIAL HISTORY OF ART, Volume II
V-116	Hauser, Arnold	THE SOCIAL HISTORY OF ART, Volume III
V-117	Hauser, Arnold	THE SOCIAL HISTORY OF ART Volume IV
V-20	Hyman, Stanley Edgar	THE ARMED VISION
V-38	Hyman, Stanley Edgar (ed.)	THE CRITICAL PERFORMANCE
V-41	James, Henry	THE FUTURE OF THE NOVEL
V-12	Jarrell, Randall	POETRY AND THE AGE
V-88	Kerman, Joseph	OPERA AS DRAMA
V-83	Kronenberger, Louis	KINGS AND DESPERATE MEN

V-167	La Rochefoucauld	MAXIMS
V-90	Levin, Harry	THE POWER OF BLACKNESS
V-81	Lowes, John Livingston	THE ROAD TO XANADU
V-55	Mann, Thomas	ESSAYS
V-720	Mirsky, D. S.	A HISTORY OF RUSSIAN LITERATURE
V-77	Mizener, Arthur	THE FAR SIDE OF PARADISE: A *Biography of F. Scott Fitzgerald*
V-47	Murray, Gilbert	THE CLASSICAL TRADITION IN POETRY
V-118	Newman, Ernest	GREAT OPERAS, Volume I
V-119	Newman, Ernest	GREAT OPERAS, Volume II
V-107	Newman, Ernest	WAGNER AS MAN AND ARTIST
V-161	Picasso, Pablo	PICASSO AND THE HUMAN COMEDY
V-24	Ransom, John Crowe	POEMS AND ESSAYS
V-89	Schorer, Mark	WILLIAM BLAKE: *The Politics of Vision*
V-108	Shahn, Ben	THE SHAPE OF CONTENT
V-186	Steiner, George	TOLSTOY OR DOSTOEVSKY
V-39	Stravinsky, Igor	THE POETICS OF MUSIC
V-100	Sullivan, J. W. N.	BEETHOVEN: *His Spiritual Development*
V-229	Sypher, Wylie	ROCOCO TO CUBISM
V-166	Sze, Mai-Mai	THE WAY OF CHINESE PAINTING
V-214	Thomson, Virgil	THE STATE OF MUSIC
V-162	Tillyard, E. M. W.	THE ELIZABETHAN WORLD PICTURE
V-35	Tindall, William York	FORCES IN MODERN BRITISH LITERATURE
V-82	Toye, Francis	VERDI: *His Life and Works*
V-62	Turnell, Martin	THE NOVEL IN FRANCE
V-194	Valéry, Paul	THE ART OF POETRY
V-122	Wilenski, R. H.	MODERN FRENCH PAINTERS, Volume I (1863-1903)
V-123	Wilenski, R. H.	MODERN FRENCH PAINTERS, Volume II (1904-1938)
V-218	Wilson, Edmund	CLASSICS & COMMERCIALS
V-181	Wilson, Edmund	THE SHORES OF LIGHT